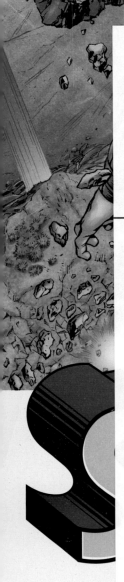

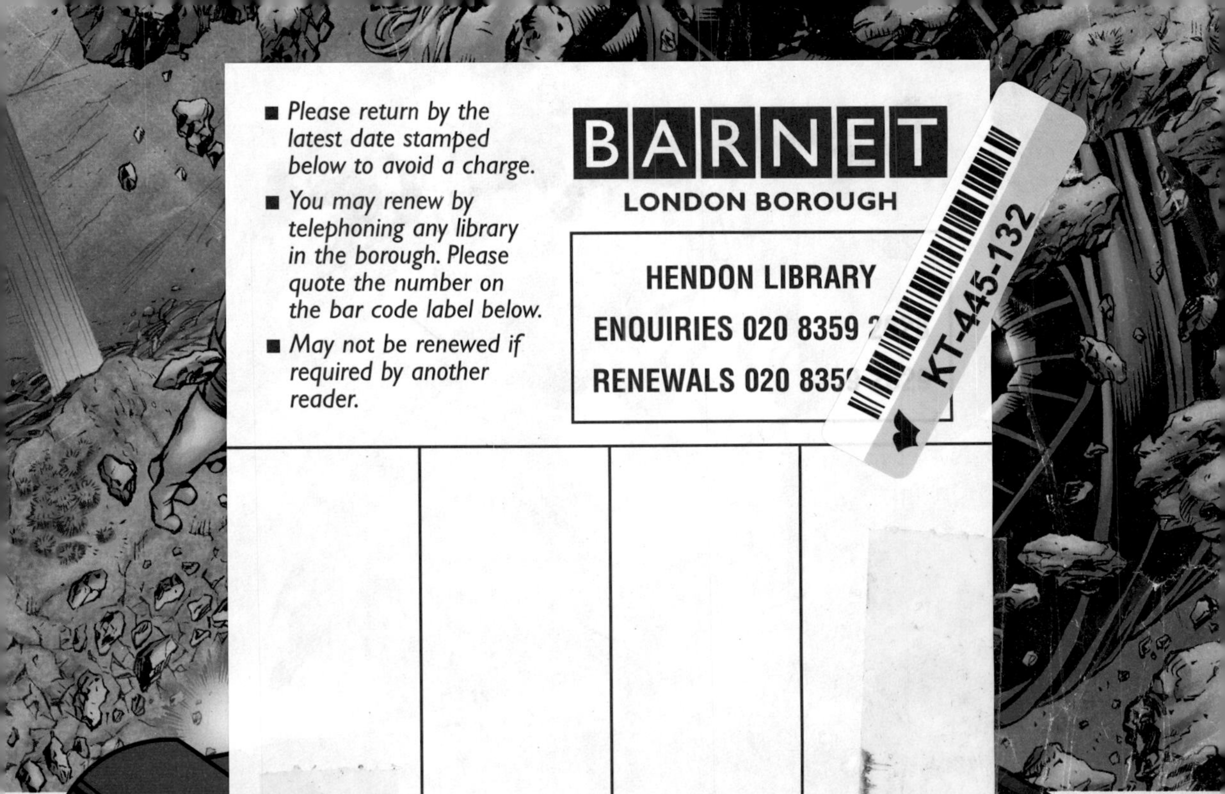

Bruno Hang *Colorist*
Richard Starkings *Letterer*

REDEMPTION

Fabian Nicieza *Writer*
Allan Goldman *Penciller*
Ron Randall *Inker*
Marta Martinez Pete Pantazis *Colorists*
Jared K. Fletcher Rob Leigh *Letterers*

THE BEAST FROM KRYPTON

Kurt Busiek *Writer*
Walter Simonson *Artist*
Alex Sinclair Lee Loughridge *Colorists*
John Workman *Letterer*

SUPERMAN created by Jerry Siegel and Joe Shuster

R E D E   I O N

Cover by Al Barrionuevo and Marta Martinez

SUPERMAN: REDEMPTION

Published by DC Comics.

DC Comics, 1700 Broadway, New York, NY 10019
A Warner Bros. Entertainment Company
Printed in Canada. First Printing.
ISBN: 978-1-4012-1636-8

Angel Cover to Superman #659 by Al Barrionuevo

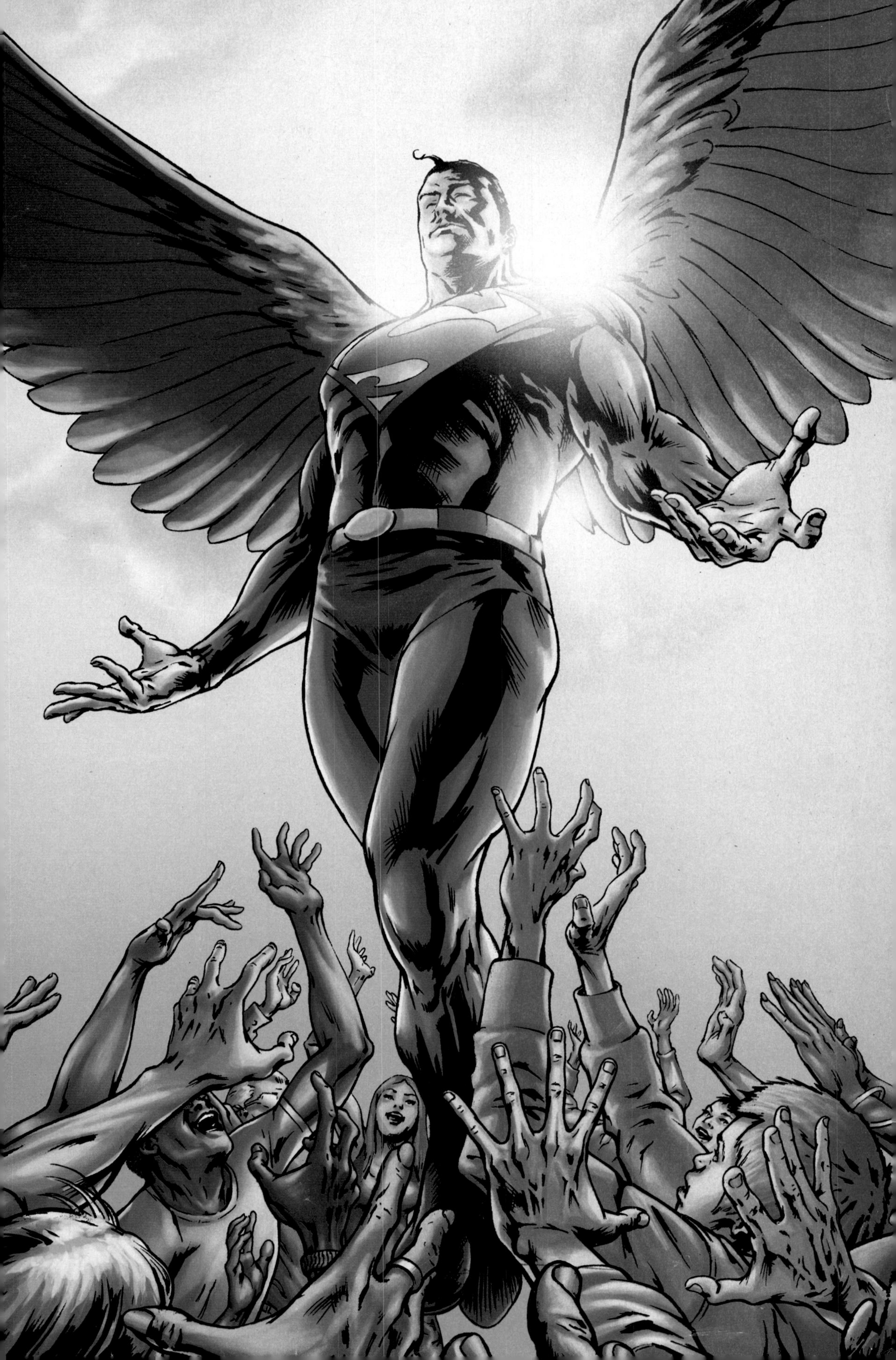

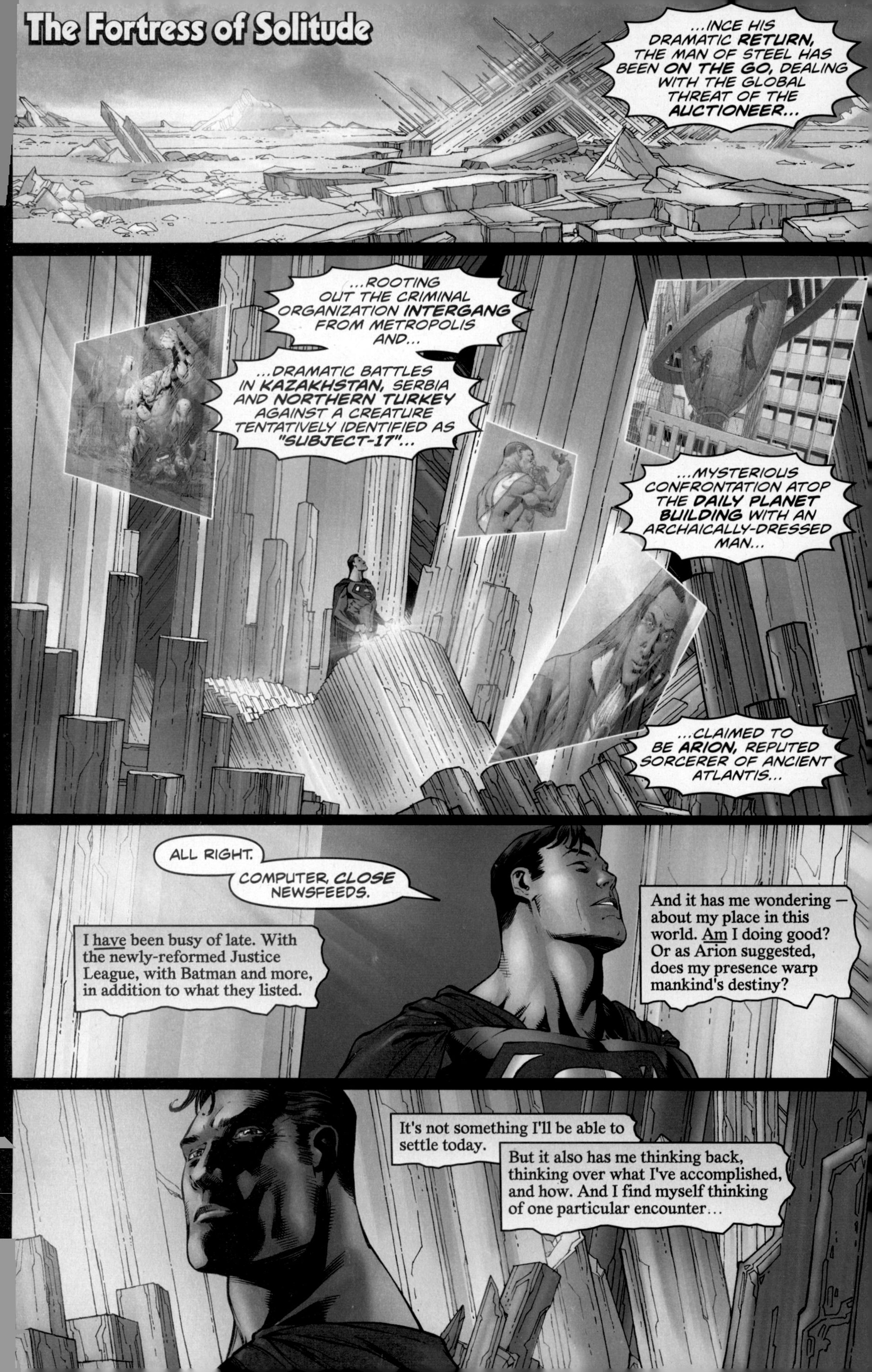
The Fortress of Solitude
...INCE HIS DRAMATIC RETURN, THE MAN OF STEEL HAS BEEN ON THE GO, DEALING WITH THE GLOBAL THREAT OF THE AUCTIONEER...
...ROOTING OUT THE CRIMINAL ORGANIZATION INTERGANG FROM METROPOLIS AND...
...DRAMATIC BATTLES IN KAZAKHSTAN, SERBIA AND NORTHERN TURKEY AGAINST A CREATURE TENTATIVELY IDENTIFIED AS "SUBJECT-17"...
...MYSTERIOUS CONFRONTATION ATOP THE DAILY PLANET BUILDING WITH AN ARCHAICALLY-DRESSED MAN...
...CLAIMED TO BE ARION, REPUTED SORCERER OF ANCIENT ATLANTIS...
ALL RIGHT.
COMPUTER, CLOSE NEWSFEEDS.
I have been busy of late. With the newly-reformed Justice League, with Batman and more, in addition to what they listed.
And it has me wondering — about my place in this world. Am I doing good? Or as Arion suggested, does my presence warp mankind's destiny?
It's not something I'll be able to settle today.
But it also has me thinking back, thinking over what I've accomplished, and how. And I find myself thinking of one particular encounter...

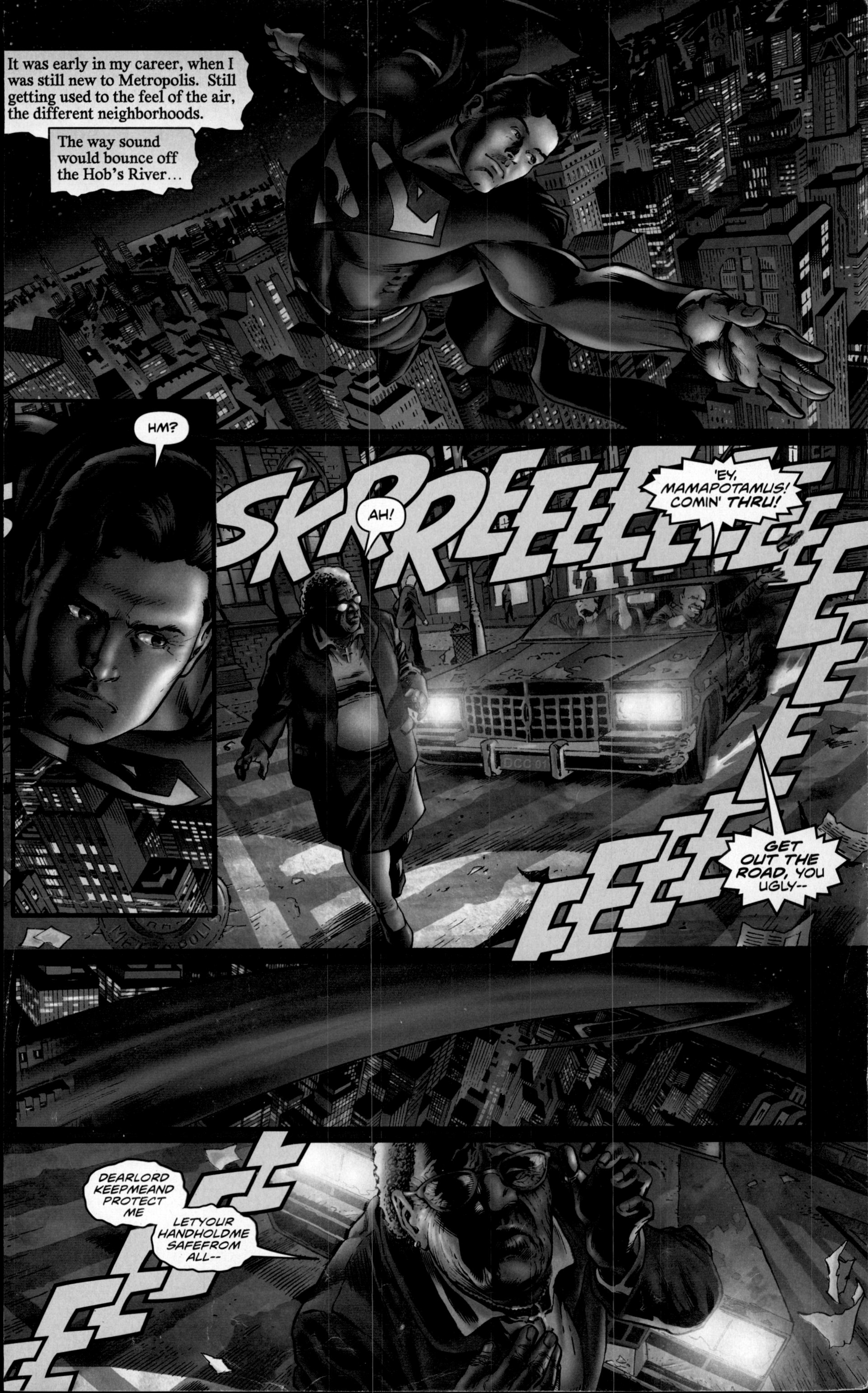
It was early in my career, when I was still new to Metropolis. Still getting used to the feel of the air, the different neighborhoods.
The way sound would bounce off the Hob's River…
HM?
SKRREEEEEEEEEEE
AH!
'EY, MAMAPOTAMUS! COMIN' THRU!
GET OUT THE ROAD, YOU UGLY--
DEARLORD KEEPMEAND PROTECT ME
LETYOUR HANDHOLDME SAFEFROM ALL--

I also wasn't all that used to stopping speeding cars yet, either.
I cushioned the impact enough to keep them alive, but wasn't sure I could whisk her out away or lift them over in time —
KSSSH
WH -- ?

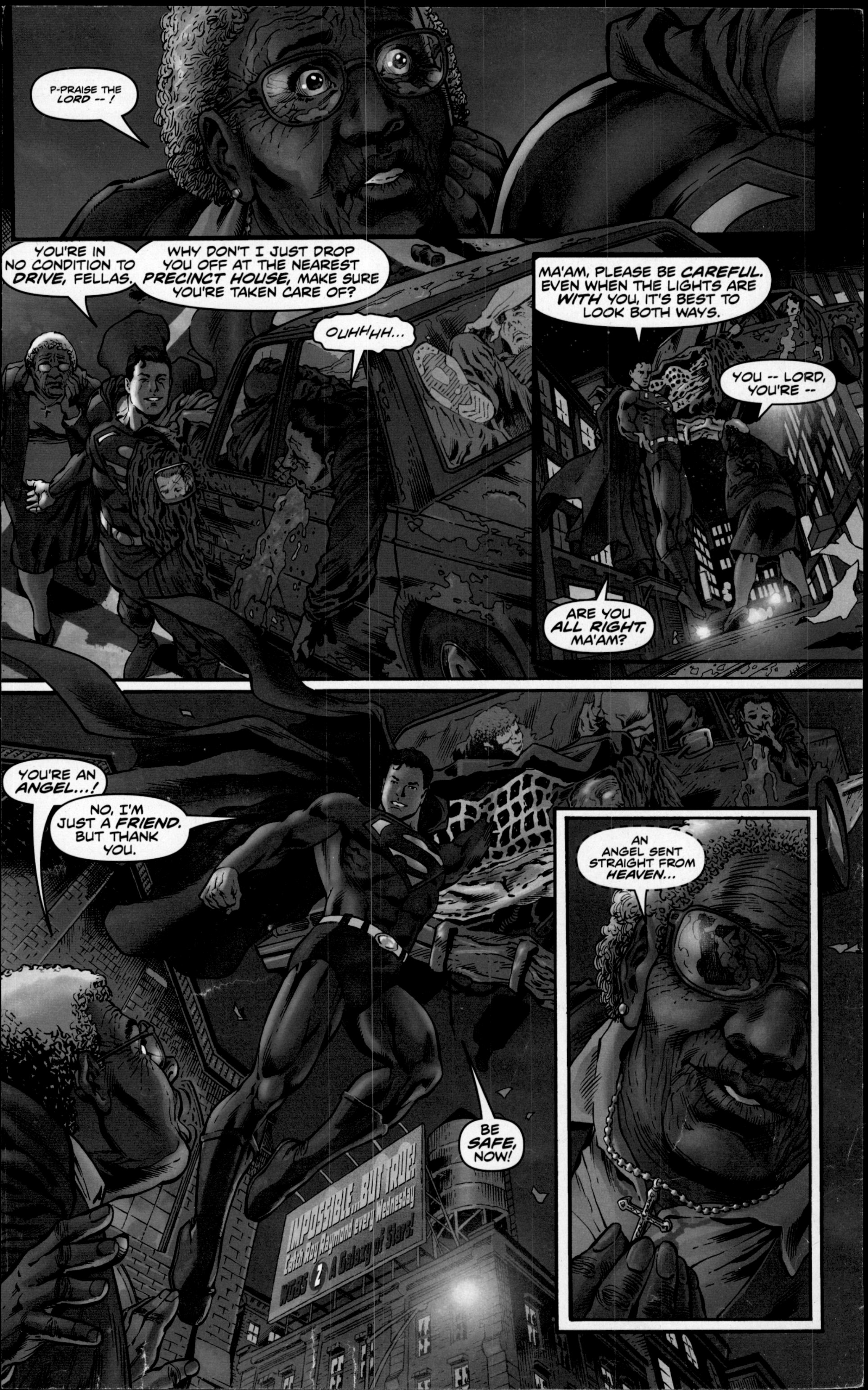
P-PRAISE THE LORD -- !
YOU'RE IN NO CONDITION TO DRIVE, FELLAS.
WHY DON'T I JUST DROP YOU OFF AT THE NEAREST PRECINCT HOUSE, MAKE SURE YOU'RE TAKEN CARE OF?
OUHHHH...
MA'AM, PLEASE BE CAREFUL. EVEN WHEN THE LIGHTS ARE WITH YOU, IT'S BEST TO LOOK BOTH WAYS.
YOU -- LORD, YOU'RE --
ARE YOU ALL RIGHT, MA'AM?
YOU'RE AN ANGEL...!
NO, I'M JUST A FRIEND. BUT THANK YOU.
AN ANGEL SENT STRAIGHT FROM HEAVEN...
BE SAFE, NOW!
IMPOSSIBLE...BUT TRUE!
Catch Ray Raymond every Wednesday
WGBS 2 A Galaxy of Stars!

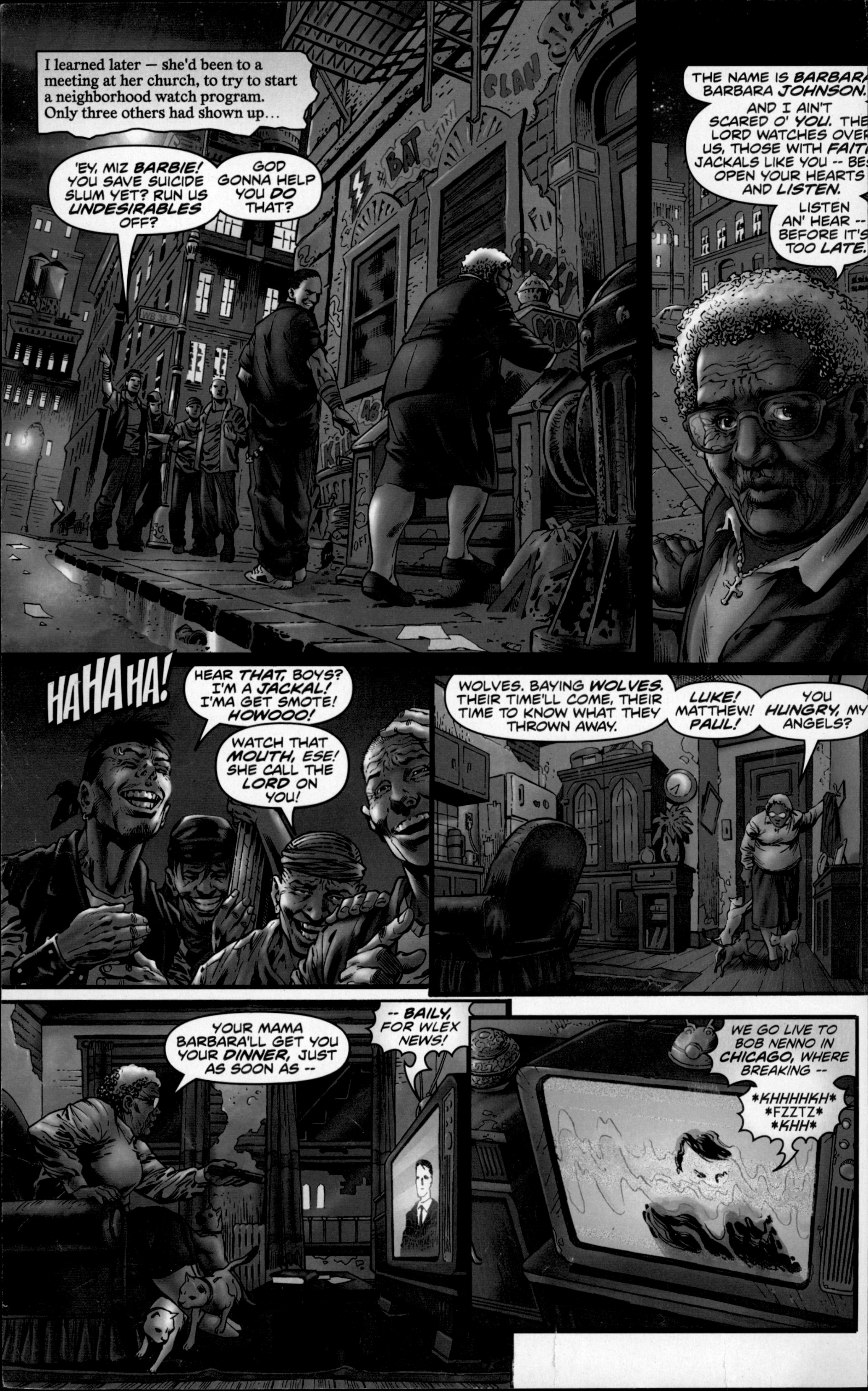
I learned later — she'd been to a meeting at her church, to try to start a neighborhood watch program. Only three others had shown up…
'EY, MIZ BARBIE! YOU SAVE SUICIDE SLUM YET? RUN US UNDESIRABLES OFF?
GOD GONNA HELP YOU DO THAT?
THE NAME IS BARBARA. BARBARA JOHNSON.
AND I AIN'T SCARED O' YOU. THE LORD WATCHES OVER US, THOSE WITH FAITH. JACKALS LIKE YOU -- BEST OPEN YOUR HEARTS AND LISTEN.
LISTEN AN' HEAR -- BEFORE IT'S TOO LATE.
HAHAHA!
HEAR THAT, BOYS? I'M A JACKAL! I'MA GET SMOTE! HOWOOO!
WATCH THAT MOUTH, ESE! SHE CALL THE LORD ON YOU!
WOLVES. BAYING WOLVES. THEIR TIME'LL COME, THEIR TIME TO KNOW WHAT THEY THROWN AWAY.
LUKE! MATTHEW! PAUL!
YOU HUNGRY, MY ANGELS?
YOUR MAMA BARBARA'LL GET YOU YOUR DINNER, JUST AS SOON AS --
-- BAILY, FOR WLEX NEWS!
WE GO LIVE TO BOB NENNO IN CHICAGO, WHERE BREAKING --
KHHHHKH *FZZTZ* *KHH*

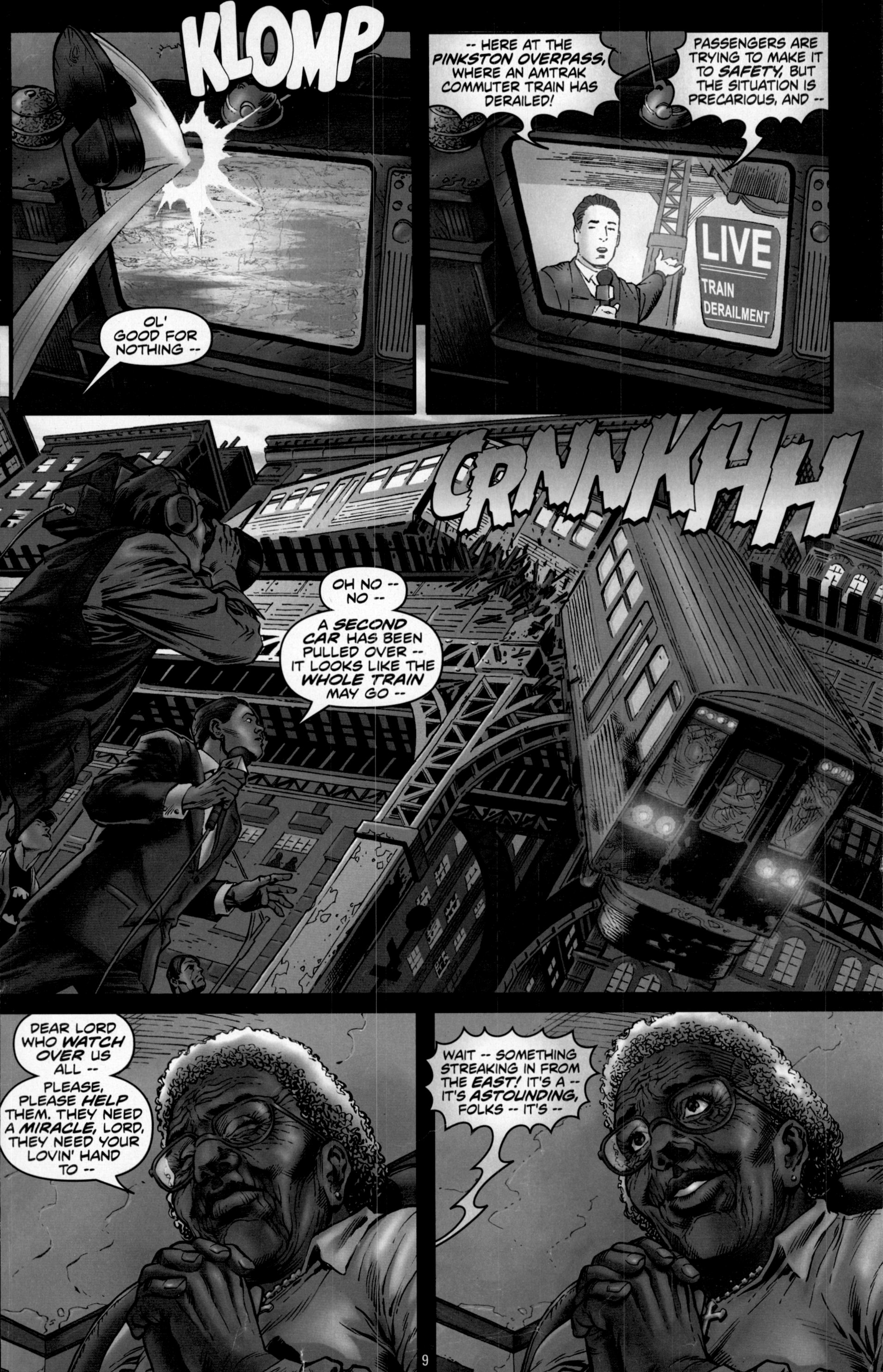
KLOMP
OL' GOOD FOR NOTHING --
-- HERE AT THE PINKSTON OVERPASS, WHERE AN AMTRAK COMMUTER TRAIN HAS DERAILED!
PASSENGERS ARE TRYING TO MAKE IT TO SAFETY, BUT THE SITUATION IS PRECARIOUS, AND --
LIVE
TRAIN DERAILMENT
CRNNKHH
OH NO -- NO --
A SECOND CAR HAS BEEN PULLED OVER -- IT LOOKS LIKE THE WHOLE TRAIN MAY GO --
DEAR LORD WHO WATCH OVER US ALL -- PLEASE, PLEASE HELP THEM. THEY NEED A MIRACLE, LORD, THEY NEED YOUR LOVIN' HAND TO --
WAIT -- SOMETHING STREAKING IN FROM THE EAST! IT'S A -- IT'S ASTOUNDING, FOLKS -- IT'S --

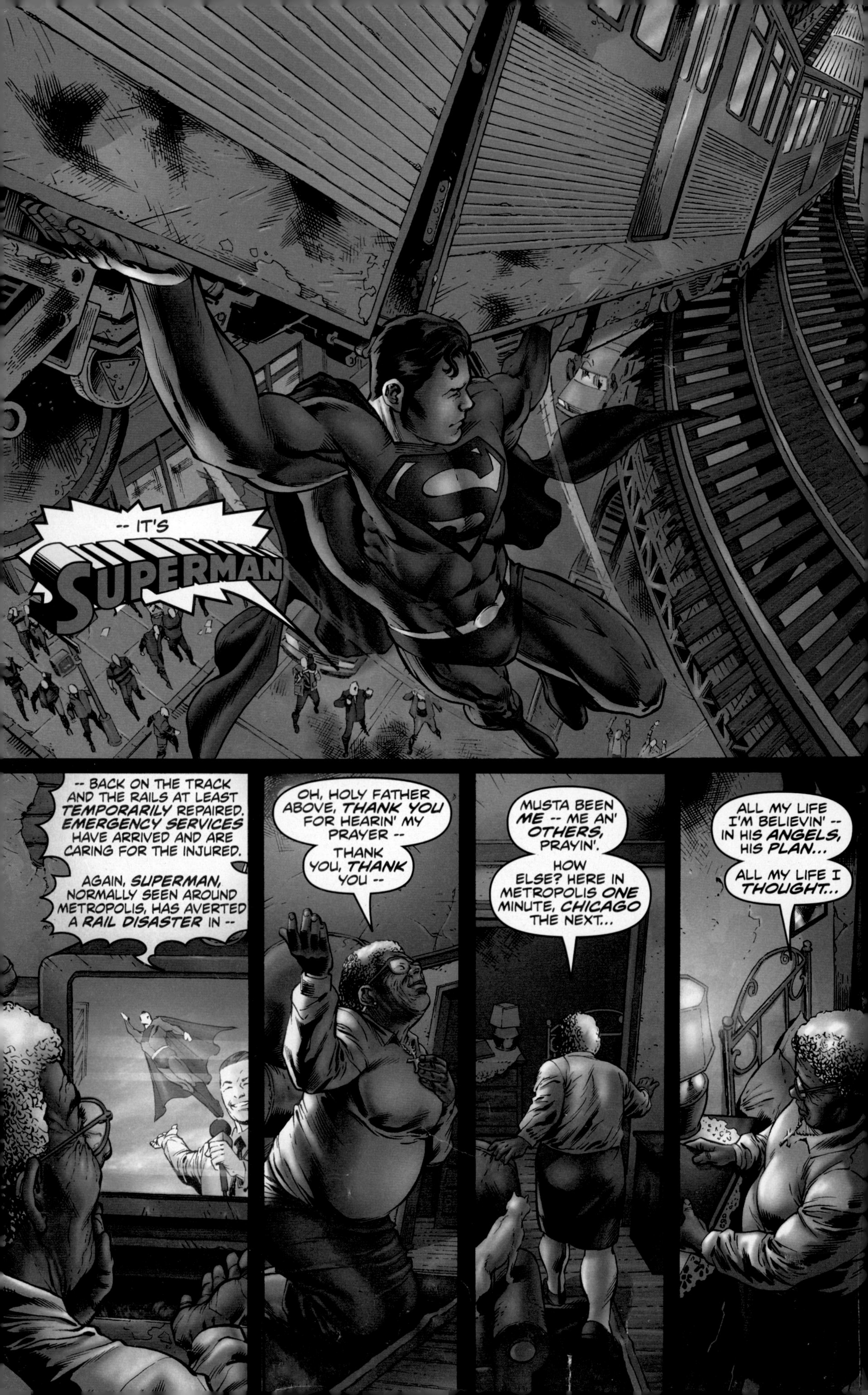
-- IT'S
SUPERMAN
-- BACK ON THE TRACK AND THE RAILS AT LEAST TEMPORARILY REPAIRED. EMERGENCY SERVICES HAVE ARRIVED AND ARE CARING FOR THE INJURED.
AGAIN, SUPERMAN, NORMALLY SEEN AROUND METROPOLIS, HAS AVERTED A RAIL DISASTER IN --
OH, HOLY FATHER ABOVE, THANK YOU FOR HEARIN' MY PRAYER --
THANK YOU, THANK YOU --
MUSTA BEEN ME -- ME AN' OTHERS, PRAYIN'.
HOW ELSE? HERE IN METROPOLIS ONE MINUTE, CHICAGO THE NEXT...
ALL MY LIFE I'M BELIEVIN' -- IN HIS ANGELS, HIS PLAN...
ALL MY LIFE I THOUGHT...

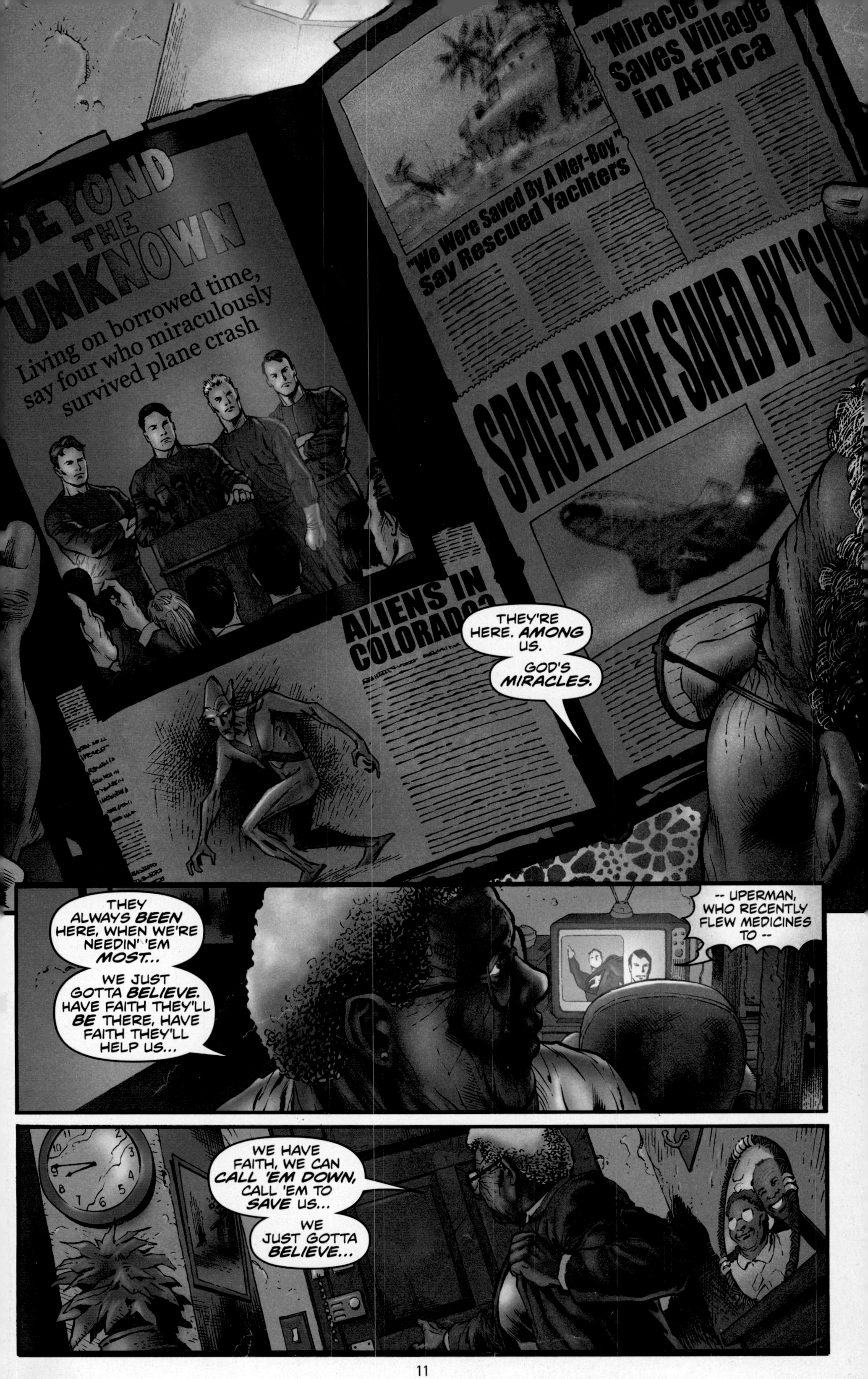
BEYOND THE UNKNOWN
Living on borrowed time, say four who miraculously survived plane crash
"We Were Saved By A Mer-Boy," Say Rescued Yachters
"Miracle
Saves Village in Africa
SPACE PLANE SAVED BY "SU
ALIENS IN COLORADO?
THEY'RE HERE. AMONG US.
GOD'S MIRACLES.
THEY ALWAYS BEEN HERE, WHEN WE'RE NEEDIN' 'EM MOST...
WE JUST GOTTA BELIEVE. HAVE FAITH THEY'LL BE THERE, HAVE FAITH THEY'LL HELP US...
-- UPERMAN, WHO RECENTLY FLEW MEDICINES TO --
WE HAVE FAITH, WE CAN CALL 'EM DOWN, CALL 'EM TO SAVE US...
WE JUST GOTTA BELIEVE...

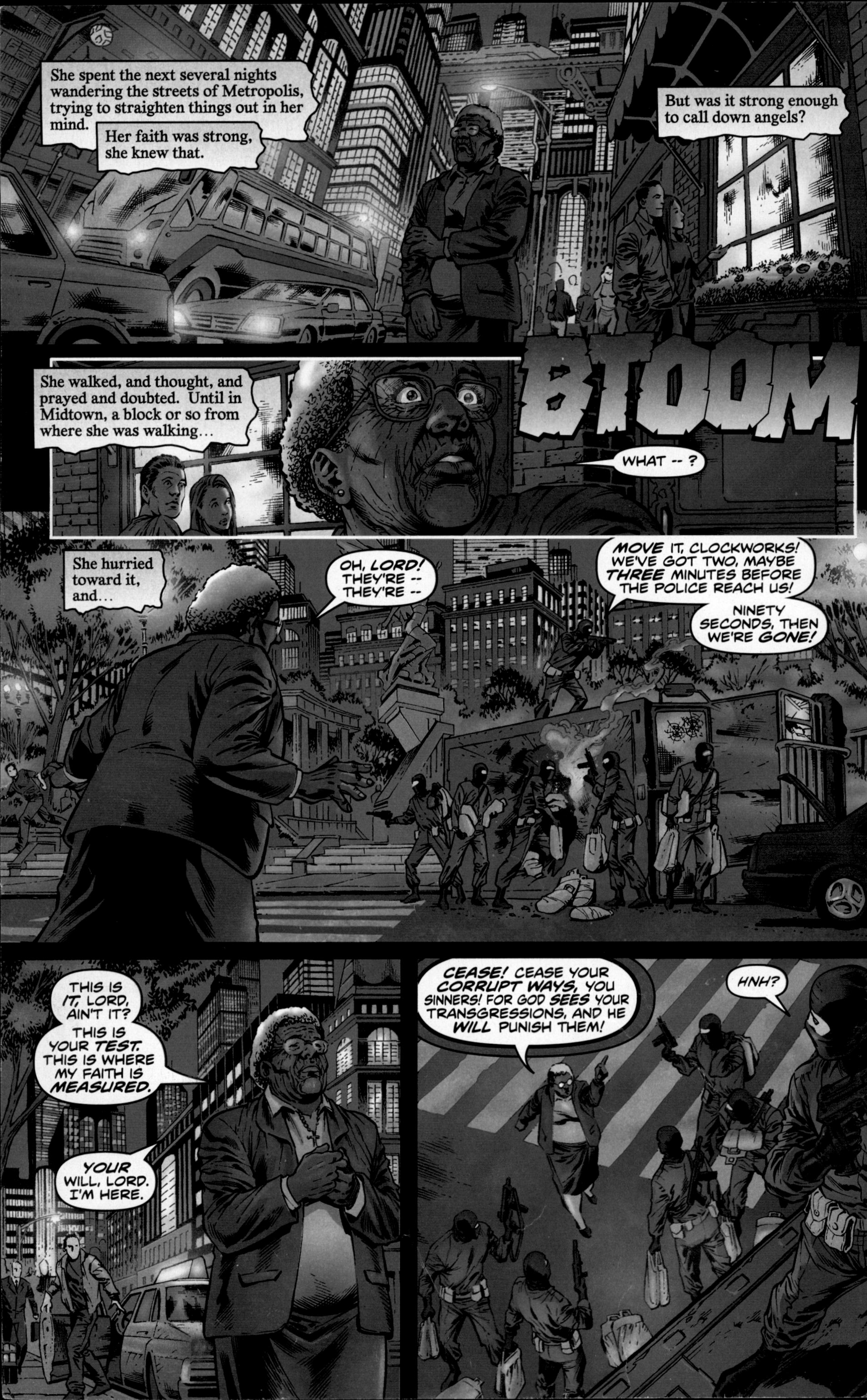

She spent the next several nights wandering the streets of Metropolis, trying to straighten things out in her mind.
Her faith was strong, she knew that.
But was it strong enough to call down angels?
She walked, and thought, and prayed and doubted. Until in Midtown, a block or so from where she was walking…
BTOOM
WHAT -- ?
She hurried toward it, and…
OH, LORD! THEY'RE -- THEY'RE --
MOVE IT, CLOCKWORKS! WE'VE GOT TWO, MAYBE THREE MINUTES BEFORE THE POLICE REACH US!
NINETY SECONDS, THEN WE'RE GONE!
THIS IS IT, LORD, AIN'T IT?
THIS IS YOUR TEST. THIS IS WHERE MY FAITH IS MEASURED.
YOUR WILL, LORD. I'M HERE.
CEASE! CEASE YOUR CORRUPT WAYS, YOU SINNERS! FOR GOD SEES YOUR TRANSGRESSIONS, AND HE WILL PUNISH THEM!
HNH?

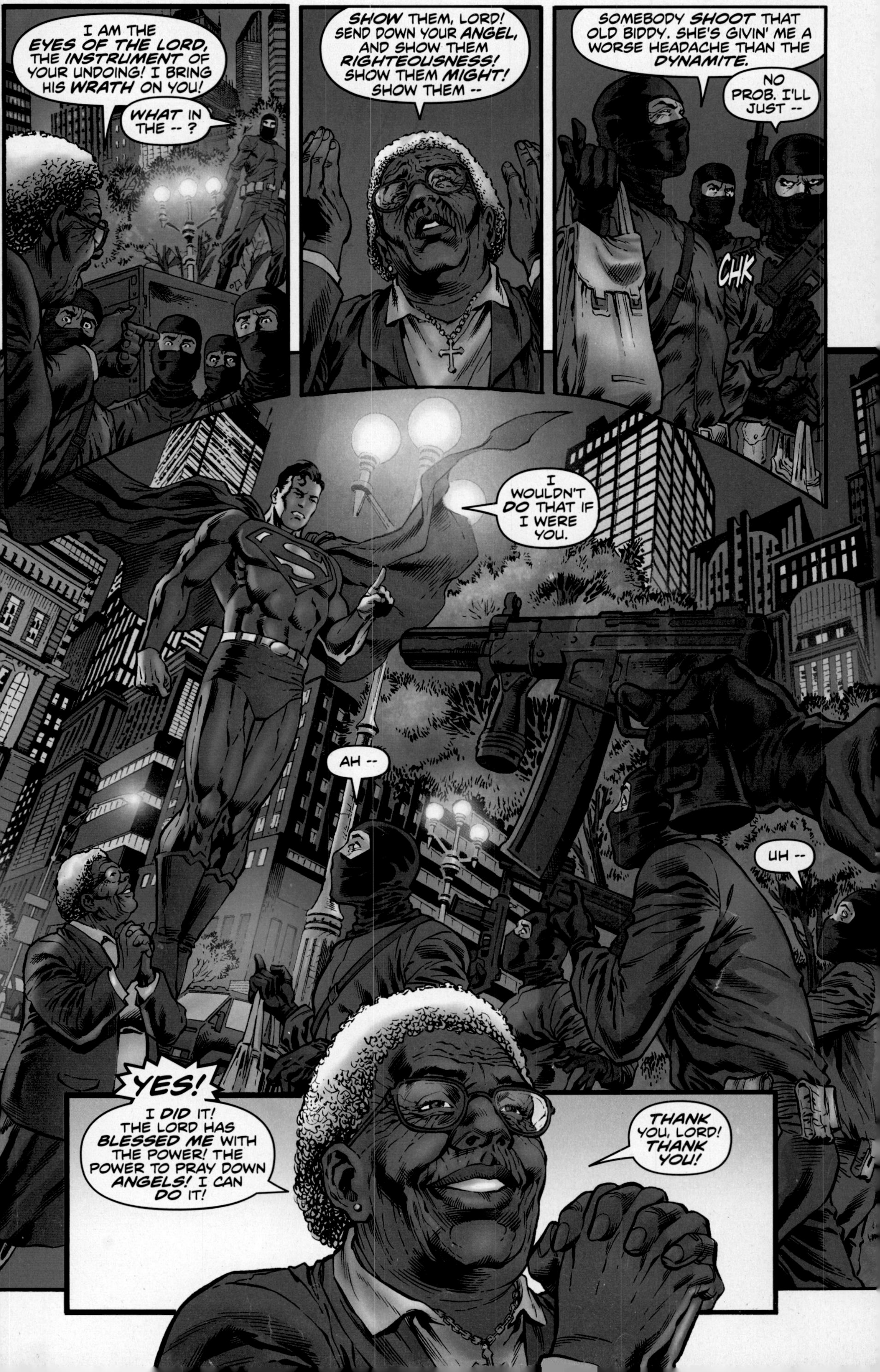
I AM THE EYES OF THE LORD, THE INSTRUMENT OF YOUR UNDOING! I BRING HIS WRATH ON YOU!
WHAT IN THE -- ?
SHOW THEM, LORD! SEND DOWN YOUR ANGEL, AND SHOW THEM RIGHTEOUSNESS! SHOW THEM MIGHT! SHOW THEM --
SOMEBODY SHOOT THAT OLD BIDDY. SHE'S GIVIN' ME A WORSE HEADACHE THAN THE DYNAMITE.
NO PROB. I'LL JUST --
CHK
I WOULDN'T DO THAT IF I WERE YOU.
AH --
UH --
YES!
I DID IT! THE LORD HAS BLESSED ME WITH THE POWER! THE POWER TO PRAY DOWN ANGELS! I CAN DO IT!
THANK YOU, LORD! THANK YOU!

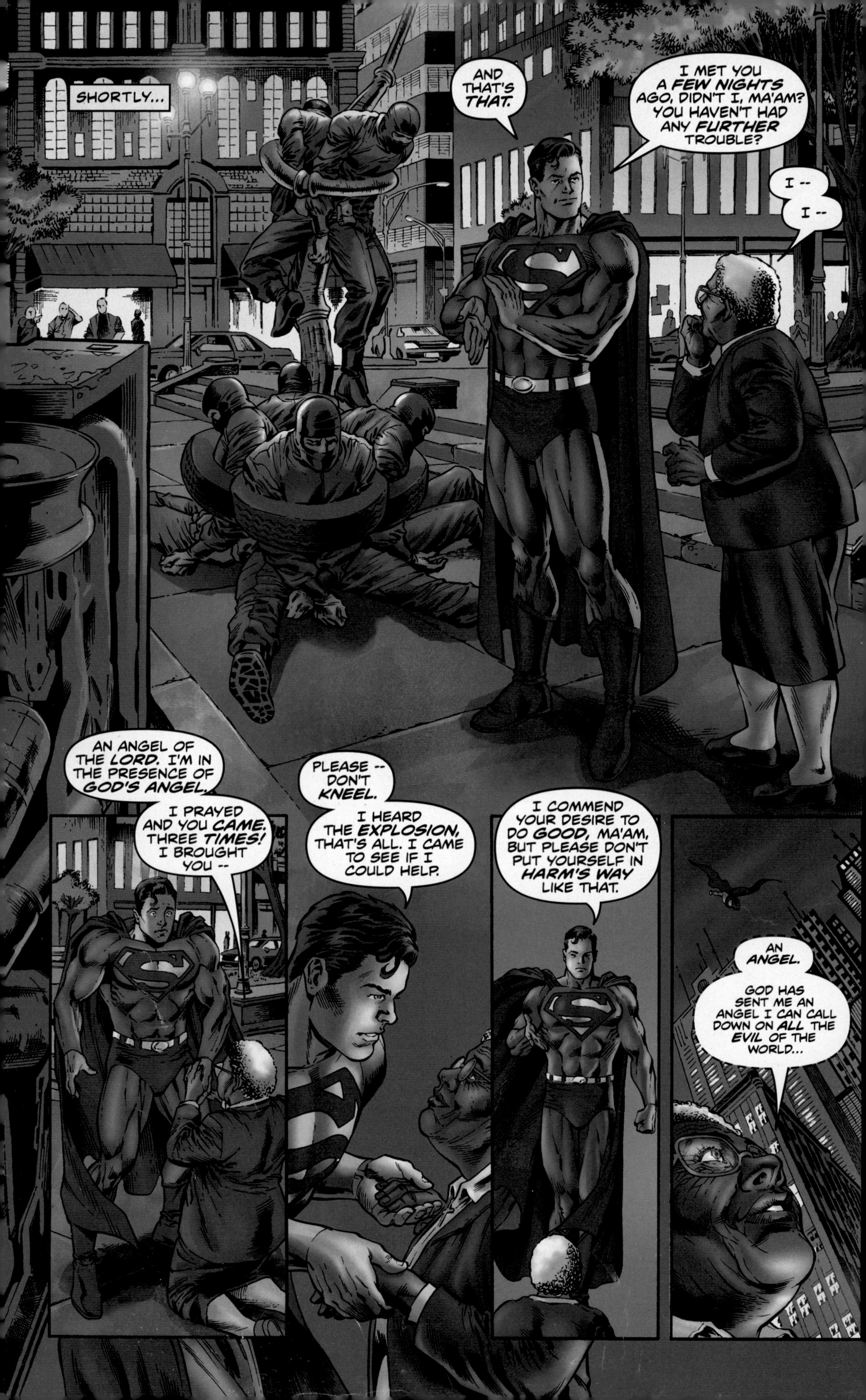

SHORTLY...
AND THAT'S THAT.
I MET YOU A FEW NIGHTS AGO, DIDN'T I, MA'AM? YOU HAVEN'T HAD ANY FURTHER TROUBLE?
I --
I --
AN ANGEL OF THE LORD. I'M IN THE PRESENCE OF GOD'S ANGEL.
I PRAYED AND YOU CAME. THREE TIMES! I BROUGHT YOU --
PLEASE -- DON'T KNEEL.
I HEARD THE EXPLOSION, THAT'S ALL. I CAME TO SEE IF I COULD HELP.
I COMMEND YOUR DESIRE TO DO GOOD, MA'AM, BUT PLEASE DON'T PUT YOURSELF IN HARM'S WAY LIKE THAT.
AN ANGEL.
GOD HAS SENT ME AN ANGEL I CAN CALL DOWN ON ALL THE EVIL OF THE WORLD...

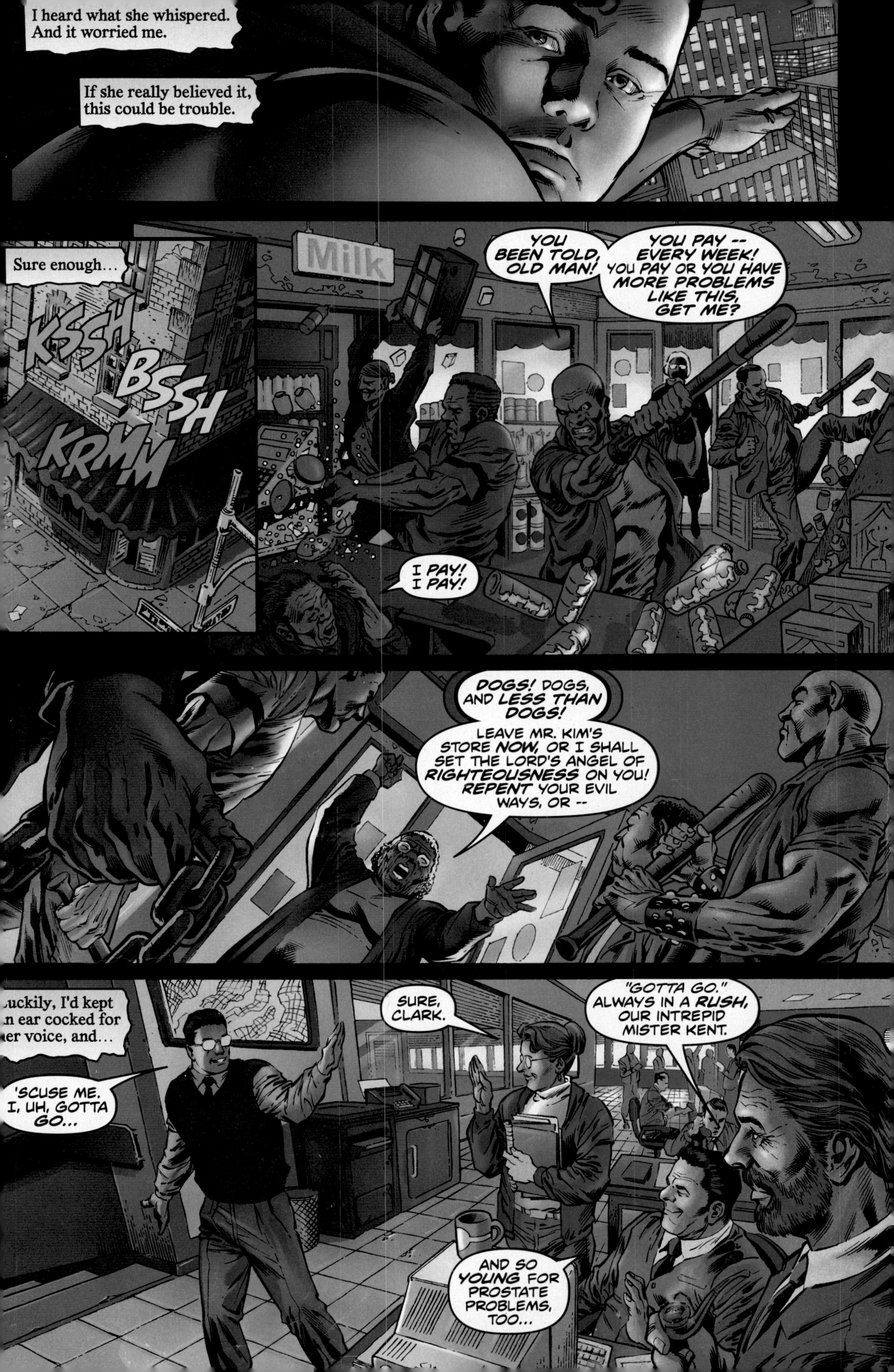

I heard what she whispered. And it worried me.
If she really believed it, this could be trouble.
Sure enough…
KSSH
BSSH
KRMM
Milk
YOU BEEN TOLD, OLD MAN!
YOU PAY -- EVERY WEEK! YOU PAY OR YOU HAVE MORE PROBLEMS LIKE THIS, GET ME?
I PAY! I PAY!
DOGS! DOGS, AND LESS THAN DOGS!
LEAVE MR. KIM'S STORE NOW, OR I SHALL SET THE LORD'S ANGEL OF RIGHTEOUSNESS ON YOU! REPENT YOUR EVIL WAYS, OR --
uckily, I'd kept n ear cocked for er voice, and…
'SCUSE ME. I, UH, GOTTA GO...
SURE, CLARK.
"GOTTA GO." ALWAYS IN A RUSH, OUR INTREPID MISTER KENT.
AND SO YOUNG FOR PROSTATE PROBLEMS, TOO...

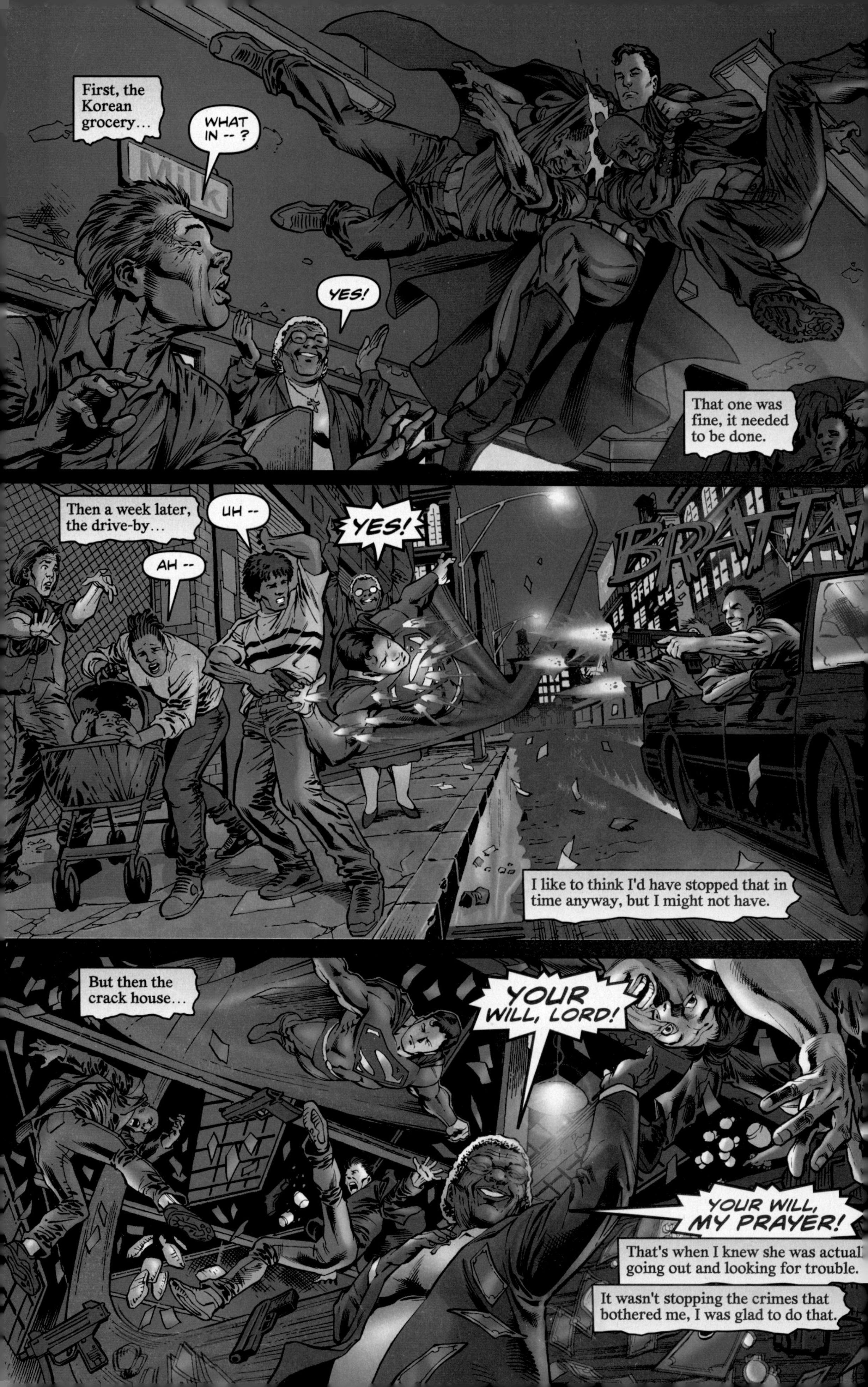
First, the Korean grocery...
WHAT IN -- ?
YES!
That one was fine, it needed to be done.
Then a week later, the drive-by...
UH --
AH --
YES!
BRATTA
I like to think I'd have stopped that in time anyway, but I might not have.
But then the crack house...
YOUR WILL, LORD!
YOUR WILL, MY PRAYER!
That's when I knew she was actual
going out and looking for trouble.
It wasn't stopping the crimes that bothered me, I was glad to do that.

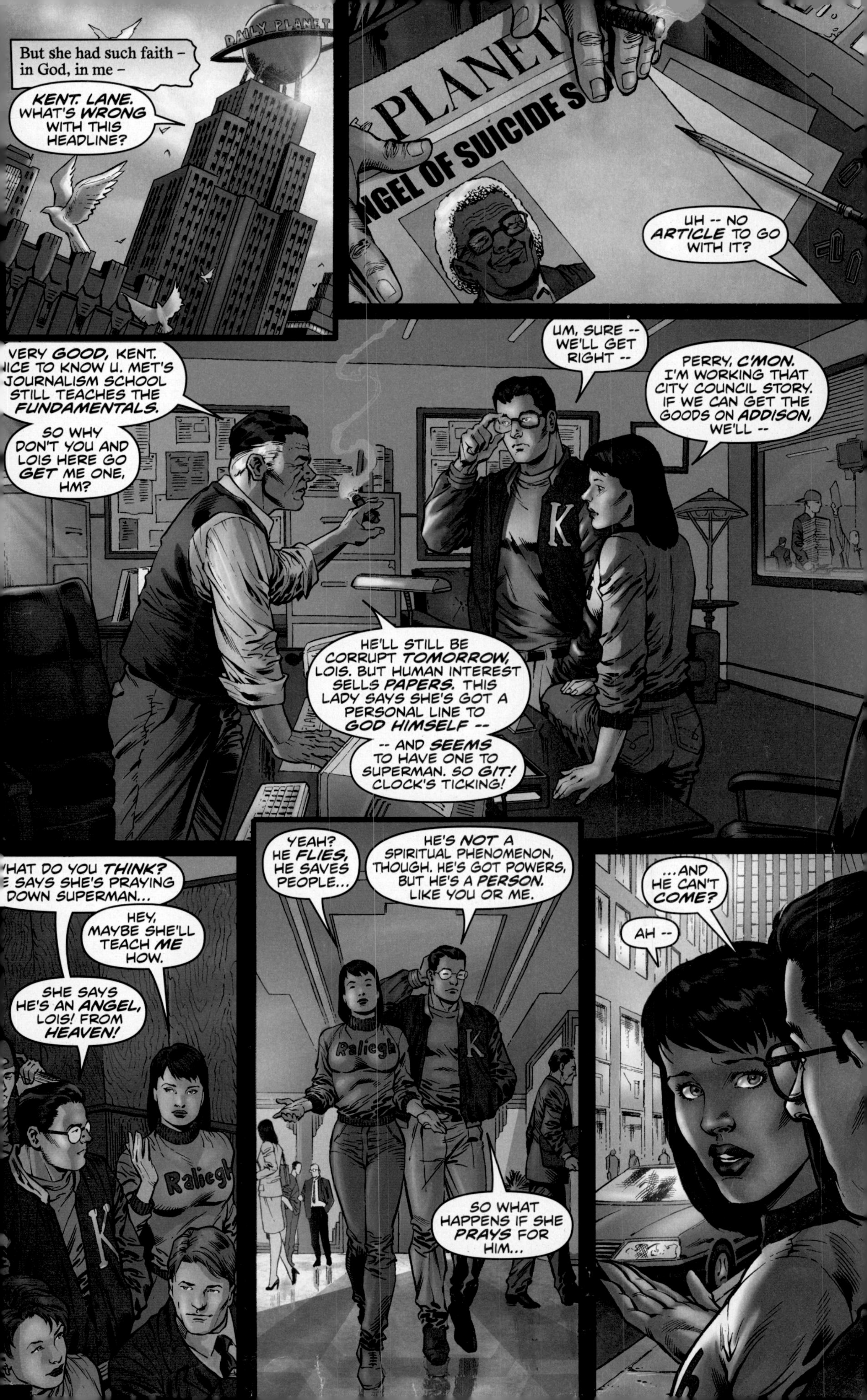
But she had such faith – in God, in me –
DAILY PLANET
KENT. LANE. WHAT'S WRONG WITH THIS HEADLINE?
PLANET
ANGEL OF SUICIDE S
UH -- NO ARTICLE TO GO WITH IT?
VERY GOOD, KENT. NICE TO KNOW U. MET'S JOURNALISM SCHOOL STILL TEACHES THE FUNDAMENTALS.
SO WHY DON'T YOU AND LOIS HERE GO GET ME ONE, HM?
UM, SURE -- WE'LL GET RIGHT --
PERRY, C'MON. I'M WORKING THAT CITY COUNCIL STORY. IF WE CAN GET THE GOODS ON ADDISON, WE'LL --
HE'LL STILL BE CORRUPT TOMORROW, LOIS. BUT HUMAN INTEREST SELLS PAPERS. THIS LADY SAYS SHE'S GOT A PERSONAL LINE TO GOD HIMSELF --
-- AND SEEMS TO HAVE ONE TO SUPERMAN. SO GIT! CLOCK'S TICKING!
WHAT DO YOU THINK? SHE SAYS SHE'S PRAYING DOWN SUPERMAN...
HEY, MAYBE SHE'LL TEACH ME HOW.
SHE SAYS HE'S AN ANGEL, LOIS! FROM HEAVEN!
Raliegh
K
YEAH? HE FLIES, HE SAVES PEOPLE...
HE'S NOT A SPIRITUAL PHENOMENON, THOUGH. HE'S GOT POWERS, BUT HE'S A PERSON. LIKE YOU OR ME.
Raliegh
K
SO WHAT HAPPENS IF SHE PRAYS FOR HIM...
...AND HE CAN'T COME?
AH --

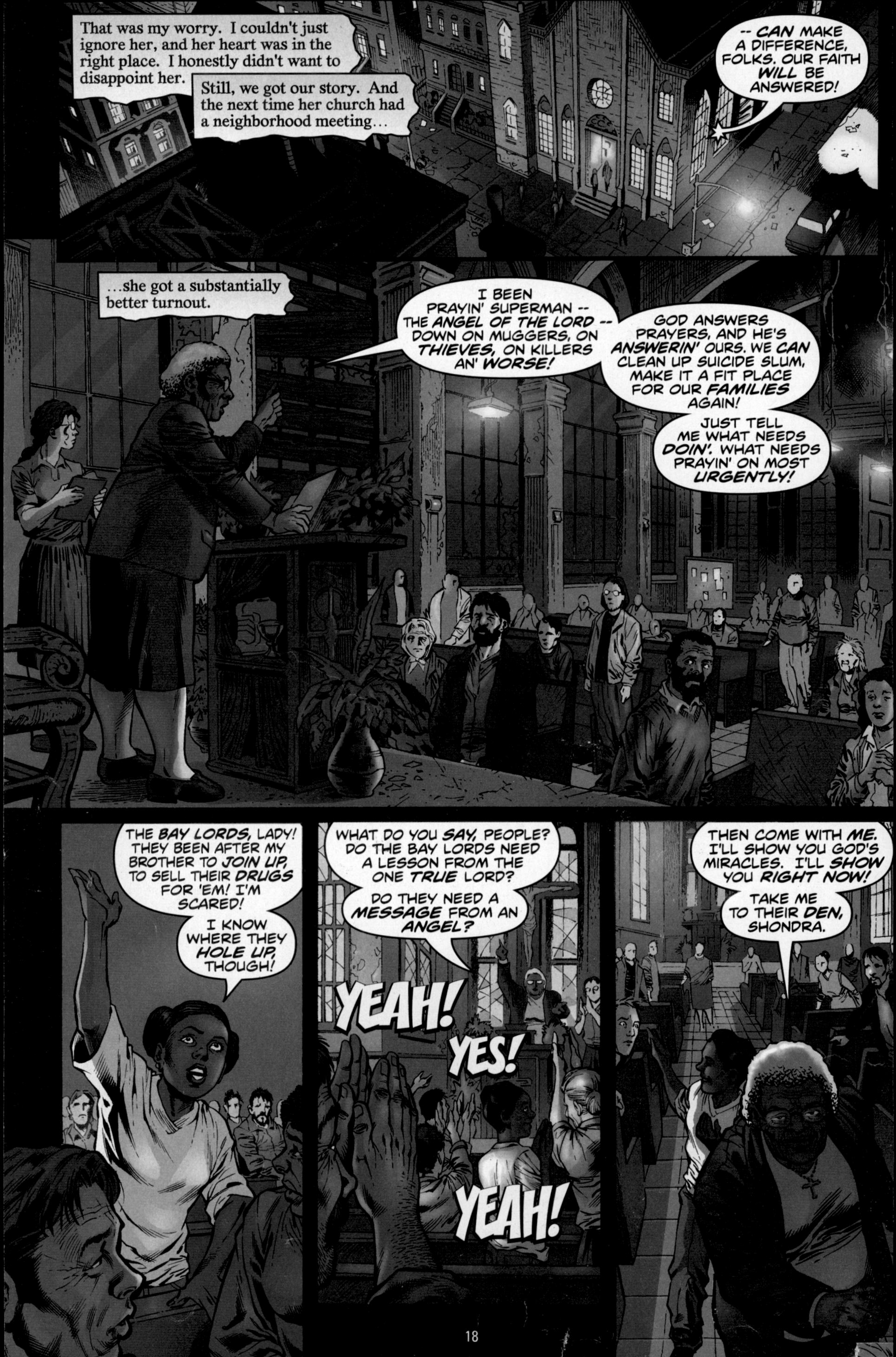
That was my worry. I couldn't just ignore her, and her heart was in the right place. I honestly didn't want to disappoint her.
Still, we got our story. And the next time her church had a neighborhood meeting…
-- CAN MAKE A DIFFERENCE, FOLKS. OUR FAITH WILL BE ANSWERED!
…she got a substantially better turnout.
I BEEN PRAYIN' SUPERMAN -- THE ANGEL OF THE LORD -- DOWN ON MUGGERS, ON THIEVES, ON KILLERS AN' WORSE!
GOD ANSWERS PRAYERS, AND HE'S ANSWERIN' OURS. WE CAN CLEAN UP SUICIDE SLUM, MAKE IT A FIT PLACE FOR OUR FAMILIES AGAIN!
JUST TELL ME WHAT NEEDS DOIN'. WHAT NEEDS PRAYIN' ON MOST URGENTLY!
THE BAY LORDS, LADY! THEY BEEN AFTER MY BROTHER TO JOIN UP, TO SELL THEIR DRUGS FOR 'EM! I'M SCARED!
I KNOW WHERE THEY HOLE UP, THOUGH!
WHAT DO YOU SAY, PEOPLE? DO THE BAY LORDS NEED A LESSON FROM THE ONE TRUE LORD?
DO THEY NEED A MESSAGE FROM AN ANGEL?
YEAH!
YES!
YEAH!
THEN COME WITH ME. I'LL SHOW YOU GOD'S MIRACLES. I'LL SHOW YOU RIGHT NOW!
TAKE ME TO THEIR DEN, SHONDRA.

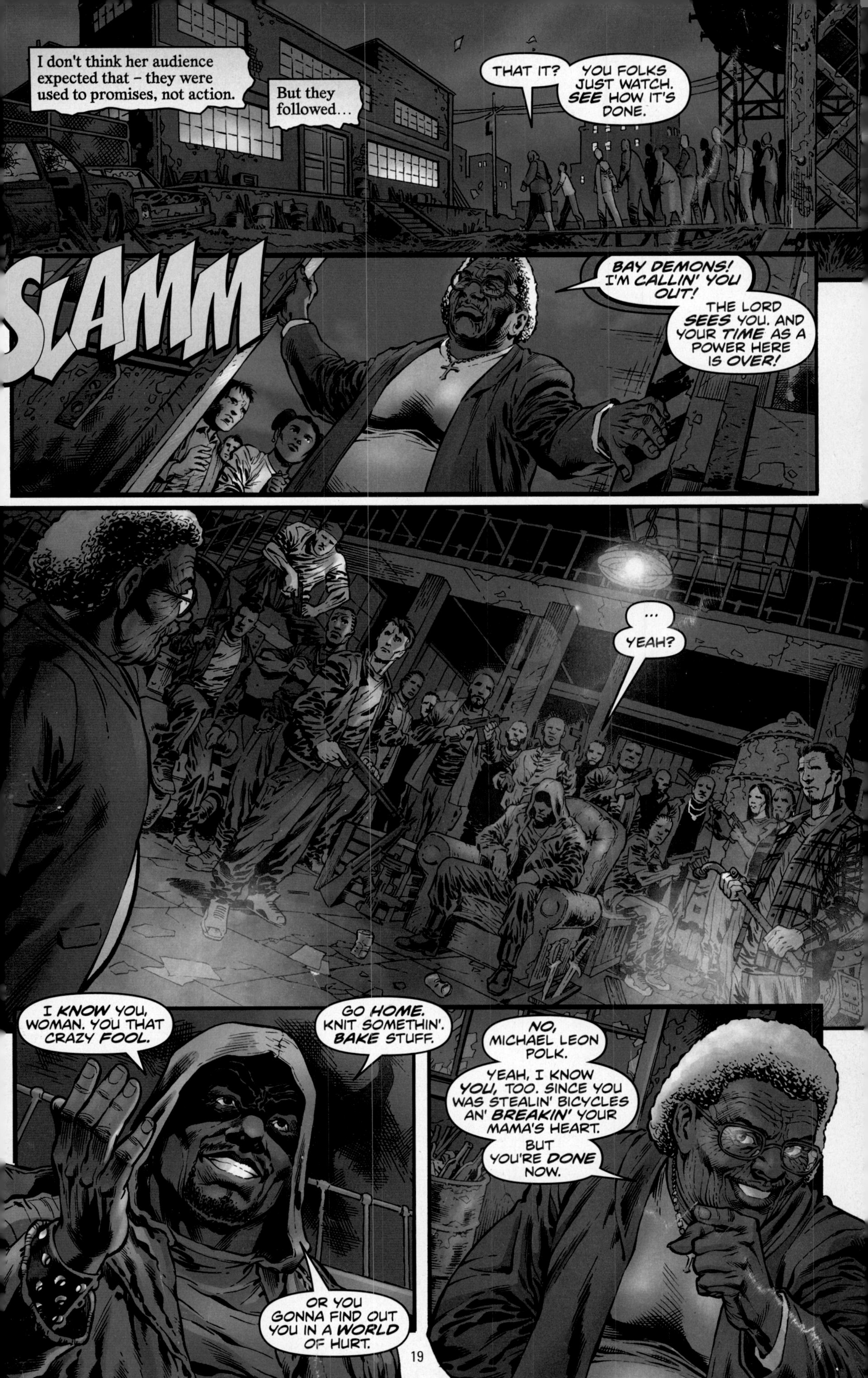
I don't think her audience expected that – they were used to promises, not action.
But they followed...
THAT IT?
YOU FOLKS JUST WATCH. SEE HOW IT'S DONE.
SLAMM
BAY DEMONS! I'M CALLIN' YOU OUT!
THE LORD SEES YOU. AND YOUR TIME AS A POWER HERE IS OVER!
... YEAH?
I KNOW YOU, WOMAN. YOU THAT CRAZY FOOL.
GO HOME. KNIT SOMETHIN'. BAKE STUFF.
OR YOU GONNA FIND OUT YOU IN A WORLD OF HURT.
NO, MICHAEL LEON POLK.
YEAH, I KNOW YOU, TOO. SINCE YOU WAS STEALIN' BICYCLES AN' BREAKIN' YOUR MAMA'S HEART.
BUT YOU'RE DONE NOW.

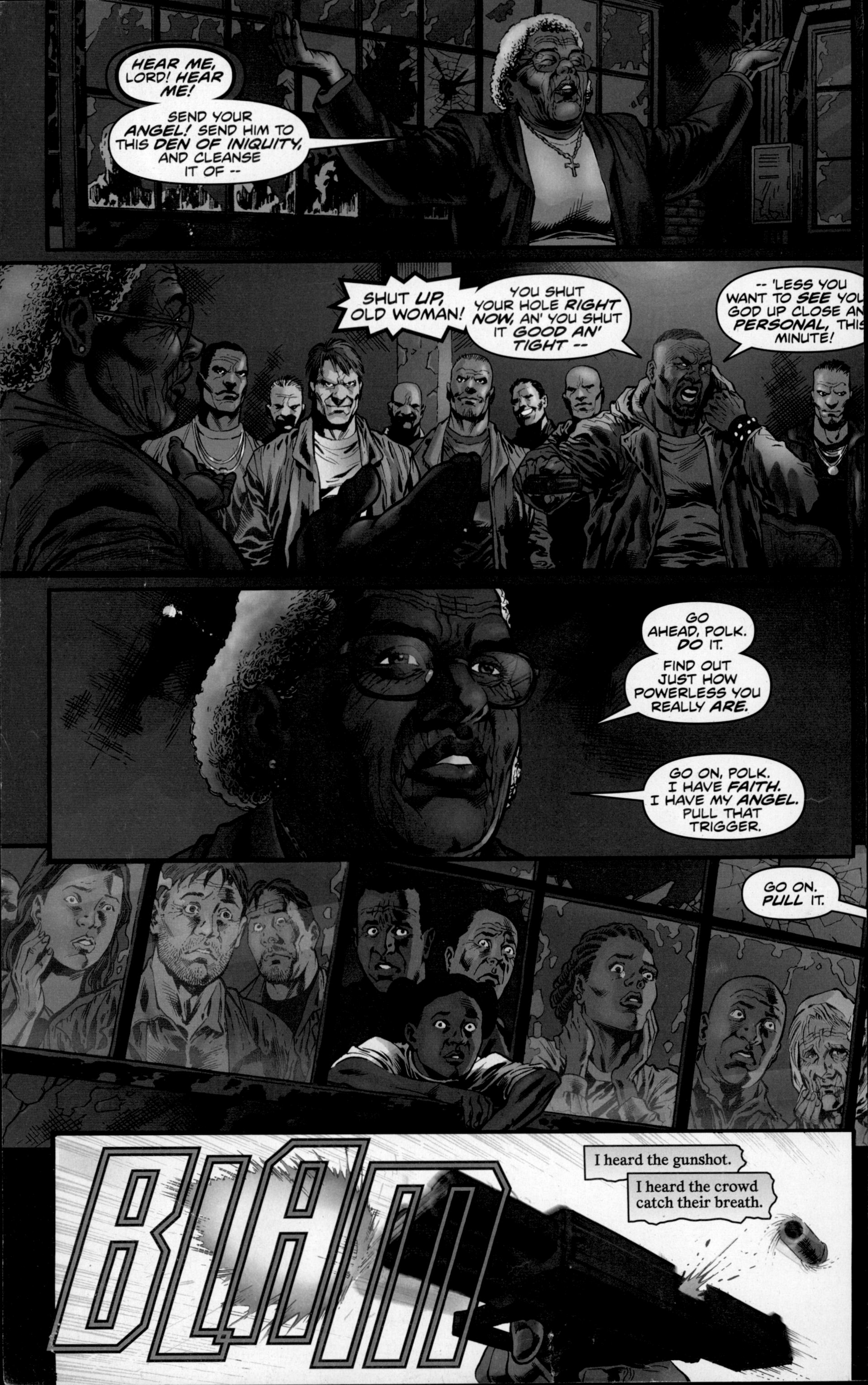
HEAR ME, LORD! HEAR ME!
SEND YOUR ANGEL! SEND HIM TO THIS DEN OF INIQUITY, AND CLEANSE IT OF --
SHUT UP, OLD WOMAN!
YOU SHUT YOUR HOLE RIGHT NOW, AN' YOU SHUT IT GOOD AN' TIGHT --
-- 'LESS YOU WANT TO SEE YOU GOD UP CLOSE AN PERSONAL, THIS MINUTE!
GO AHEAD, POLK. DO IT.
FIND OUT JUST HOW POWERLESS YOU REALLY ARE.
GO ON, POLK. I HAVE FAITH. I HAVE MY ANGEL. PULL THAT TRIGGER.
GO ON. PULL IT.
BLAM
I heard the gunshot.
I heard the crowd catch their breath.

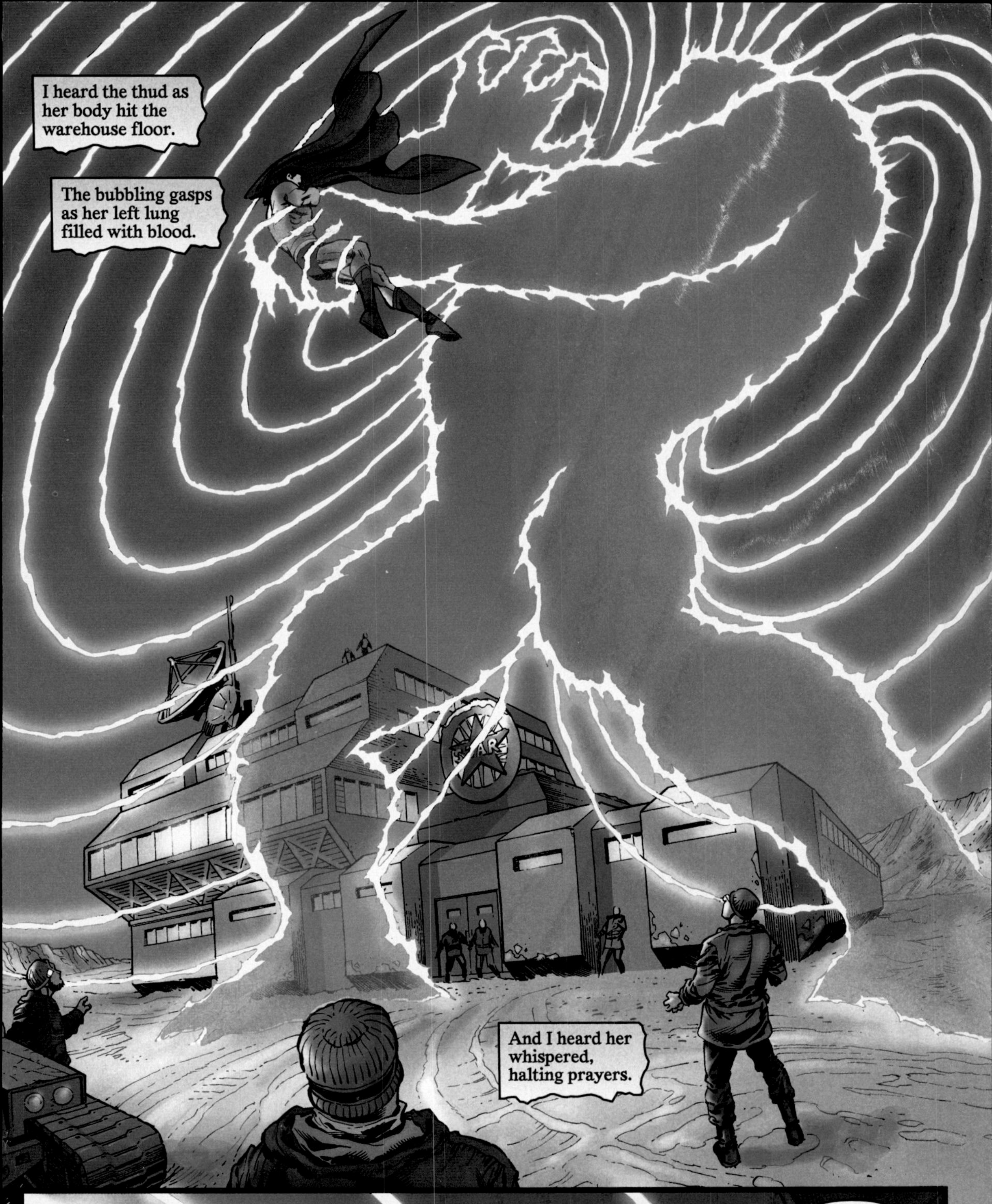
I heard the thud as her body hit the warehouse floor.
The bubbling gasps as her left lung filled with blood.
And I heard her whispered, halting prayers.

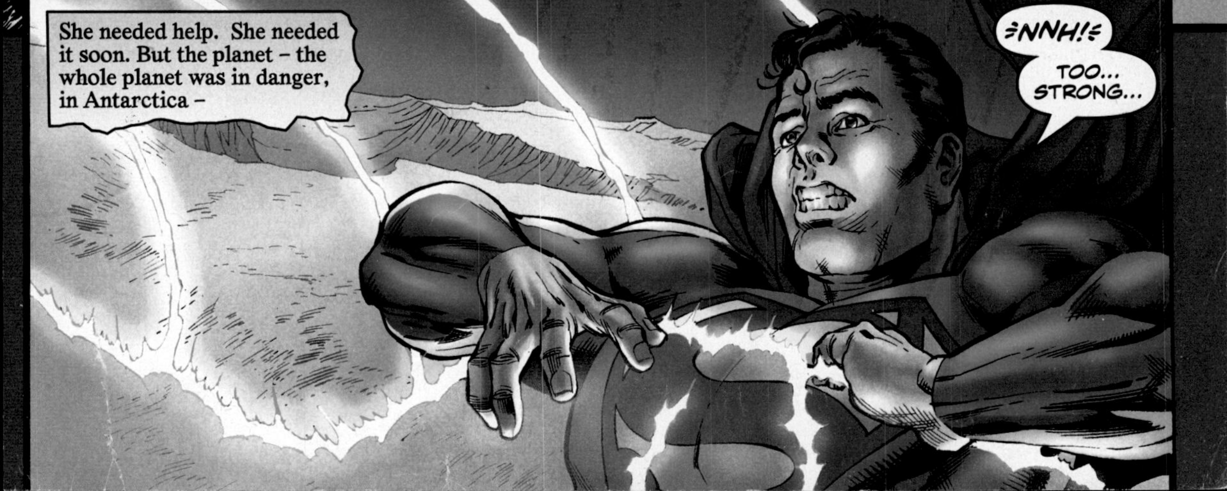
She needed help. She needed it soon. But the planet – the whole planet was in danger, in Antarctica –
NNH!
TOO... STRONG...

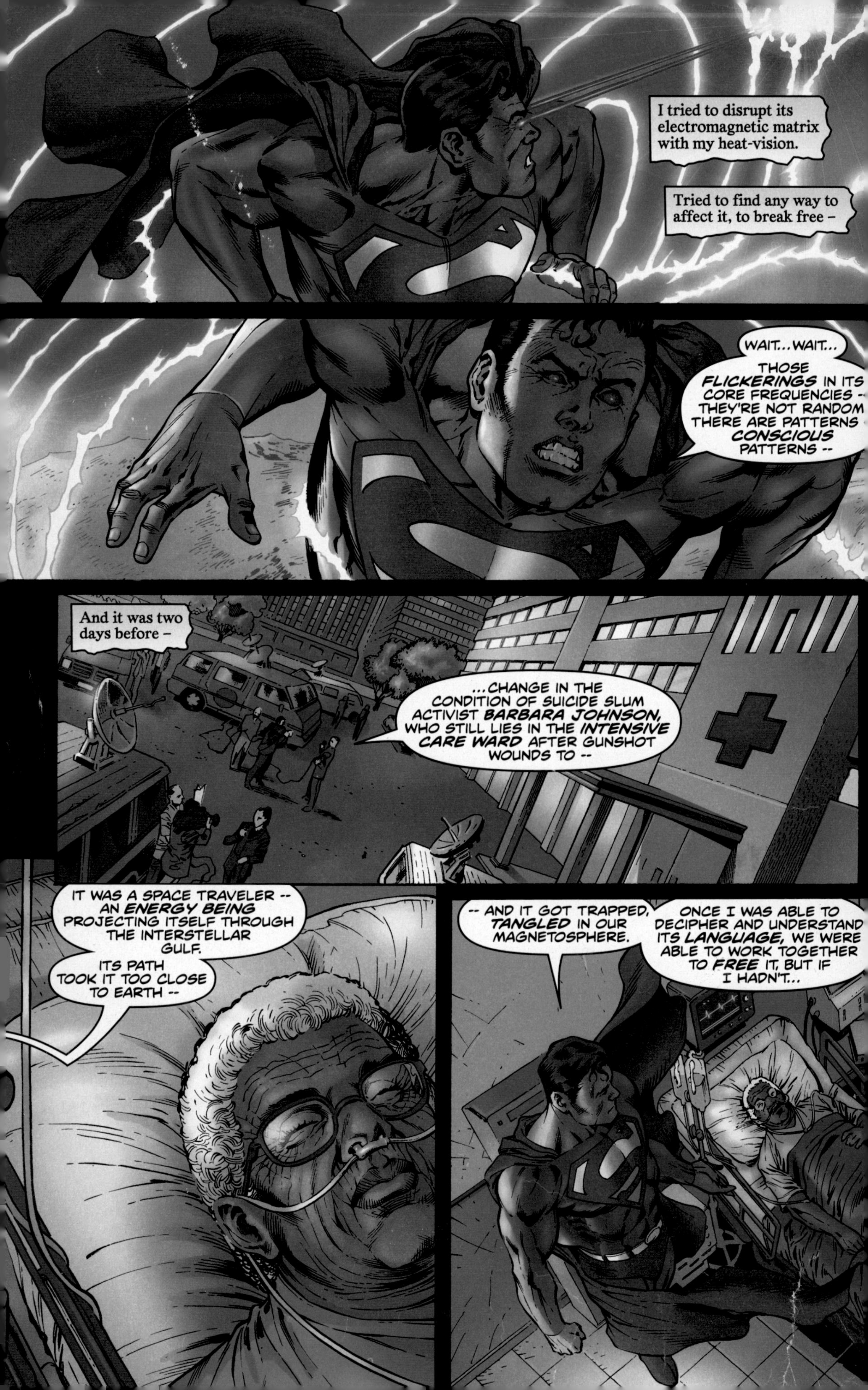
I tried to disrupt its electromagnetic matrix with my heat-vision.
Tried to find any way to affect it, to break free –
WAIT... WAIT... THOSE FLICKERINGS IN ITS CORE FREQUENCIES -- THEY'RE NOT RANDOM THERE ARE PATTERNS CONSCIOUS PATTERNS --
And it was two days before –
...CHANGE IN THE CONDITION OF SUICIDE SLUM ACTIVIST BARBARA JOHNSON, WHO STILL LIES IN THE INTENSIVE CARE WARD AFTER GUNSHOT WOUNDS TO --
IT WAS A SPACE TRAVELER -- AN ENERGY BEING PROJECTING ITSELF THROUGH THE INTERSTELLAR GULF.
ITS PATH TOOK IT TOO CLOSE TO EARTH --
-- AND IT GOT TRAPPED, TANGLED IN OUR MAGNETOSPHERE.
ONCE I WAS ABLE TO DECIPHER AND UNDERSTAND ITS LANGUAGE, WE WERE ABLE TO WORK TOGETHER TO FREE IT, BUT IF I HADN'T...

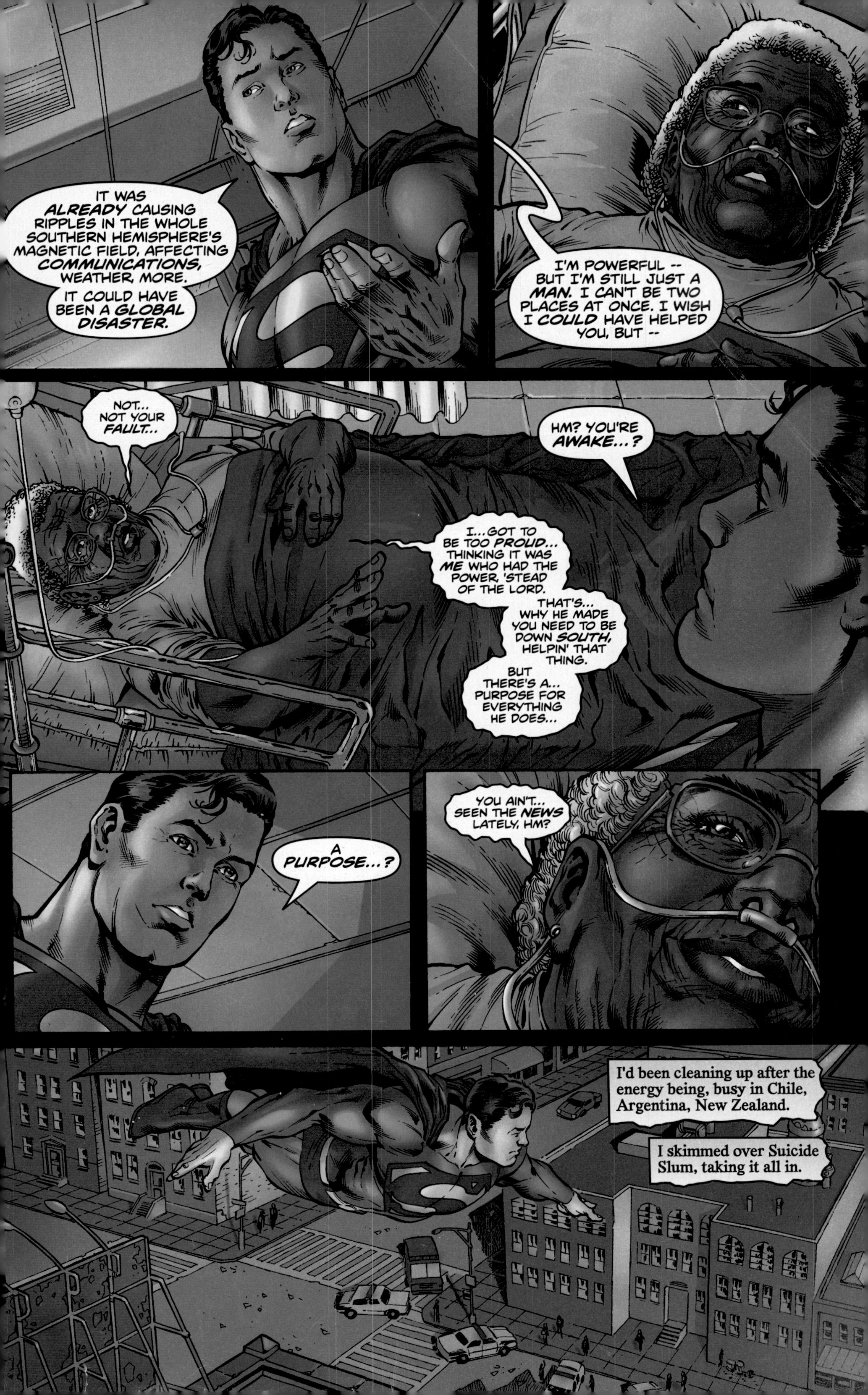
IT WAS ALREADY CAUSING RIPPLES IN THE WHOLE SOUTHERN HEMISPHERE'S MAGNETIC FIELD, AFFECTING COMMUNICATIONS, WEATHER, MORE.
IT COULD HAVE BEEN A GLOBAL DISASTER.
I'M POWERFUL -- BUT I'M STILL JUST A MAN. I CAN'T BE TWO PLACES AT ONCE. I WISH I COULD HAVE HELPED YOU, BUT --
NOT... NOT YOUR FAULT...
HM? YOU'RE AWAKE...?
I...GOT TO BE TOO PROUD... THINKING IT WAS ME WHO HAD THE POWER, 'STEAD OF THE LORD.
THAT'S... WHY HE MADE YOU NEED TO BE DOWN SOUTH, HELPIN' THAT THING.
BUT THERE'S A... PURPOSE FOR EVERYTHING HE DOES...
A PURPOSE...?
YOU AIN'T... SEEN THE NEWS LATELY, HM?
I'd been cleaning up after the energy being, busy in Chile, Argentina, New Zealand.
I skimmed over Suicide Slum, taking it all in.

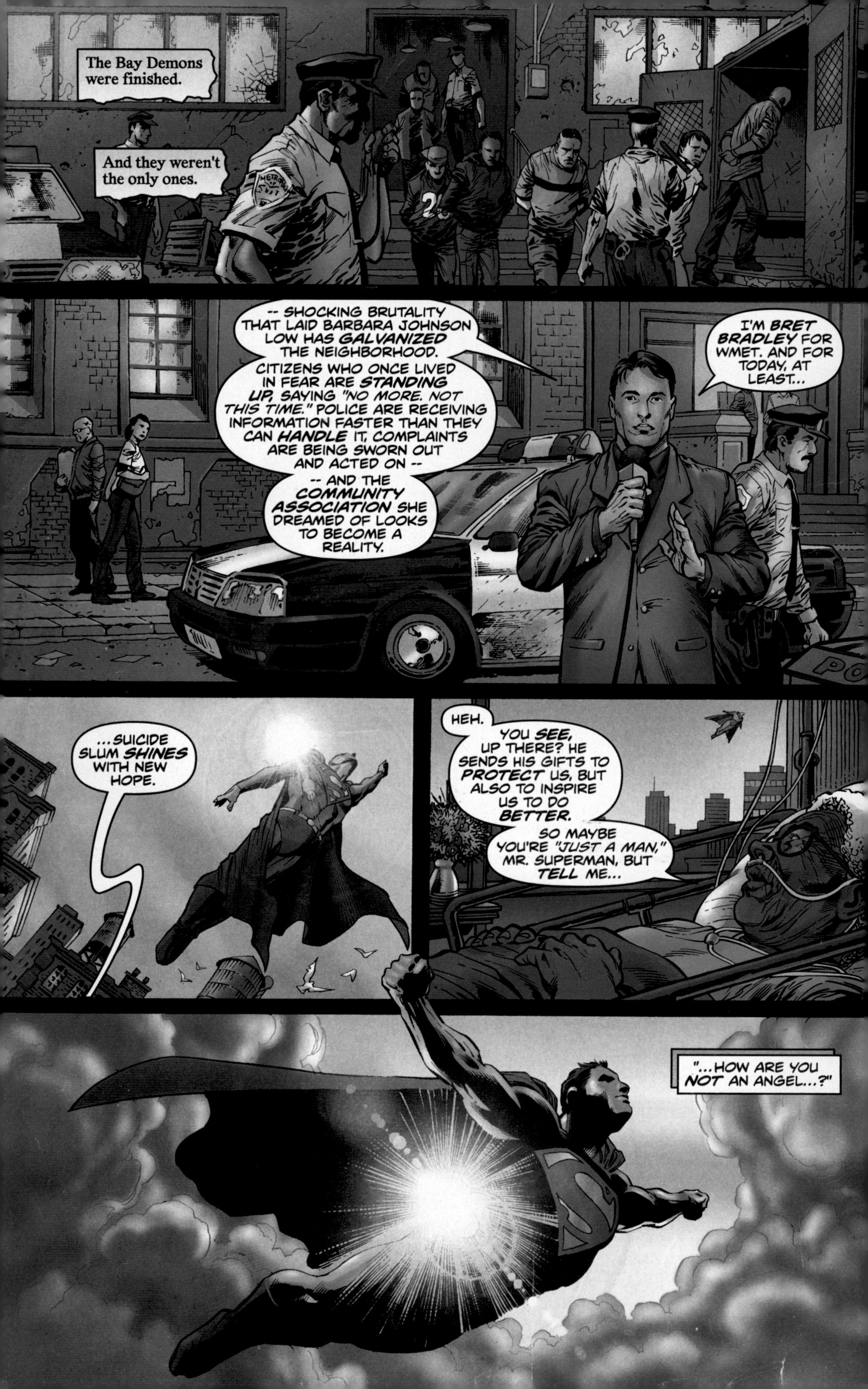
The Bay Demons were finished.
And they weren't the only ones.
-- SHOCKING BRUTALITY THAT LAID BARBARA JOHNSON LOW HAS GALVANIZED THE NEIGHBORHOOD.
CITIZENS WHO ONCE LIVED IN FEAR ARE STANDING UP, SAYING "NO MORE. NOT THIS TIME." POLICE ARE RECEIVING INFORMATION FASTER THAN THEY CAN HANDLE IT, COMPLAINTS ARE BEING SWORN OUT AND ACTED ON --
-- AND THE COMMUNITY ASSOCIATION SHE DREAMED OF LOOKS TO BECOME A REALITY.
I'M BRET BRADLEY FOR WMET. AND FOR TODAY, AT LEAST...
...SUICIDE SLUM SHINES WITH NEW HOPE.
HEH.
YOU SEE, UP THERE? HE SENDS HIS GIFTS TO PROTECT US, BUT ALSO TO INSPIRE US TO DO BETTER.
SO MAYBE YOU'RE "JUST A MAN," MR. SUPERMAN, BUT TELL ME...
"...HOW ARE YOU NOT AN ANGEL...?"

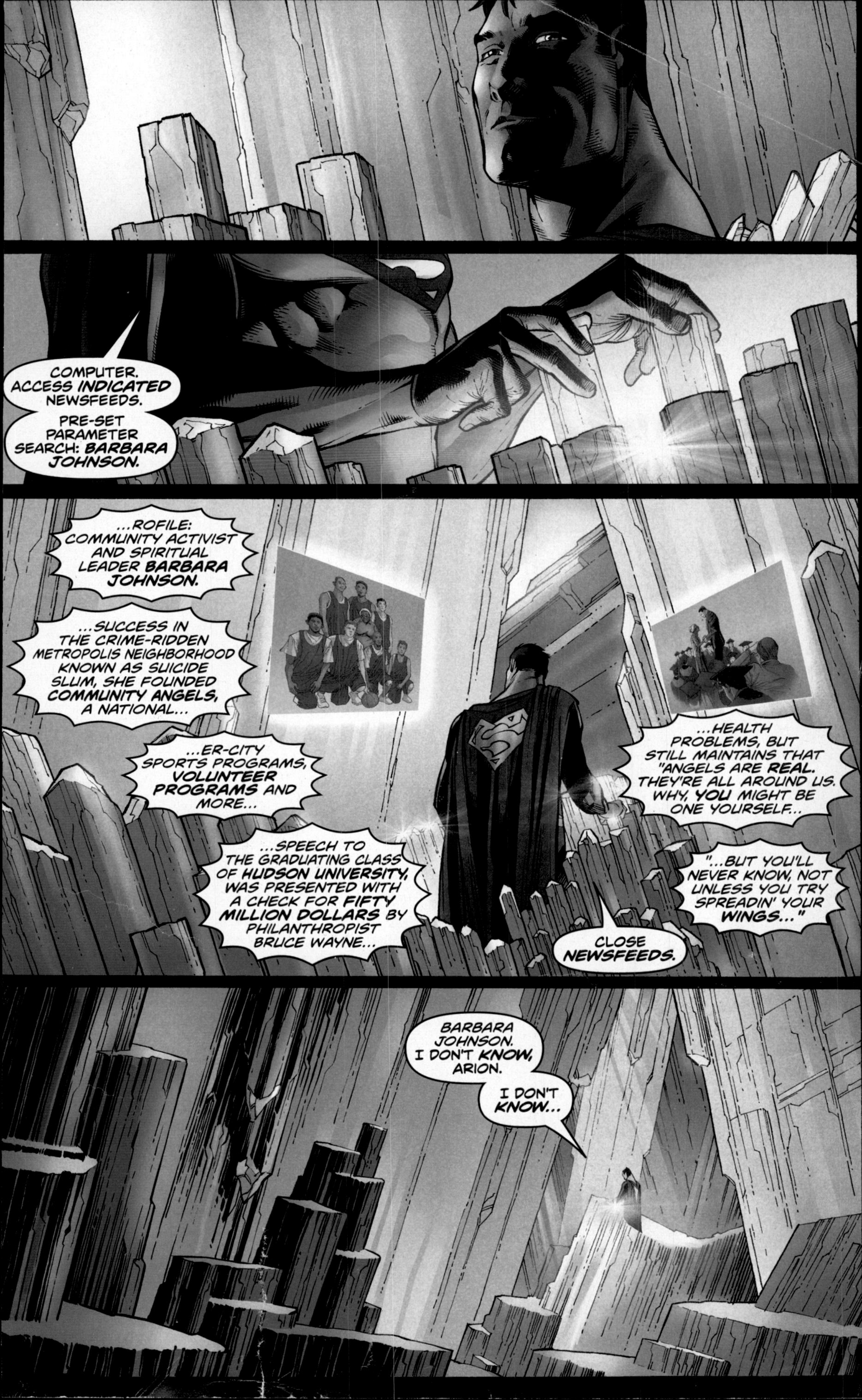
COMPUTER. ACCESS INDICATED NEWSFEEDS.
PRE-SET PARAMETER SEARCH: BARBARA JOHNSON.
...ROFILE: COMMUNITY ACTIVIST AND SPIRITUAL LEADER BARBARA JOHNSON.
...SUCCESS IN THE CRIME-RIDDEN METROPOLIS NEIGHBORHOOD KNOWN AS SUICIDE SLUM, SHE FOUNDED COMMUNITY ANGELS, A NATIONAL...
...ER-CITY SPORTS PROGRAMS, VOLUNTEER PROGRAMS AND MORE...
...SPEECH TO THE GRADUATING CLASS OF HUDSON UNIVERSITY, WAS PRESENTED WITH A CHECK FOR FIFTY MILLION DOLLARS BY PHILANTHROPIST BRUCE WAYNE...
...HEALTH PROBLEMS, BUT STILL MAINTAINS THAT "ANGELS ARE REAL. THEY'RE ALL AROUND US. WHY, YOU MIGHT BE ONE YOURSELF...
"...BUT YOU'LL NEVER KNOW, NOT UNLESS YOU TRY SPREADIN' YOUR WINGS..."
CLOSE NEWSFEEDS.
BARBARA JOHNSON. I DON'T KNOW, ARION.
I DON'T KNOW...

Redemption Chapter One Cover to Action Comics 848 by Brad Walker and Robin Riggs

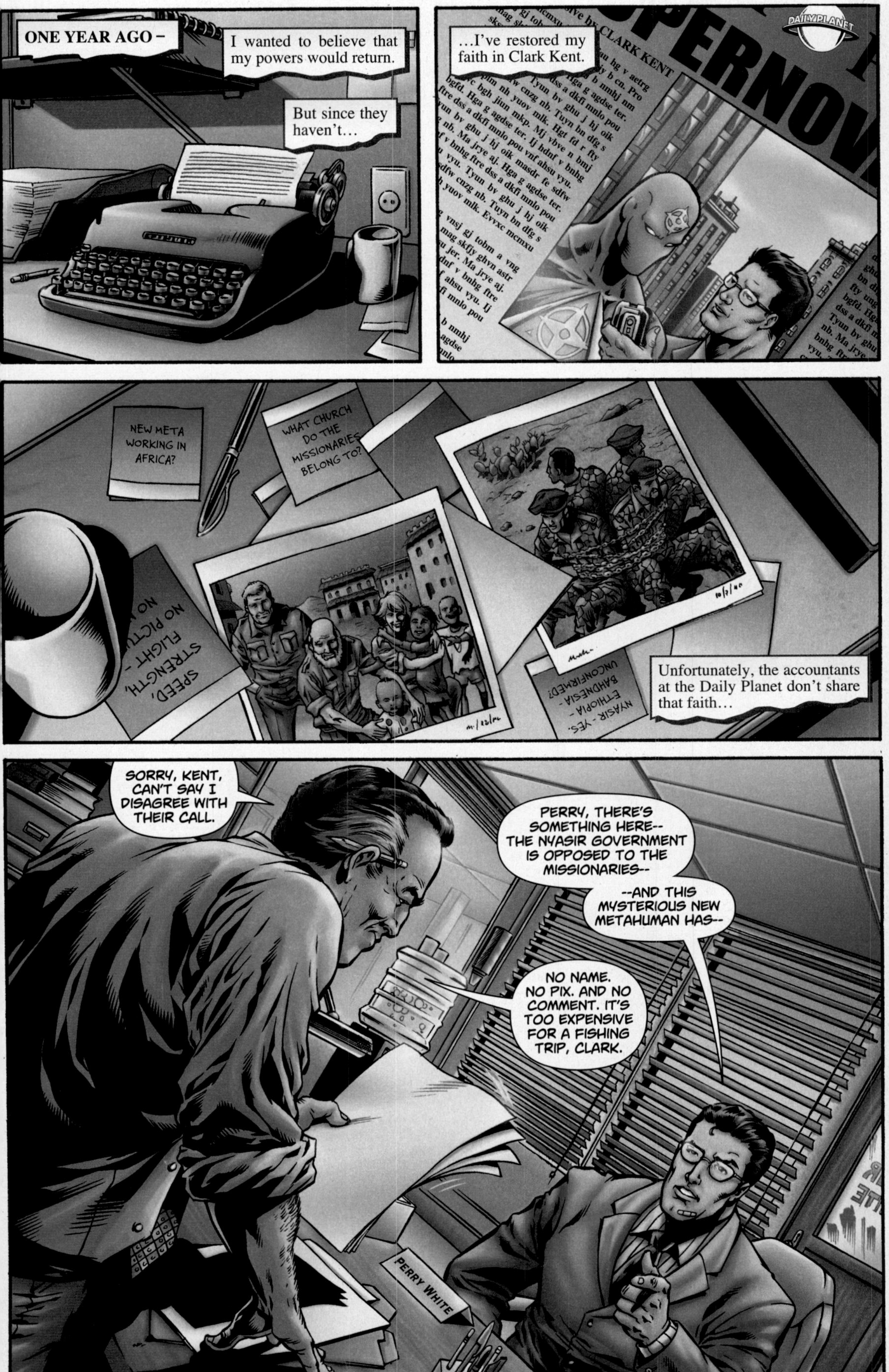
ONE YEAR AGO –
I wanted to believe that my powers would return.
But since they haven't…
DAILY PLANET
by CLARK KENT
…I've restored my faith in Clark Kent.
NEW META WORKING IN AFRICA?
WHAT CHURCH DO THE MISSIONARIES BELONG TO?
SPEED, STRENGTH, FLIGHT -
NYASIR - YES. ETHIOPIA - BANDENSIA UNCONFIRMED?
Unfortunately, the accountants at the Daily Planet don't share that faith…
SORRY, KENT, CAN'T SAY I DISAGREE WITH THEIR CALL.
PERRY, THERE'S SOMETHING HERE-- THE NYASIR GOVERNMENT IS OPPOSED TO THE MISSIONARIES--
--AND THIS MYSTERIOUS NEW METAHUMAN HAS--
NO NAME. NO PIX. AND NO COMMENT. IT'S TOO EXPENSIVE FOR A FISHING TRIP, CLARK.
PERRY WHITE

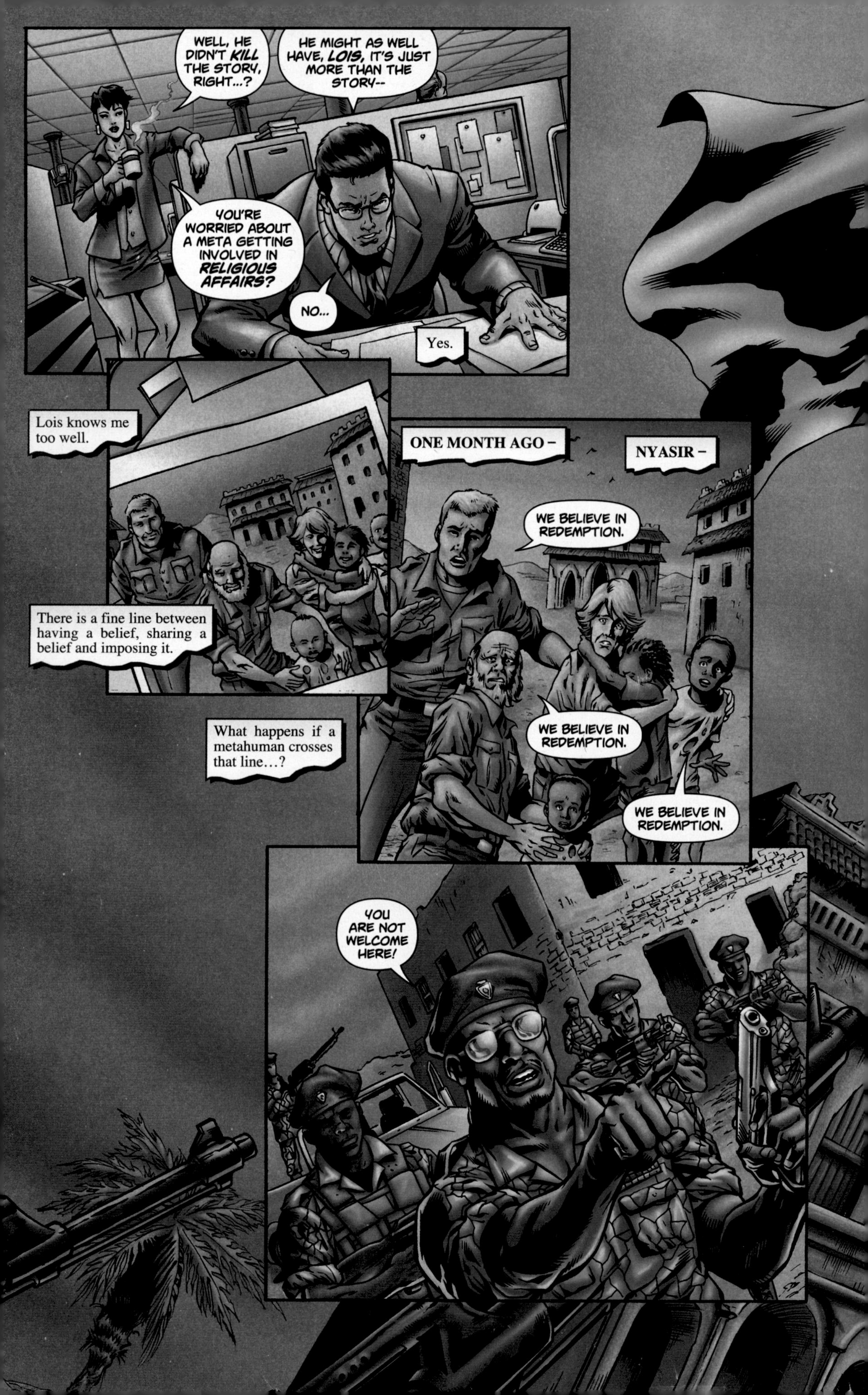
WELL, HE DIDN'T KILL THE STORY, RIGHT...?
HE MIGHT AS WELL HAVE, LOIS, IT'S JUST MORE THAN THE STORY--
YOU'RE WORRIED ABOUT A META GETTING INVOLVED IN RELIGIOUS AFFAIRS?
NO...
Yes.
Lois knows me too well.
There is a fine line between having a belief, sharing a belief and imposing it.
ONE MONTH AGO –
NYASIR –
WE BELIEVE IN REDEMPTION.
WE BELIEVE IN REDEMPTION.
WE BELIEVE IN REDEMPTION.
What happens if a metahuman crosses that line...?
YOU ARE NOT WELCOME HERE!

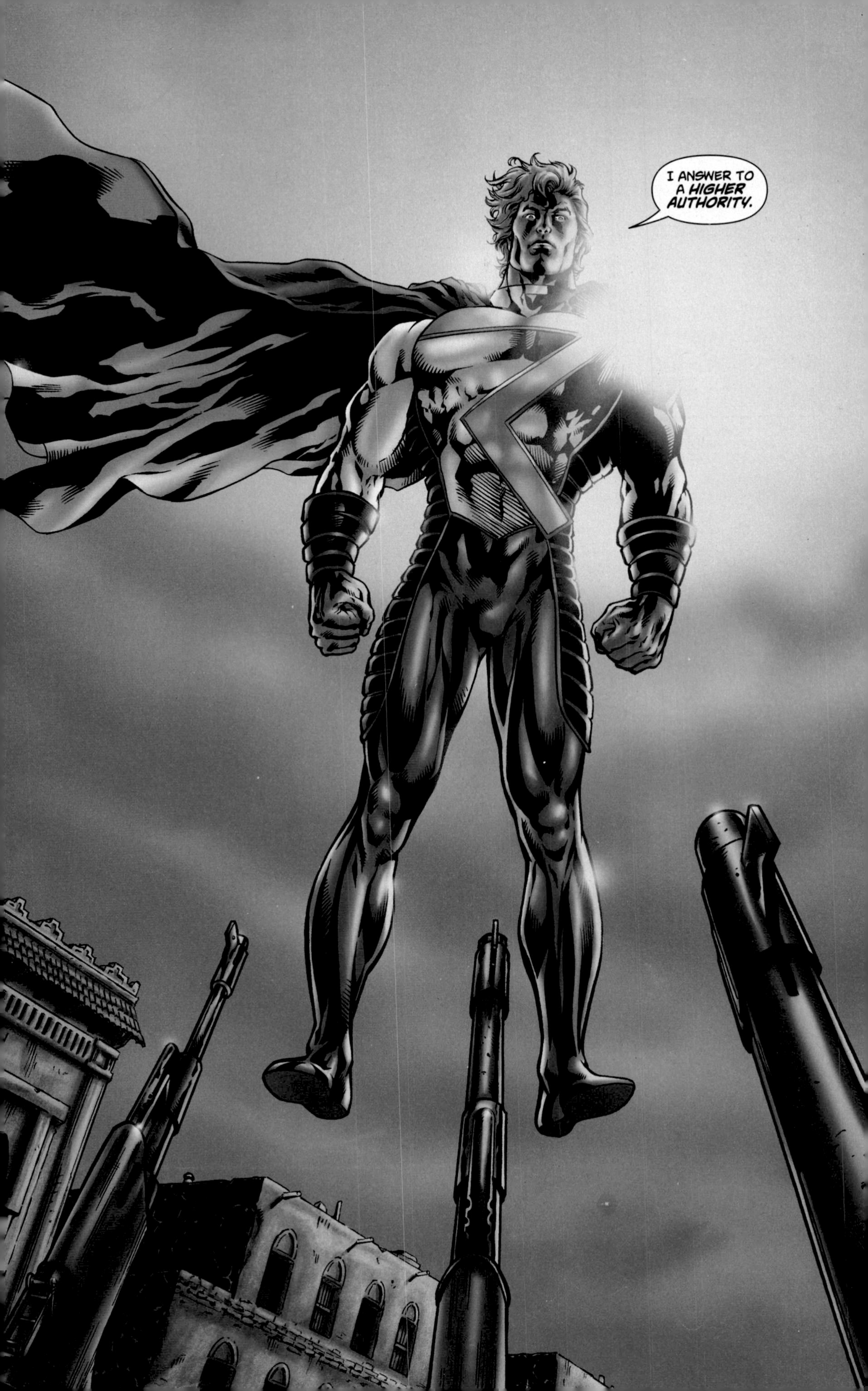
I ANSWER TO A HIGHER AUTHORITY.

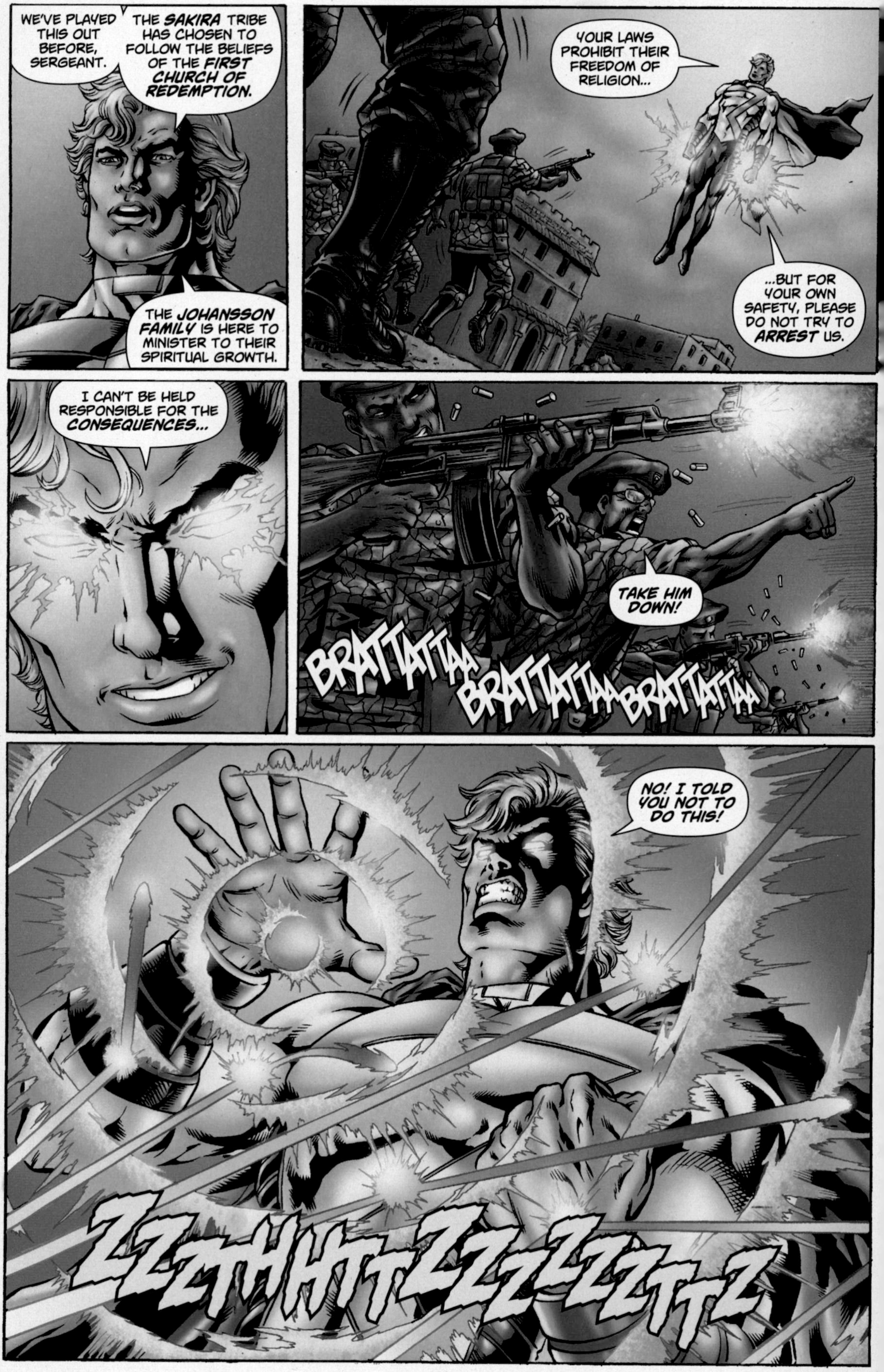
WE'VE PLAYED THIS OUT BEFORE, SERGEANT.
THE SAKIRA TRIBE HAS CHOSEN TO FOLLOW THE BELIEFS OF THE FIRST CHURCH OF REDEMPTION.
THE JOHANSSON FAMILY IS HERE TO MINISTER TO THEIR SPIRITUAL GROWTH.
YOUR LAWS PROHIBIT THEIR FREEDOM OF RELIGION...
...BUT FOR YOUR OWN SAFETY, PLEASE DO NOT TRY TO ARREST US.
I CAN'T BE HELD RESPONSIBLE FOR THE CONSEQUENCES...
TAKE HIM DOWN!
BRATTATTAA BRATTATTAA BRATTATTAA
NO! I TOLD YOU NOT TO DO THIS!
ZZZTHHTTZZZZZZZTTTZ

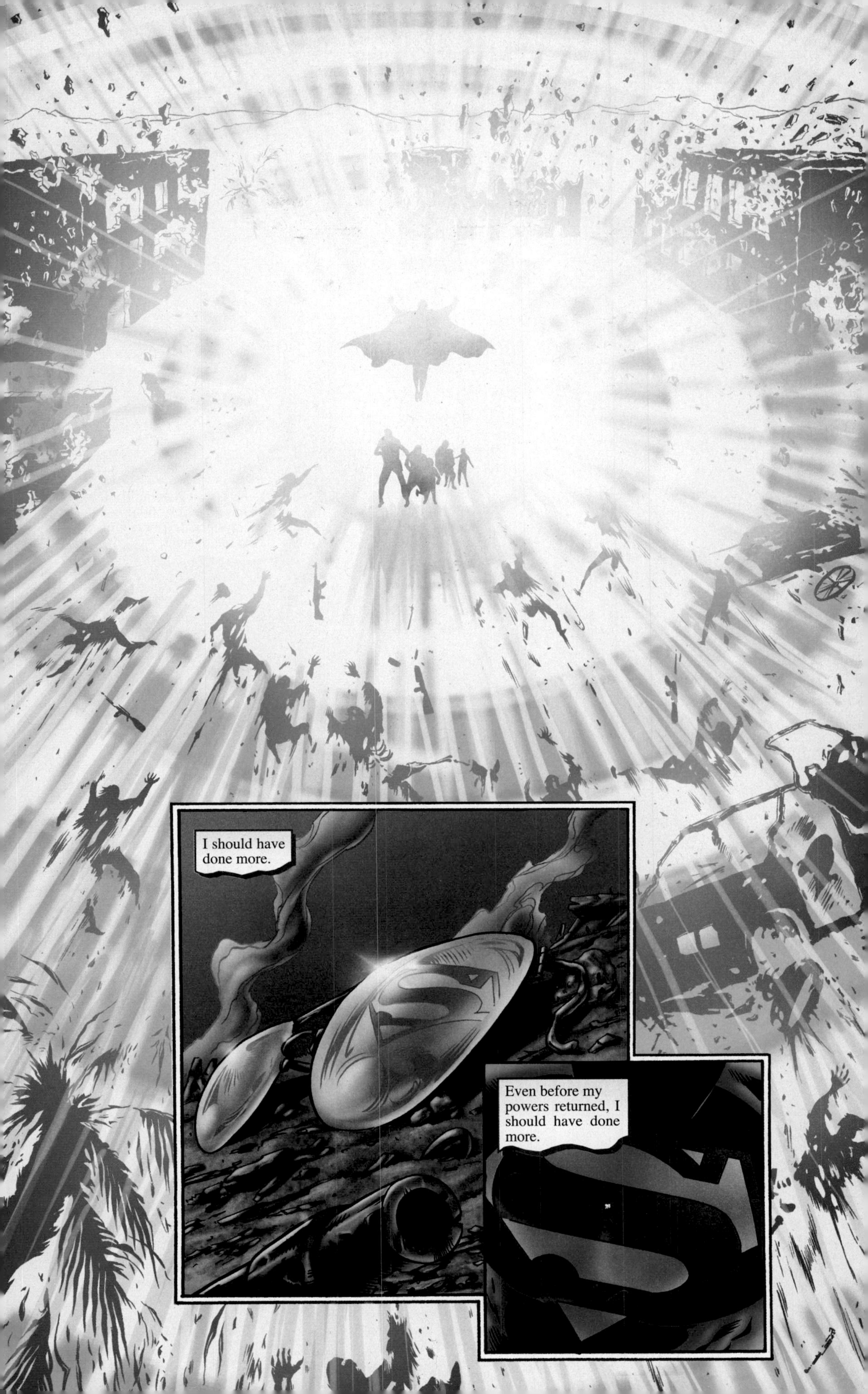
I should have done more.
Even before my powers returned, I should have done more.

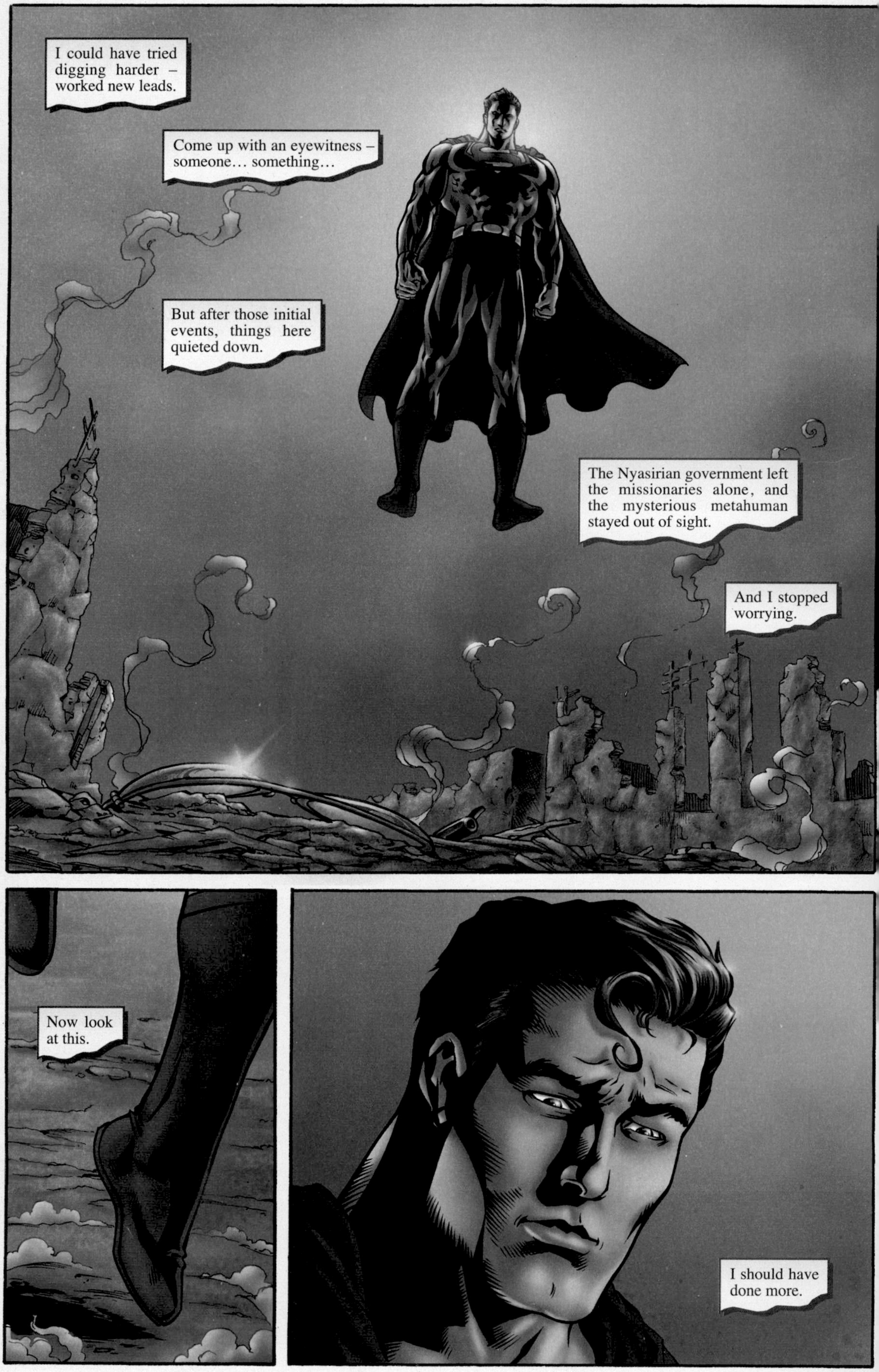
I could have tried digging harder – worked new leads.
Come up with an eyewitness – someone… something…
But after those initial events, things here quieted down.
The Nyasirian government left the missionaries alone, and the mysterious metahuman stayed out of sight.
And I stopped worrying.
Now look at this.
I should have done more.

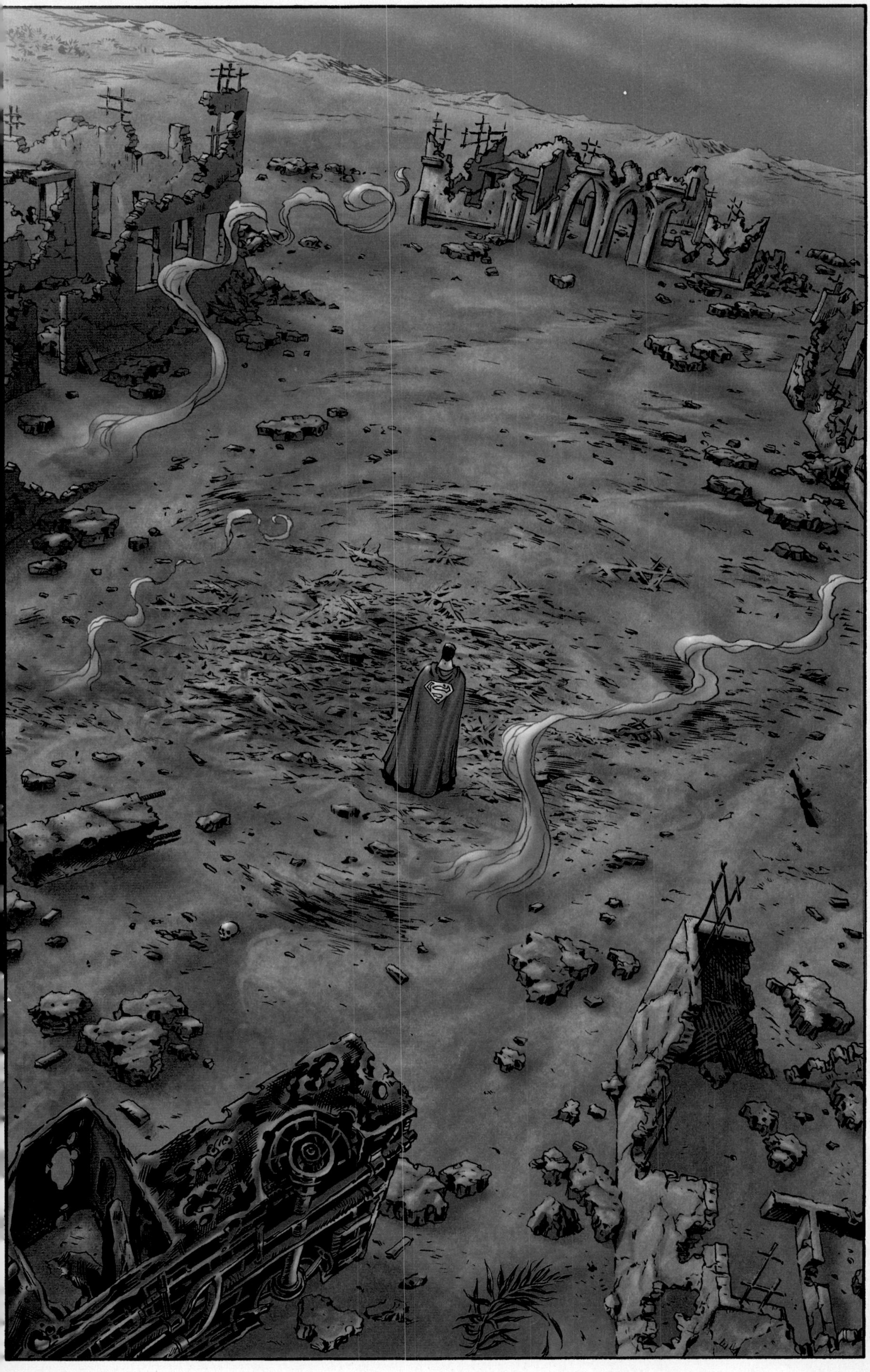

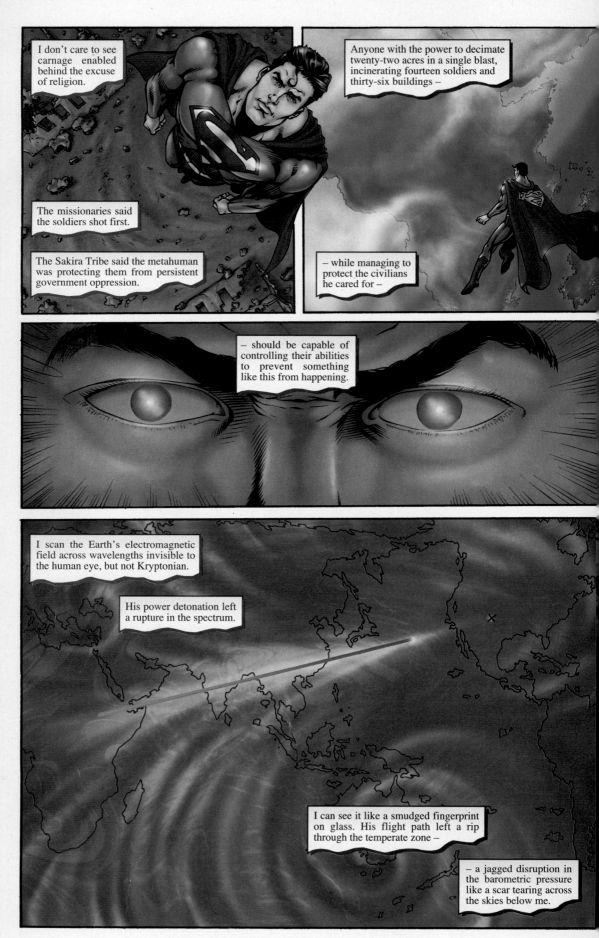

I don't care to see carnage enabled behind the excuse of religion.

The missionaries said the soldiers shot first.

The Sakira Tribe said the metahuman was protecting them from persistent government oppression.

Anyone with the power to decimate twenty-two acres in a single blast, incinerating fourteen soldiers and thirty-six buildings –

– while managing to protect the civilians he cared for –

– should be capable of controlling their abilities to prevent something like this from happening.

I scan the Earth's electromagnetic field across wavelengths invisible to the human eye, but not Kryptonian.

His power detonation left a rupture in the spectrum.

I can see it like a smudged fingerprint on glass. His flight path left a rip through the temperate zone –

– a jagged disruption in the barometric pressure like a scar tearing across the skies below me.

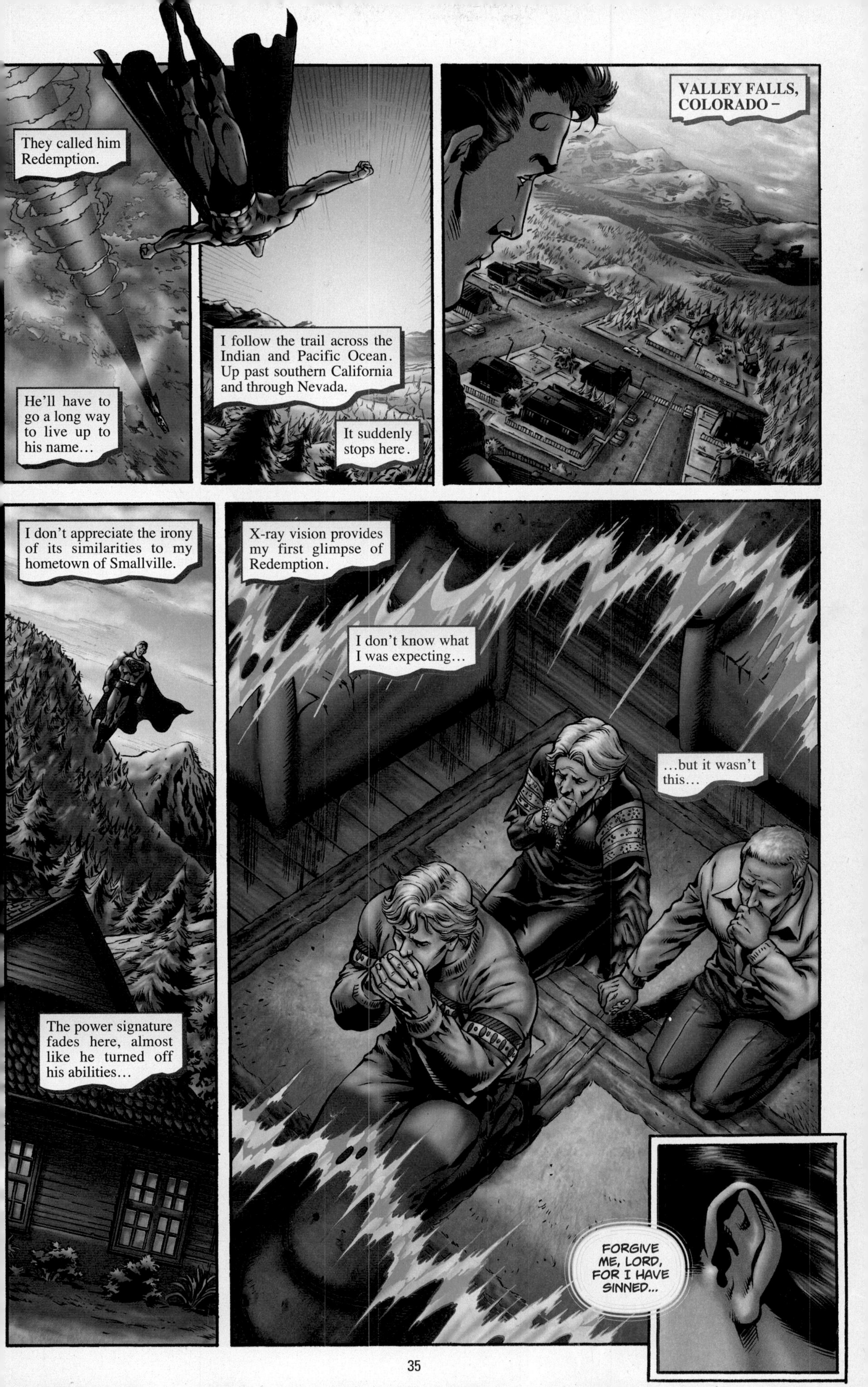
They called him Redemption.
He'll have to go a long way to live up to his name...
I follow the trail across the Indian and Pacific Ocean. Up past southern California and through Nevada.
It suddenly stops here.
VALLEY FALLS, COLORADO –
I don't appreciate the irony of its similarities to my hometown of Smallville.
The power signature fades here, almost like he turned off his abilities...
X-ray vision provides my first glimpse of Redemption.
I don't know what I was expecting...
...but it wasn't this...
FORGIVE ME, LORD, FOR I HAVE SINNED...

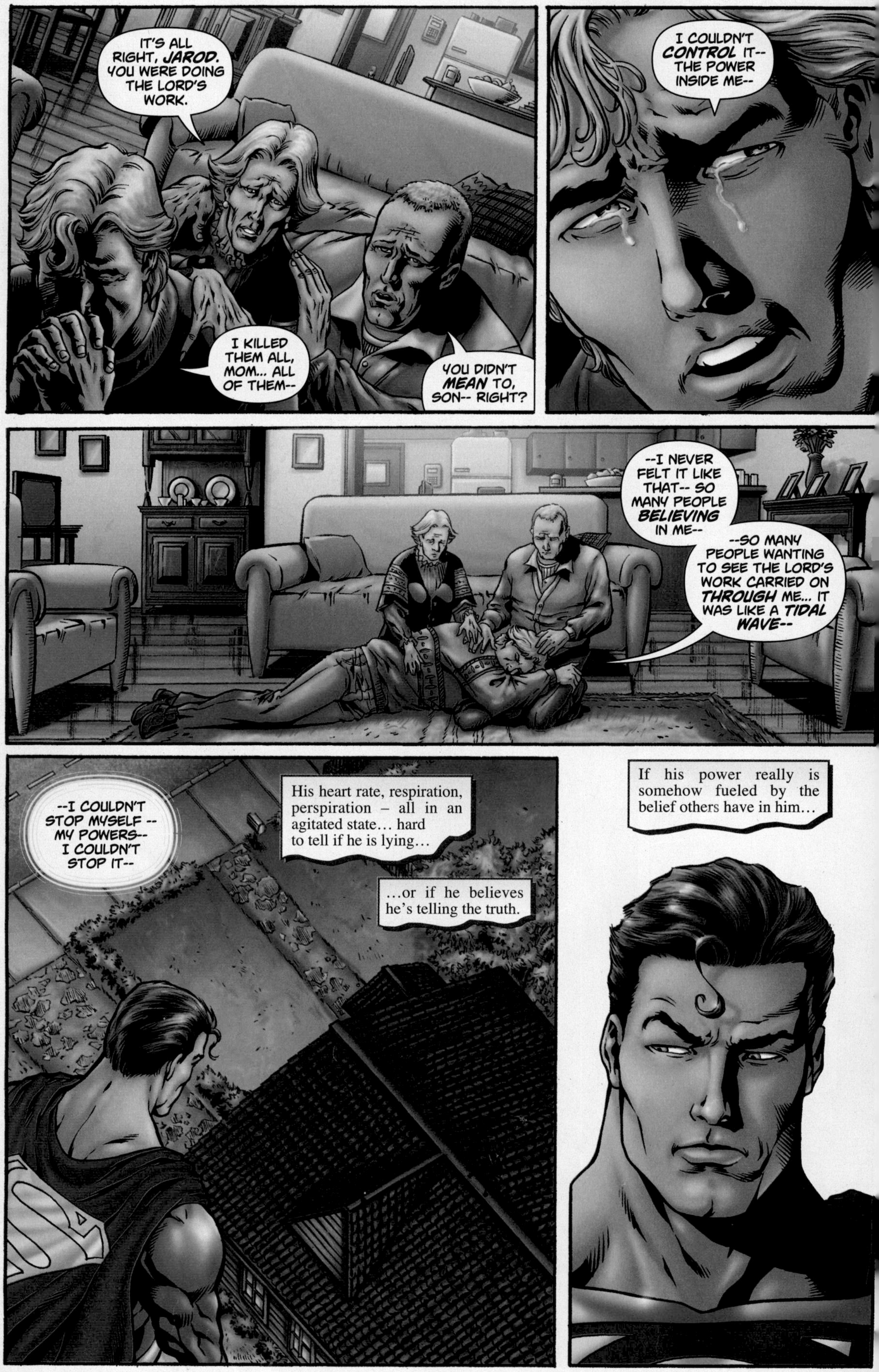
IT'S ALL RIGHT, JAROD. YOU WERE DOING THE LORD'S WORK.
I KILLED THEM ALL, MOM... ALL OF THEM--
YOU DIDN'T MEAN TO, SON-- RIGHT?
I COULDN'T CONTROL IT-- THE POWER INSIDE ME--
--I NEVER FELT IT LIKE THAT-- SO MANY PEOPLE BELIEVING IN ME--
--SO MANY PEOPLE WANTING TO SEE THE LORD'S WORK CARRIED ON THROUGH ME... IT WAS LIKE A TIDAL WAVE--
--I COULDN'T STOP MYSELF -- MY POWERS-- I COULDN'T STOP IT--
His heart rate, respiration, perspiration – all in an agitated state… hard to tell if he is lying…
…or if he believes he's telling the truth.
If his power really is somehow fueled by the belief others have in him…

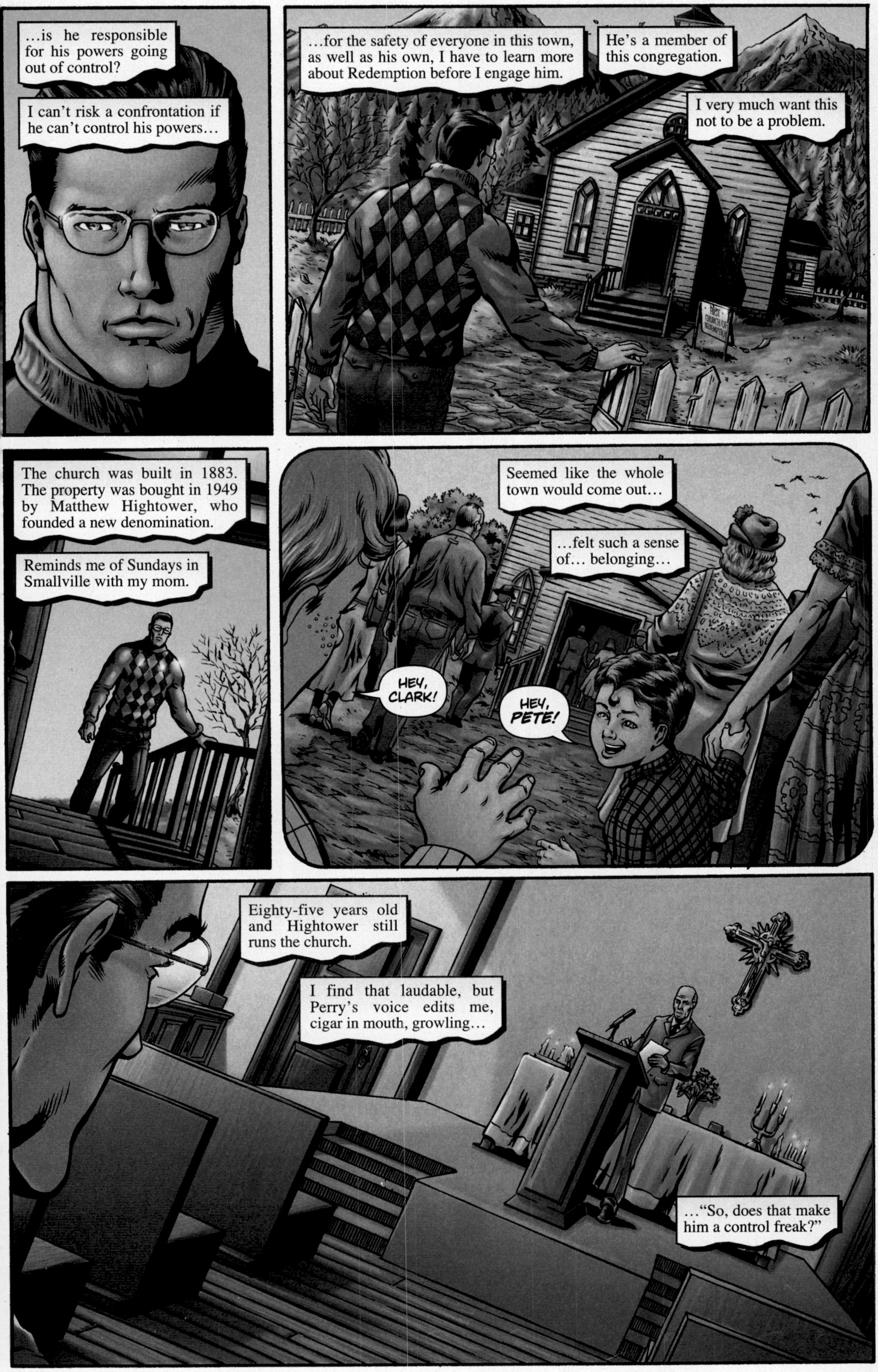
...is he responsible for his powers going out of control?
I can't risk a confrontation if he can't control his powers...
...for the safety of everyone in this town, as well as his own, I have to learn more about Redemption before I engage him.
He's a member of this congregation.
I very much want this not to be a problem.
The church was built in 1883. The property was bought in 1949 by Matthew Hightower, who founded a new denomination.
Reminds me of Sundays in Smallville with my mom.
Seemed like the whole town would come out...
...felt such a sense of... belonging...
HEY, CLARK!
HEY, PETE!
Eighty-five years old and Hightower still runs the church.
I find that laudable, but Perry's voice edits me, cigar in mouth, growling...
..."So, does that make him a control freak?"

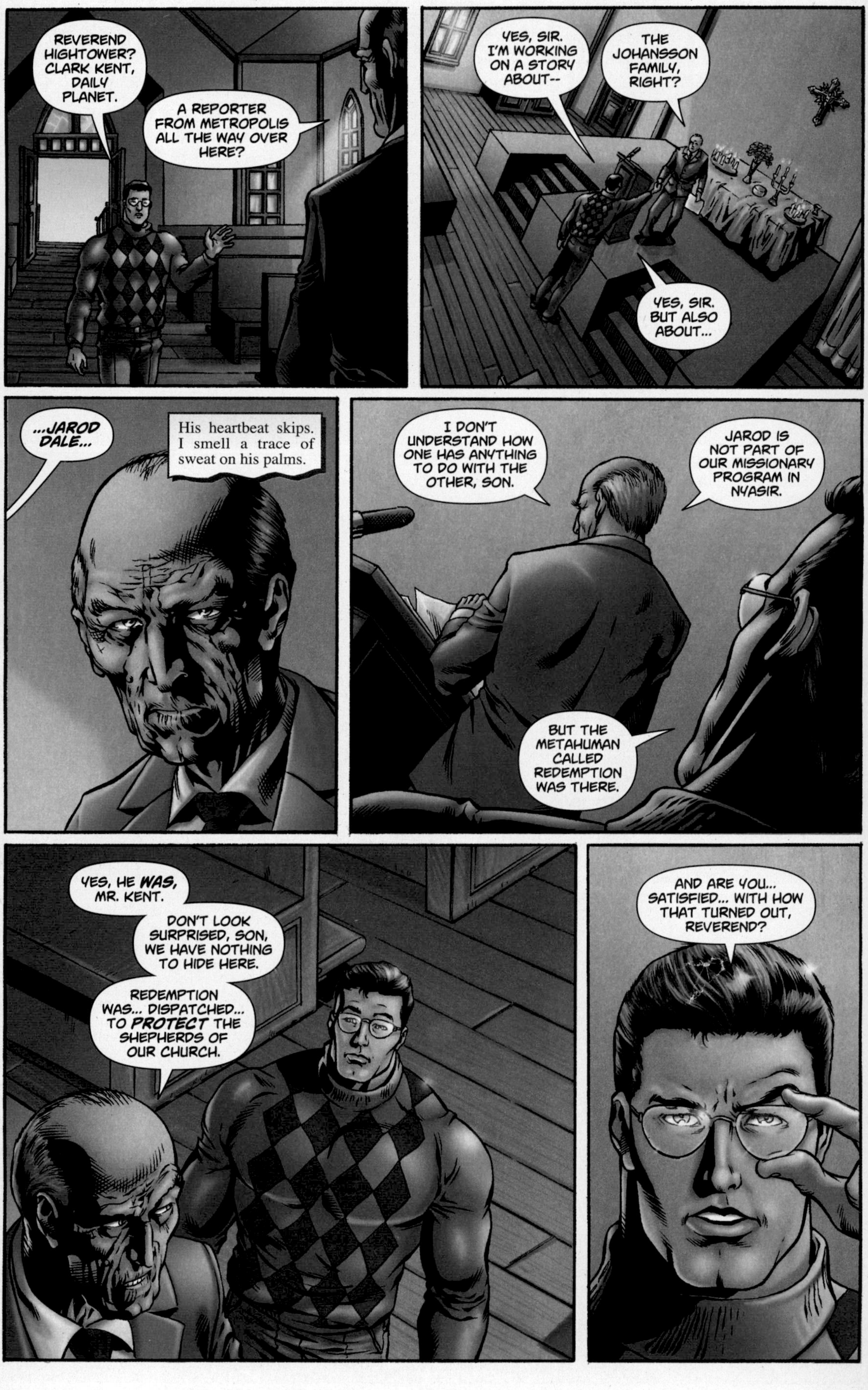
REVEREND HIGHTOWER? CLARK KENT, DAILY PLANET.
A REPORTER FROM METROPOLIS ALL THE WAY OVER HERE?
YES, SIR. I'M WORKING ON A STORY ABOUT--
THE JOHANSSON FAMILY, RIGHT?
YES, SIR. BUT ALSO ABOUT...
...JAROD DALE...
His heartbeat skips. I smell a trace of sweat on his palms.
I DON'T UNDERSTAND HOW ONE HAS ANYTHING TO DO WITH THE OTHER, SON.
JAROD IS NOT PART OF OUR MISSIONARY PROGRAM IN NYASIR.
BUT THE METAHUMAN CALLED REDEMPTION WAS THERE.
YES, HE WAS, MR. KENT.
DON'T LOOK SURPRISED, SON, WE HAVE NOTHING TO HIDE HERE.
REDEMPTION WAS... DISPATCHED... TO PROTECT THE SHEPHERDS OF OUR CHURCH.
AND ARE YOU... SATISFIED... WITH HOW THAT TURNED OUT, REVEREND?

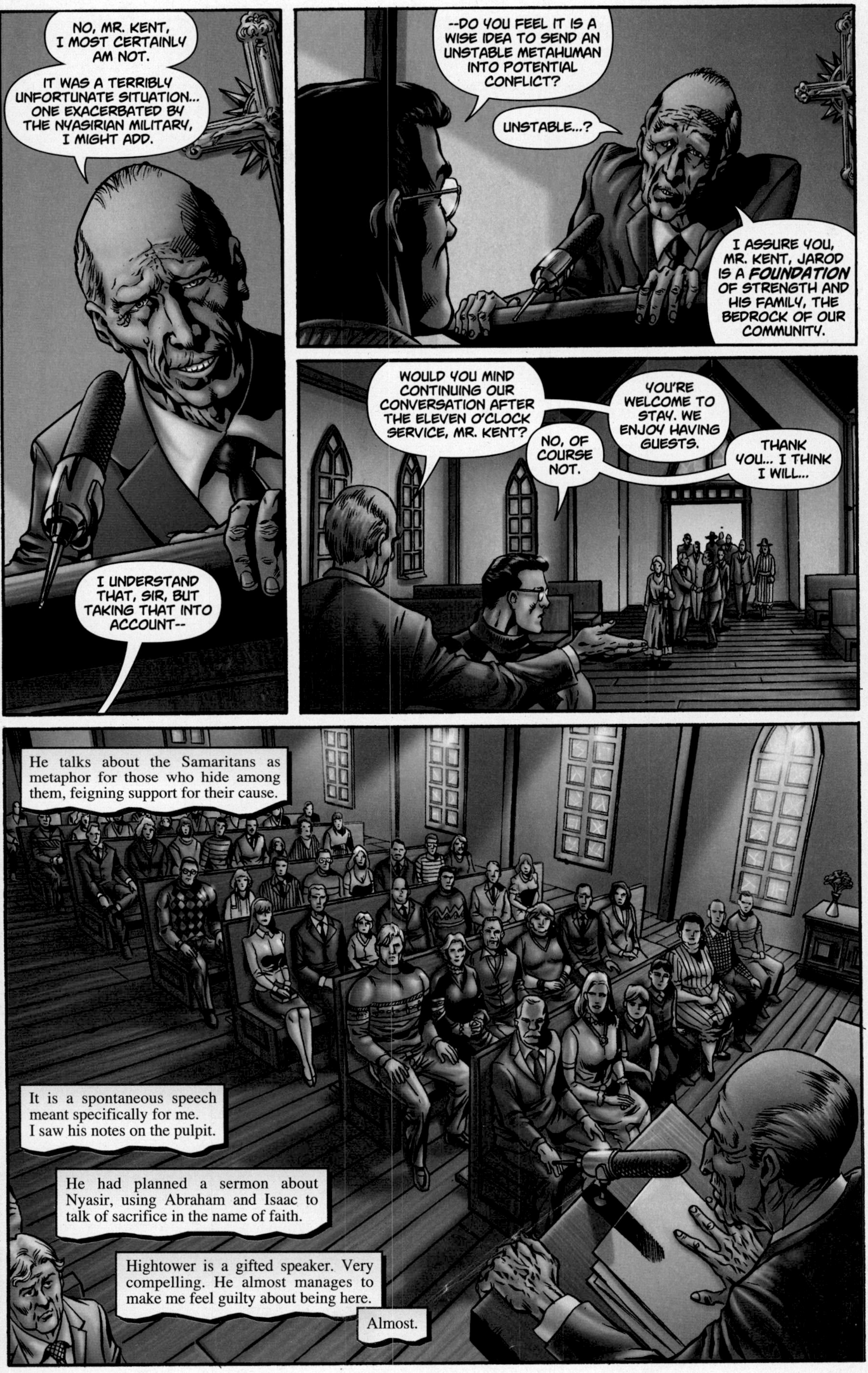
NO, MR. KENT, I MOST CERTAINLY AM NOT.
IT WAS A TERRIBLY UNFORTUNATE SITUATION... ONE EXACERBATED BY THE NYASIRIAN MILITARY, I MIGHT ADD.
I UNDERSTAND THAT, SIR, BUT TAKING THAT INTO ACCOUNT--
--DO YOU FEEL IT IS A WISE IDEA TO SEND AN UNSTABLE METAHUMAN INTO POTENTIAL CONFLICT?
UNSTABLE...?
I ASSURE YOU, MR. KENT, JAROD IS A FOUNDATION OF STRENGTH AND HIS FAMILY, THE BEDROCK OF OUR COMMUNITY.
WOULD YOU MIND CONTINUING OUR CONVERSATION AFTER THE ELEVEN O'CLOCK SERVICE, MR. KENT?
NO, OF COURSE NOT.
YOU'RE WELCOME TO STAY. WE ENJOY HAVING GUESTS.
THANK YOU... I THINK I WILL...
He talks about the Samaritans as metaphor for those who hide among them, feigning support for their cause.
It is a spontaneous speech meant specifically for me. I saw his notes on the pulpit.
He had planned a sermon about Nyasir, using Abraham and Isaac to talk of sacrifice in the name of faith.
Hightower is a gifted speaker. Very compelling. He almost manages to make me feel guilty about being here.
Almost.

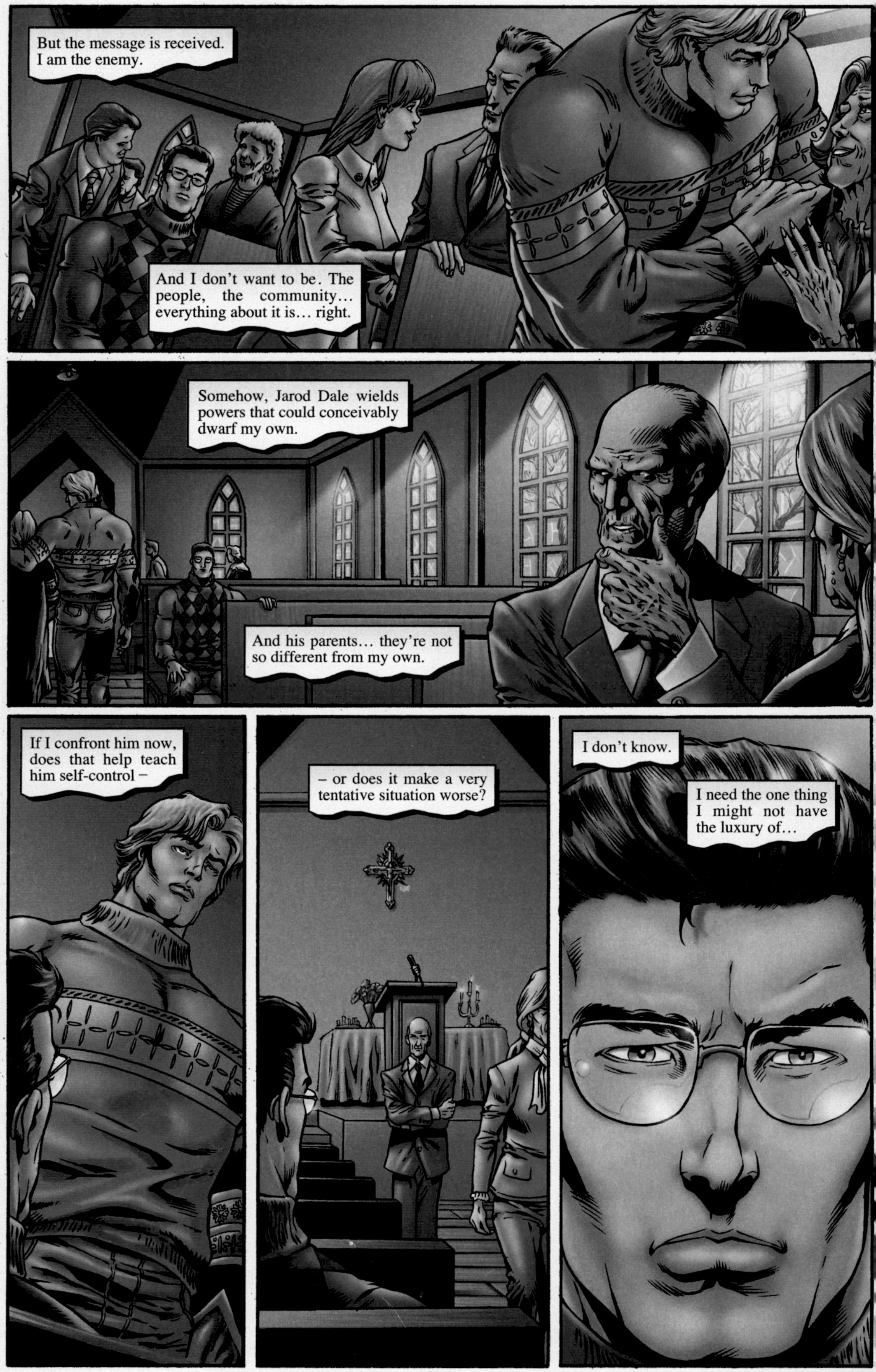
But the message is received. I am the enemy.
And I don't want to be. The people, the community... everything about it is... right.
Somehow, Jarod Dale wields powers that could conceivably dwarf my own.
And his parents... they're not so different from my own.
If I confront him now, does that help teach him self-control –
– or does it make a very tentative situation worse?
I don't know.
I need the one thing I might not have the luxury of...

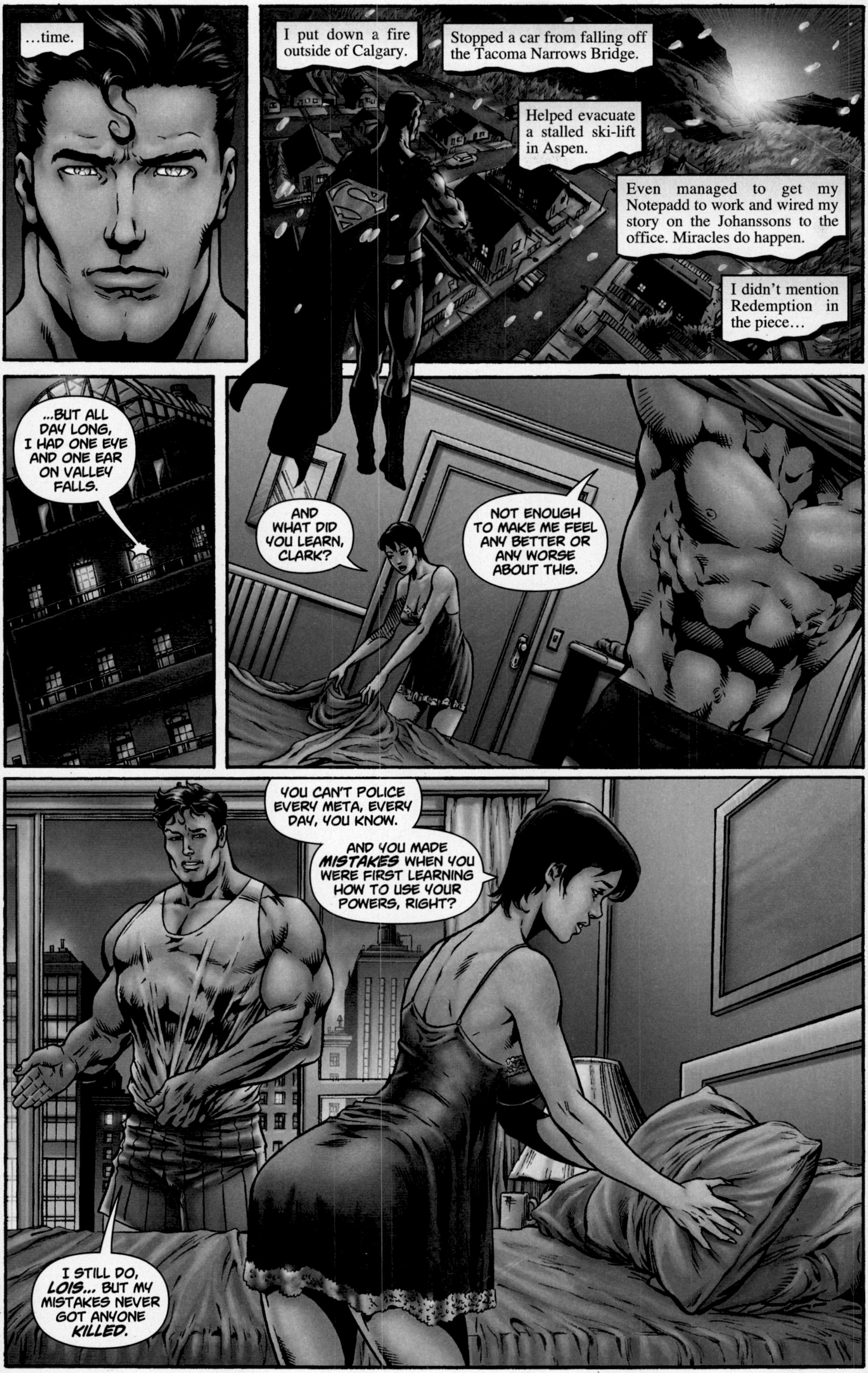

...time.
I put down a fire outside of Calgary.
Stopped a car from falling off the Tacoma Narrows Bridge.
Helped evacuate a stalled ski-lift in Aspen.
Even managed to get my Notepadd to work and wired my story on the Johanssons to the office. Miracles do happen.
I didn't mention Redemption in the piece...
...BUT ALL DAY LONG, I HAD ONE EYE AND ONE EAR ON VALLEY FALLS.
AND WHAT DID YOU LEARN, CLARK?
NOT ENOUGH TO MAKE ME FEEL ANY BETTER OR ANY WORSE ABOUT THIS.
YOU CAN'T POLICE EVERY META, EVERY DAY, YOU KNOW.
AND YOU MADE MISTAKES WHEN YOU WERE FIRST LEARNING HOW TO USE YOUR POWERS, RIGHT?
I STILL DO, LOIS... BUT MY MISTAKES NEVER GOT ANYONE KILLED.

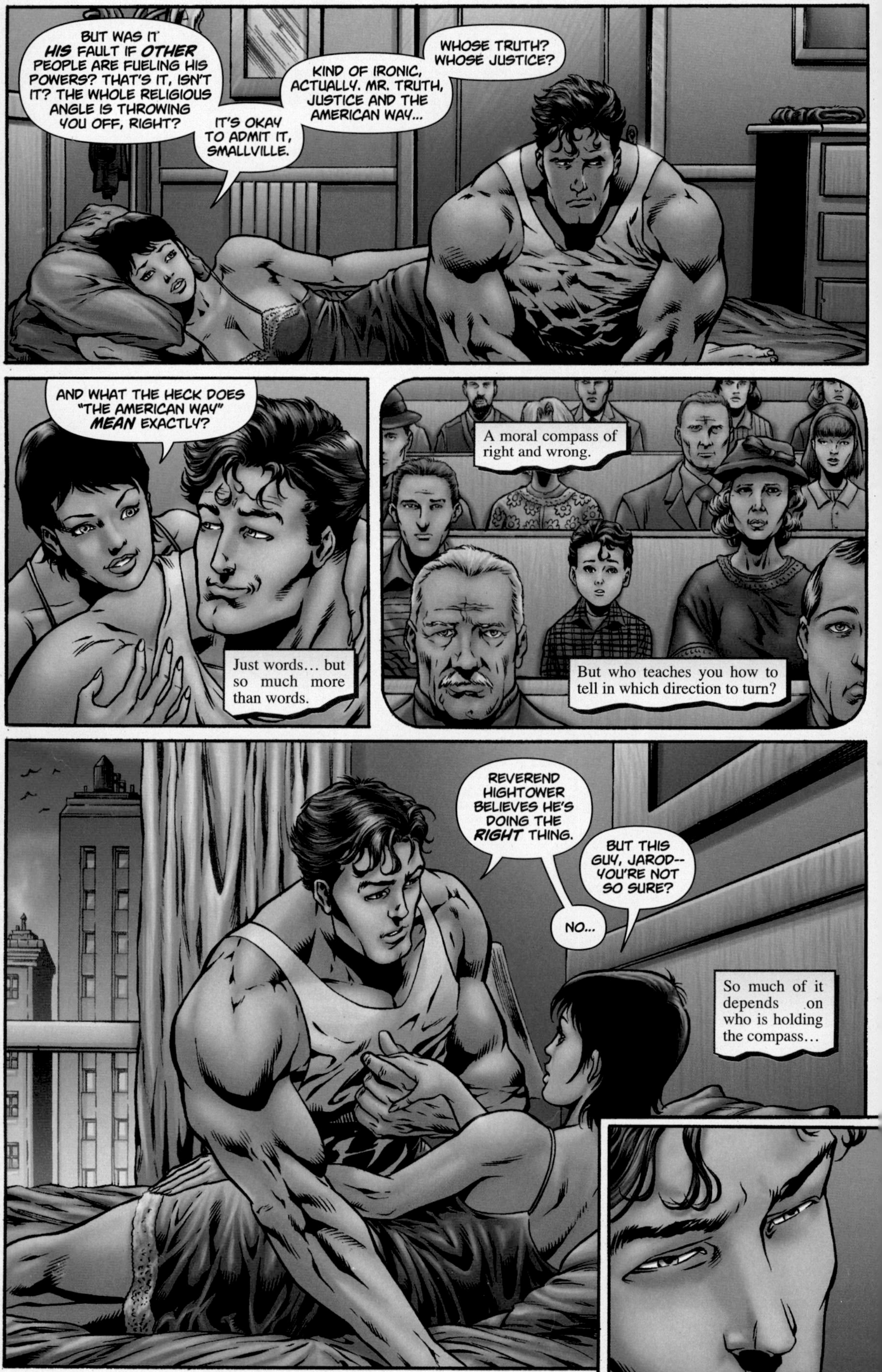
BUT WAS IT HIS FAULT IF OTHER PEOPLE ARE FUELING HIS POWERS? THAT'S IT, ISN'T IT? THE WHOLE RELIGIOUS ANGLE IS THROWING YOU OFF, RIGHT?
IT'S OKAY TO ADMIT IT, SMALLVILLE.
KIND OF IRONIC, ACTUALLY. MR. TRUTH, JUSTICE AND THE AMERICAN WAY...
WHOSE TRUTH? WHOSE JUSTICE?
AND WHAT THE HECK DOES "THE AMERICAN WAY" MEAN EXACTLY?
Just words… but so much more than words.
A moral compass of right and wrong.
But who teaches you how to tell in which direction to turn?
REVEREND HIGHTOWER BELIEVES HE'S DOING THE RIGHT THING.
BUT THIS GUY, JAROD-- YOU'RE NOT SO SURE?
NO...
So much of it depends on who is holding the compass…

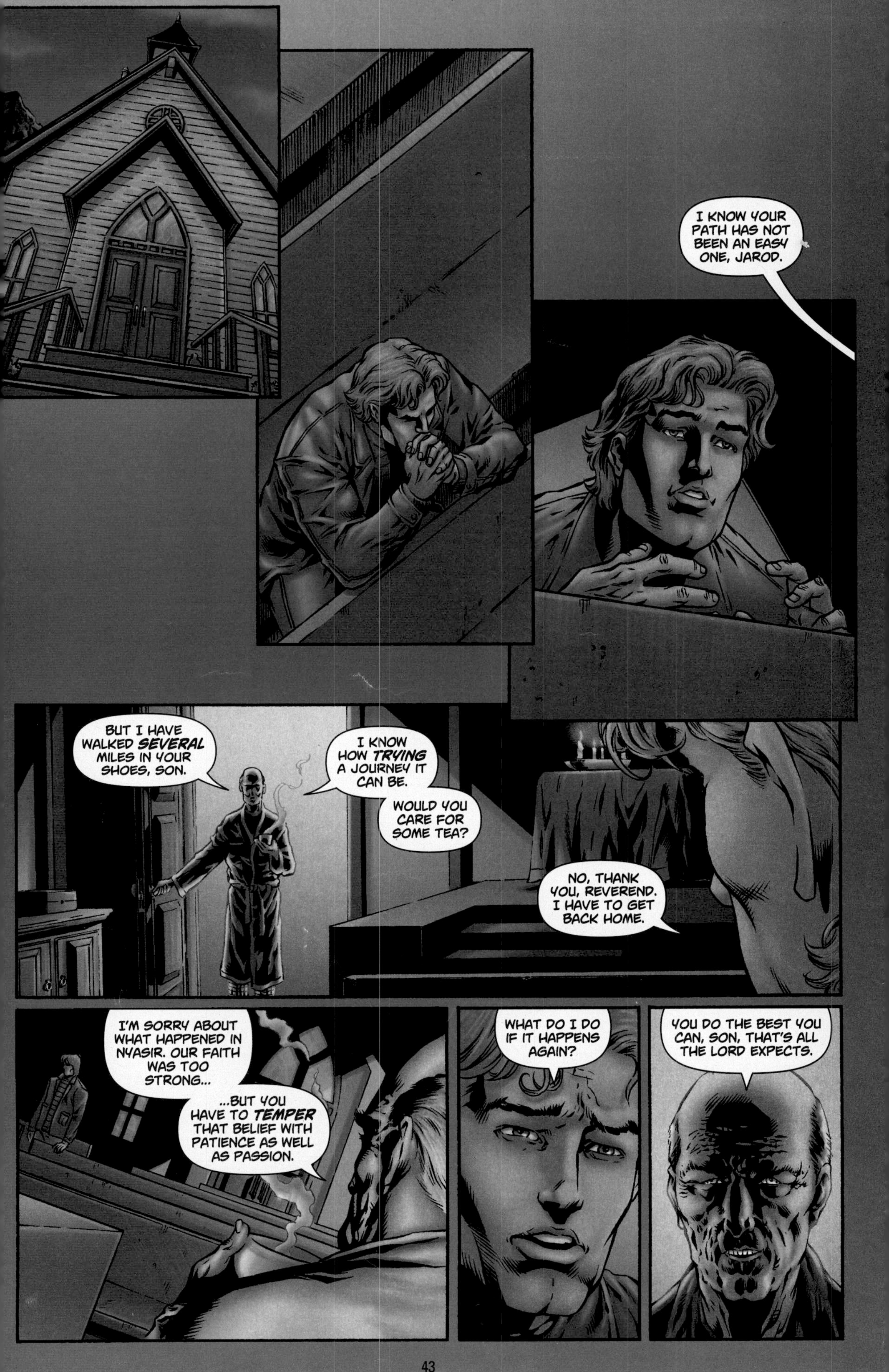
I KNOW YOUR PATH HAS NOT BEEN AN EASY ONE, JAROD.
BUT I HAVE WALKED SEVERAL MILES IN YOUR SHOES, SON.
I KNOW HOW TRYING A JOURNEY IT CAN BE.
WOULD YOU CARE FOR SOME TEA?
NO, THANK YOU, REVEREND. I HAVE TO GET BACK HOME.
I'M SORRY ABOUT WHAT HAPPENED IN NYASIR. OUR FAITH WAS TOO STRONG...
...BUT YOU HAVE TO TEMPER THAT BELIEF WITH PATIENCE AS WELL AS PASSION.
WHAT DO I DO IF IT HAPPENS AGAIN?
YOU DO THE BEST YOU CAN, SON. THAT'S ALL THE LORD EXPECTS.

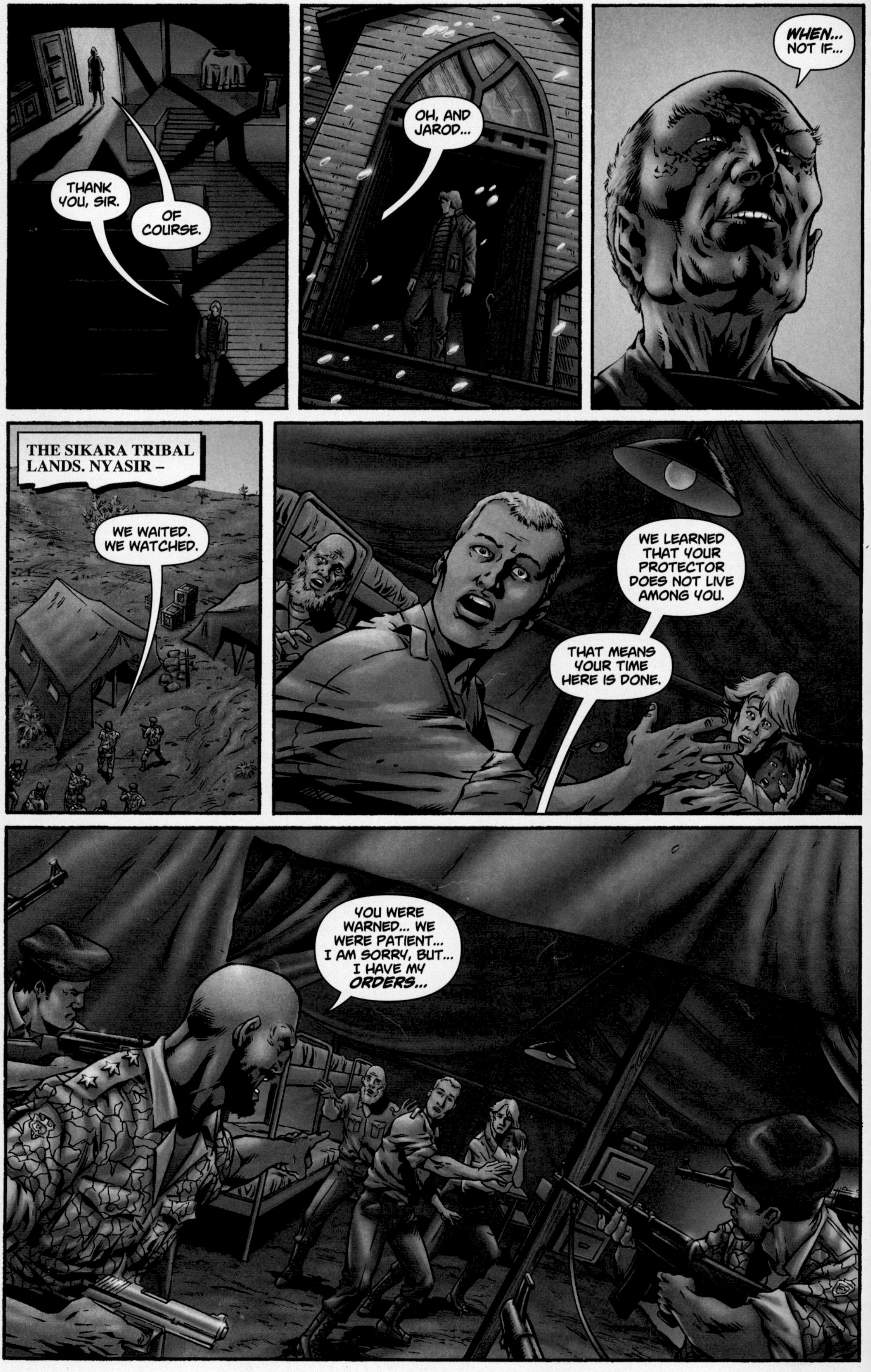

THANK YOU, SIR.
OF COURSE.
OH, AND JAROD...
WHEN... NOT IF...
THE SIKARA TRIBAL LANDS. NYASIR –
WE WAITED. WE WATCHED.
WE LEARNED THAT YOUR PROTECTOR DOES NOT LIVE AMONG YOU.
THAT MEANS YOUR TIME HERE IS DONE.
YOU WERE WARNED... WE WERE PATIENT... I AM SORRY, BUT... I HAVE MY ORDERS...

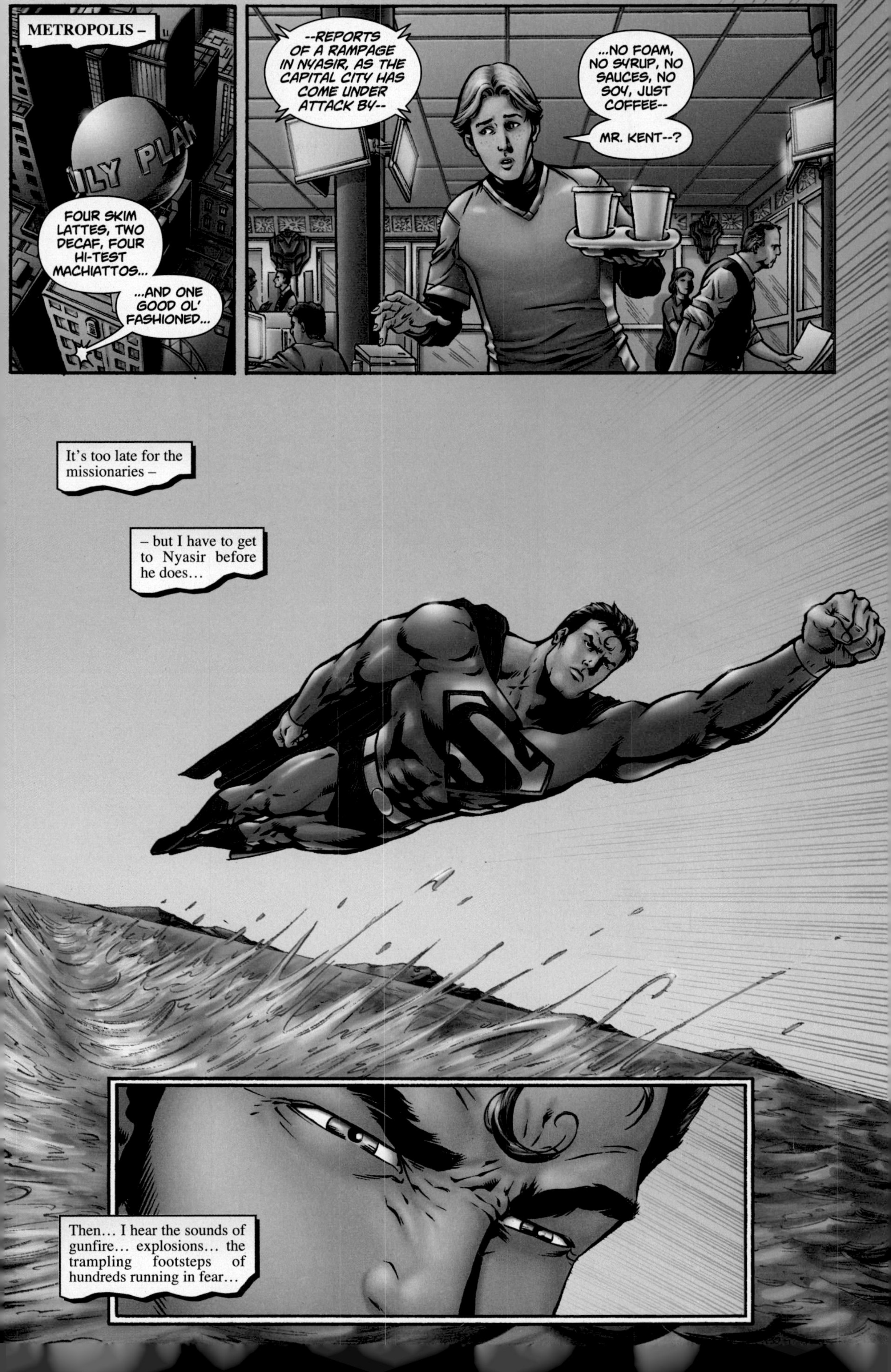
METROPOLIS –
FOUR SKIM LATTES, TWO DECAF, FOUR HI-TEST MACHIATTOS...
...AND ONE GOOD OL' FASHIONED...
--REPORTS OF A RAMPAGE IN NYASIR, AS THE CAPITAL CITY HAS COME UNDER ATTACK BY--
...NO FOAM, NO SYRUP, NO SAUCES, NO SOY, JUST COFFEE--
MR. KENT--?
It's too late for the missionaries –
– but I have to get to Nyasir before he does…
Then… I hear the sounds of gunfire… explosions… the trampling footsteps of hundreds running in fear…

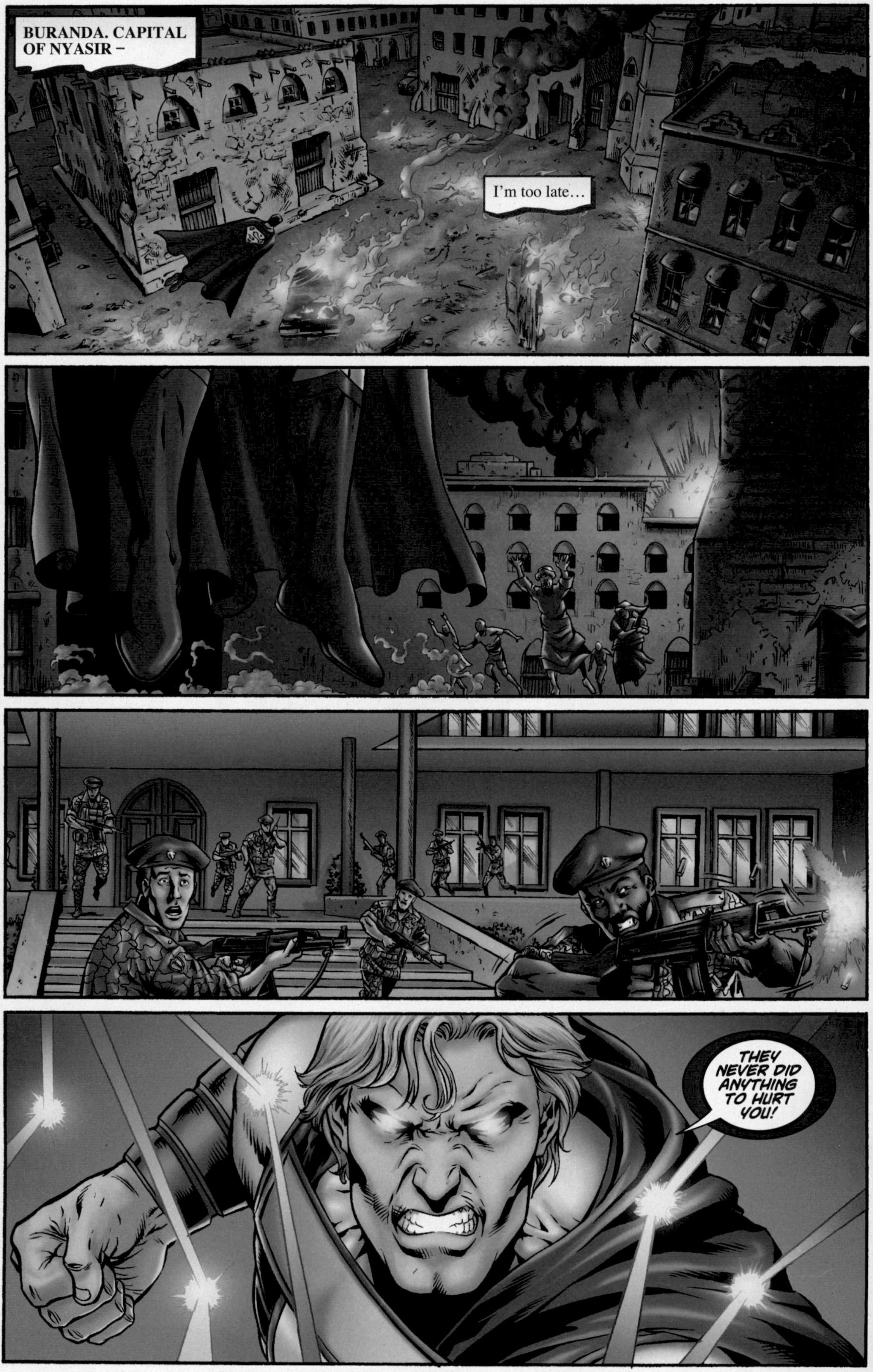
BURANDA. CAPITAL OF NYASIR –
I'm too late…
THEY NEVER DID ANYTHING TO HURT YOU!

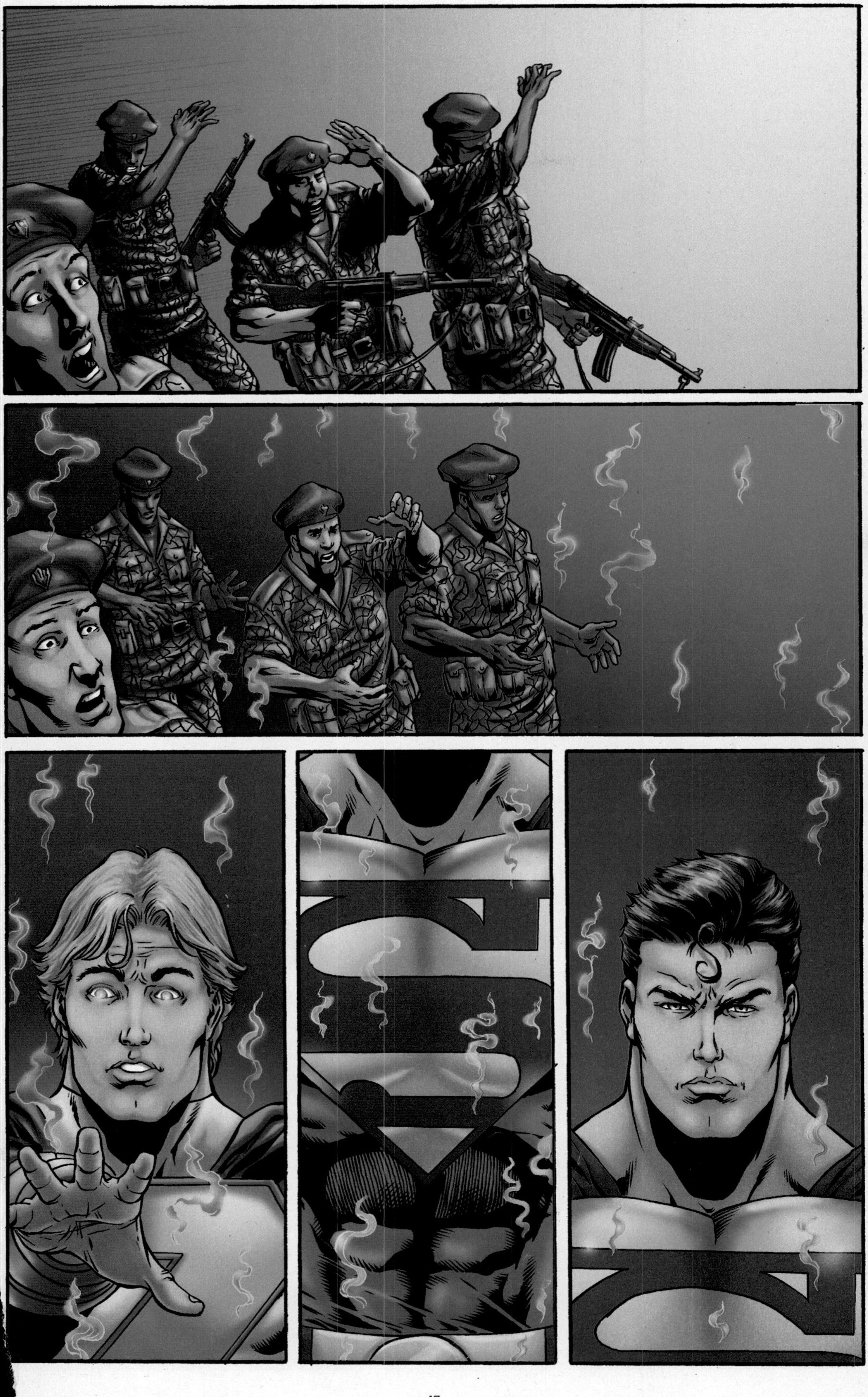

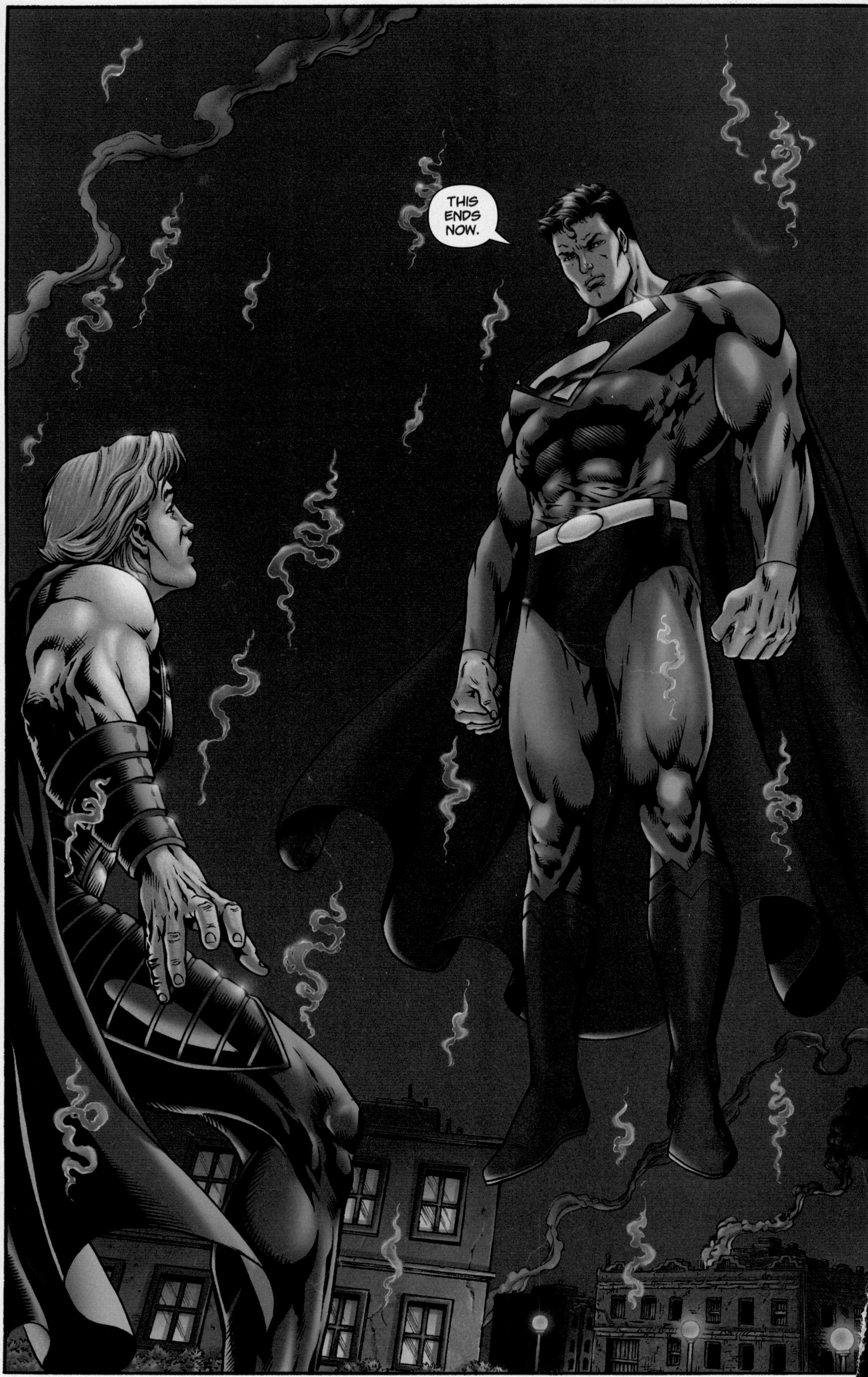
THIS ENDS NOW.

Redemption Chapter Two Cover to Action Comics 849 by Brad Walker and Robin Riggs

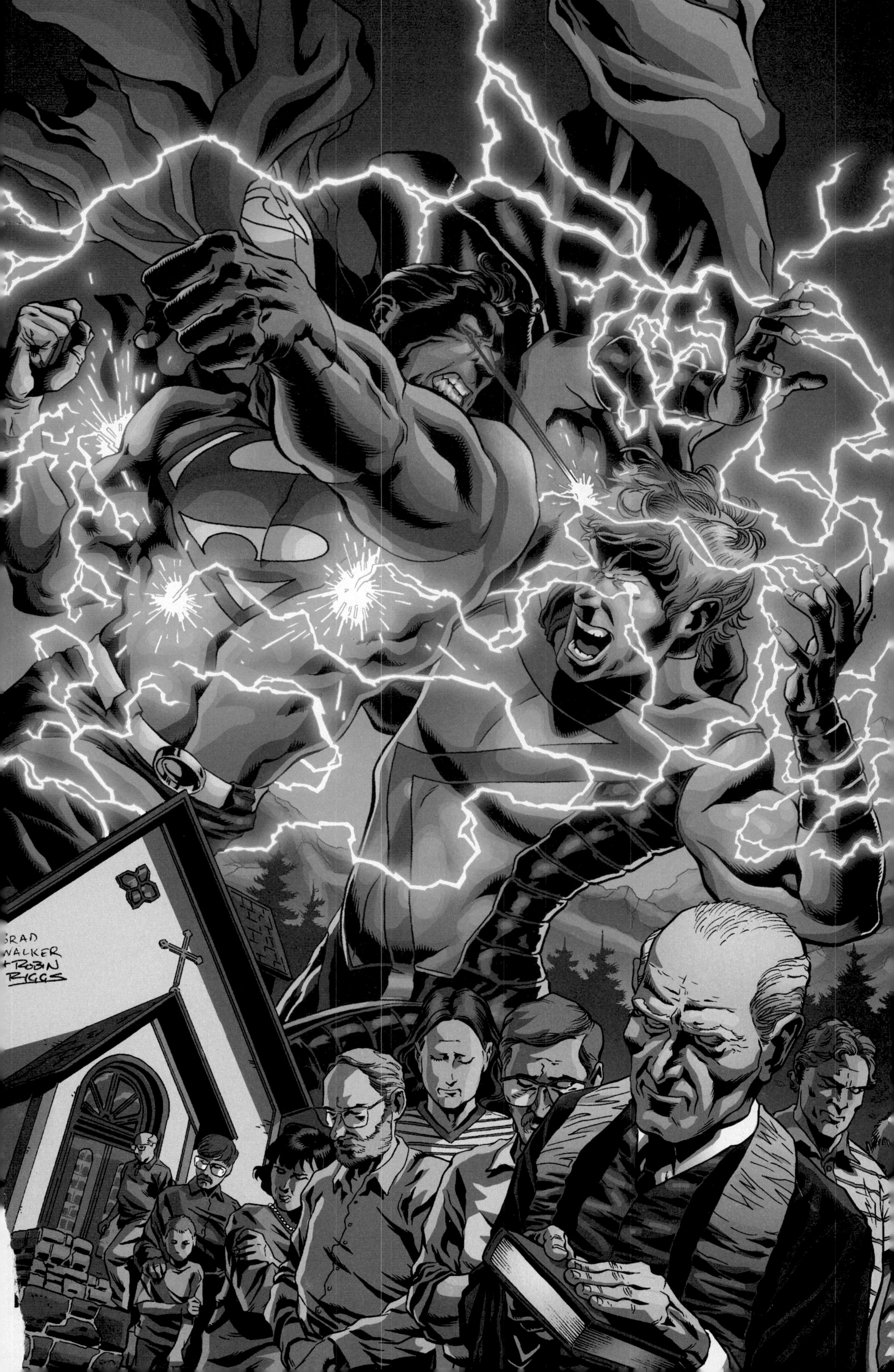

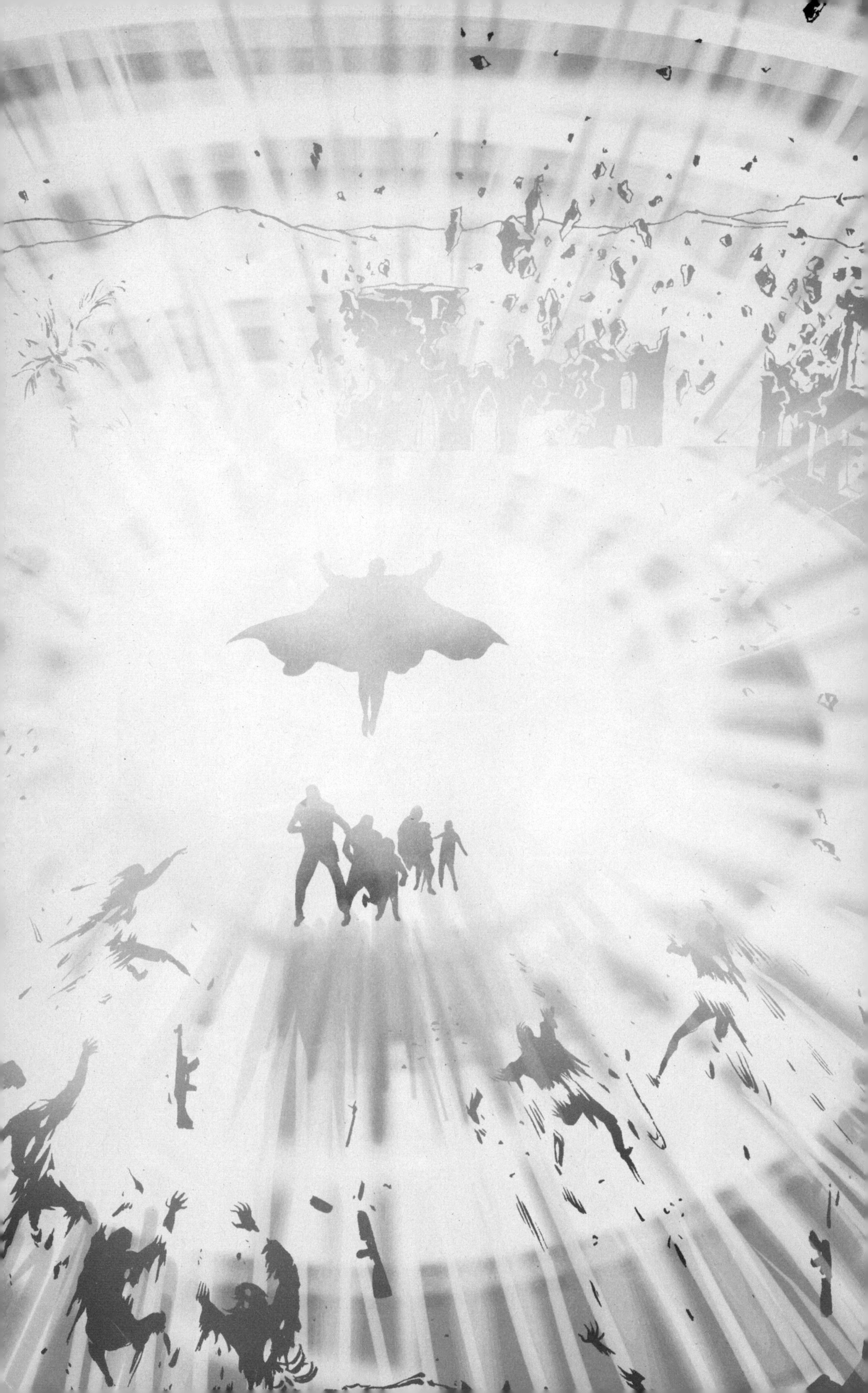

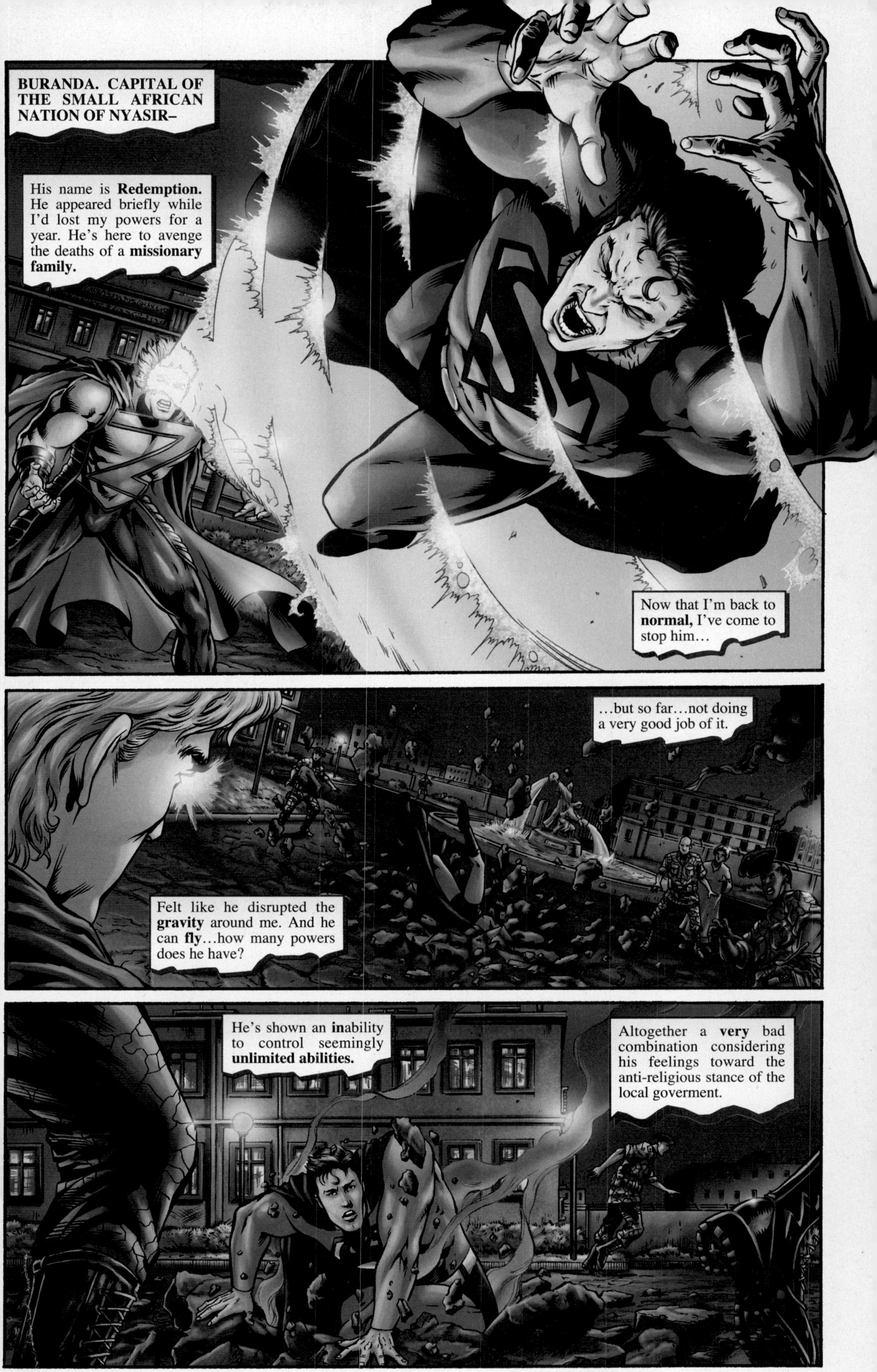
BURANDA. CAPITAL OF THE SMALL AFRICAN NATION OF NYASIR–
His name is **Redemption.** He appeared briefly while I'd lost my powers for a year. He's here to avenge the deaths of a **missionary family.**
Now that I'm back to **normal,** I've come to stop him…
…but so far…not doing a very good job of it.
Felt like he disrupted the **gravity** around me. And he can **fly**…how many powers does he have?
He's shown an **in**ability to control seemingly **unlimited abilities.**
Altogether a **very** bad combination considering his feelings toward the anti-religious stance of the local goverment.

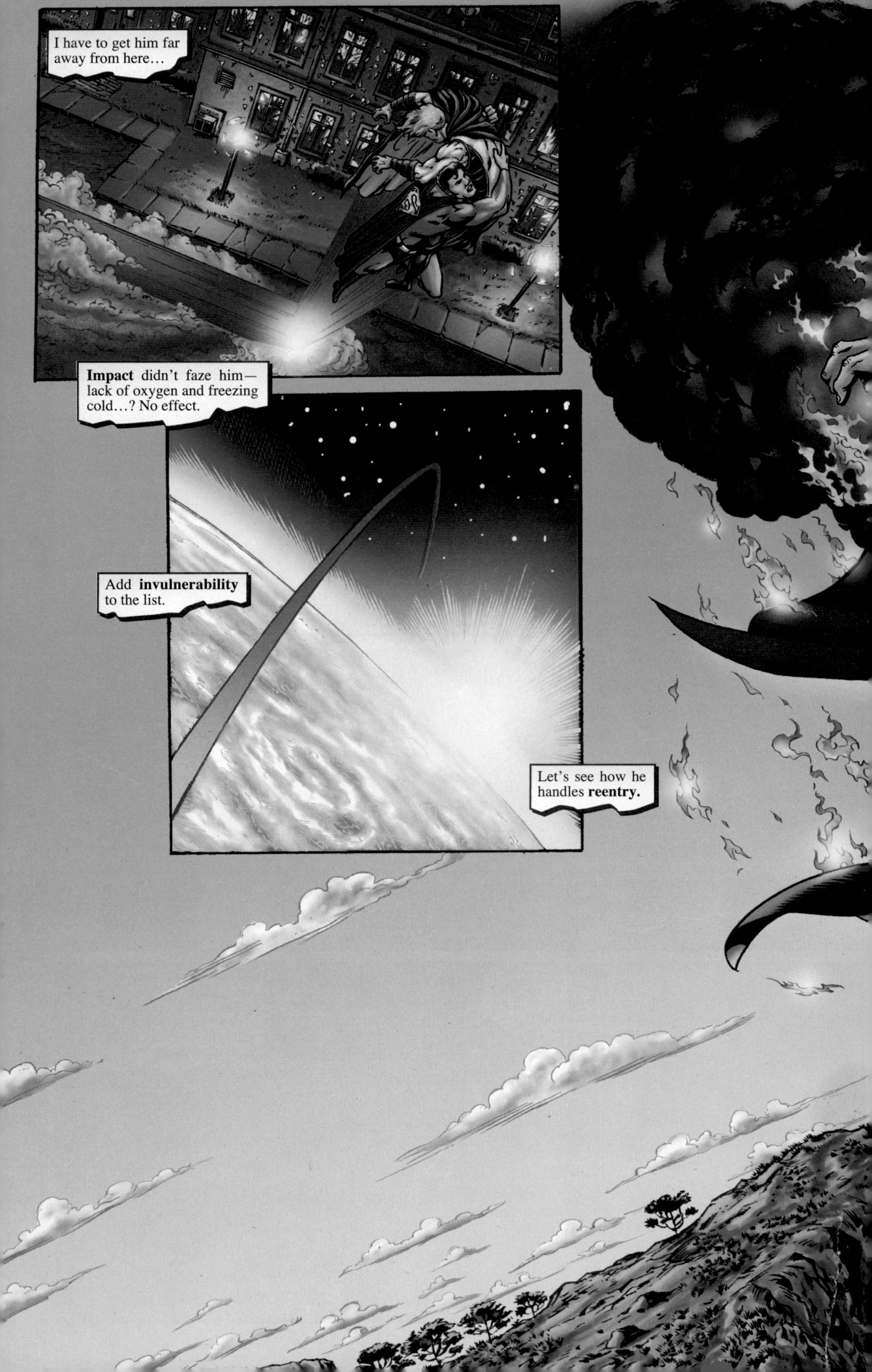
I have to get him far away from here…
Impact didn't faze him—lack of oxygen and freezing cold…? No effect.
Add **invulnerability** to the list.
Let's see how he handles **reentry.**

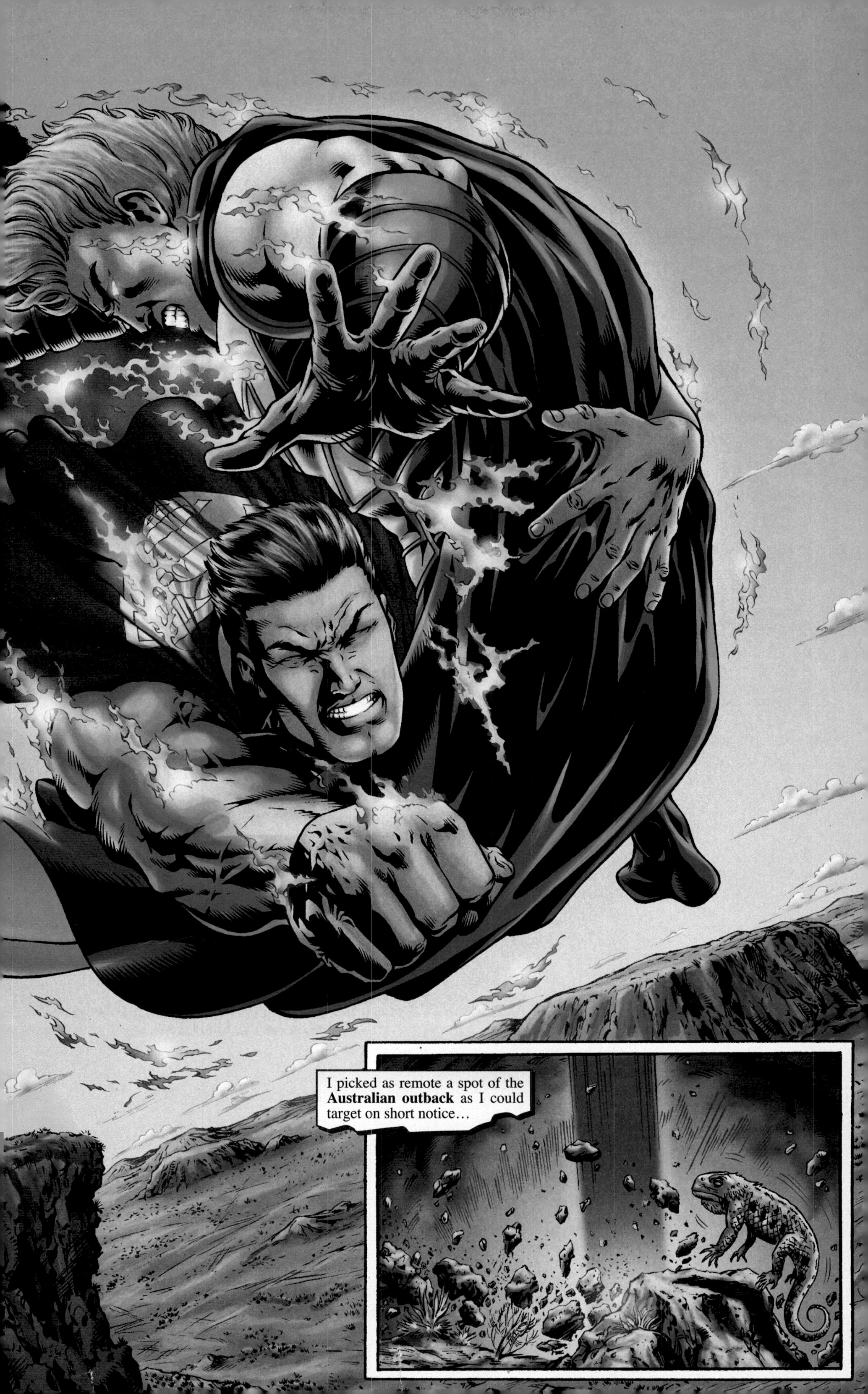
I picked as remote a spot of the **Australian outback** as I could target on short notice…

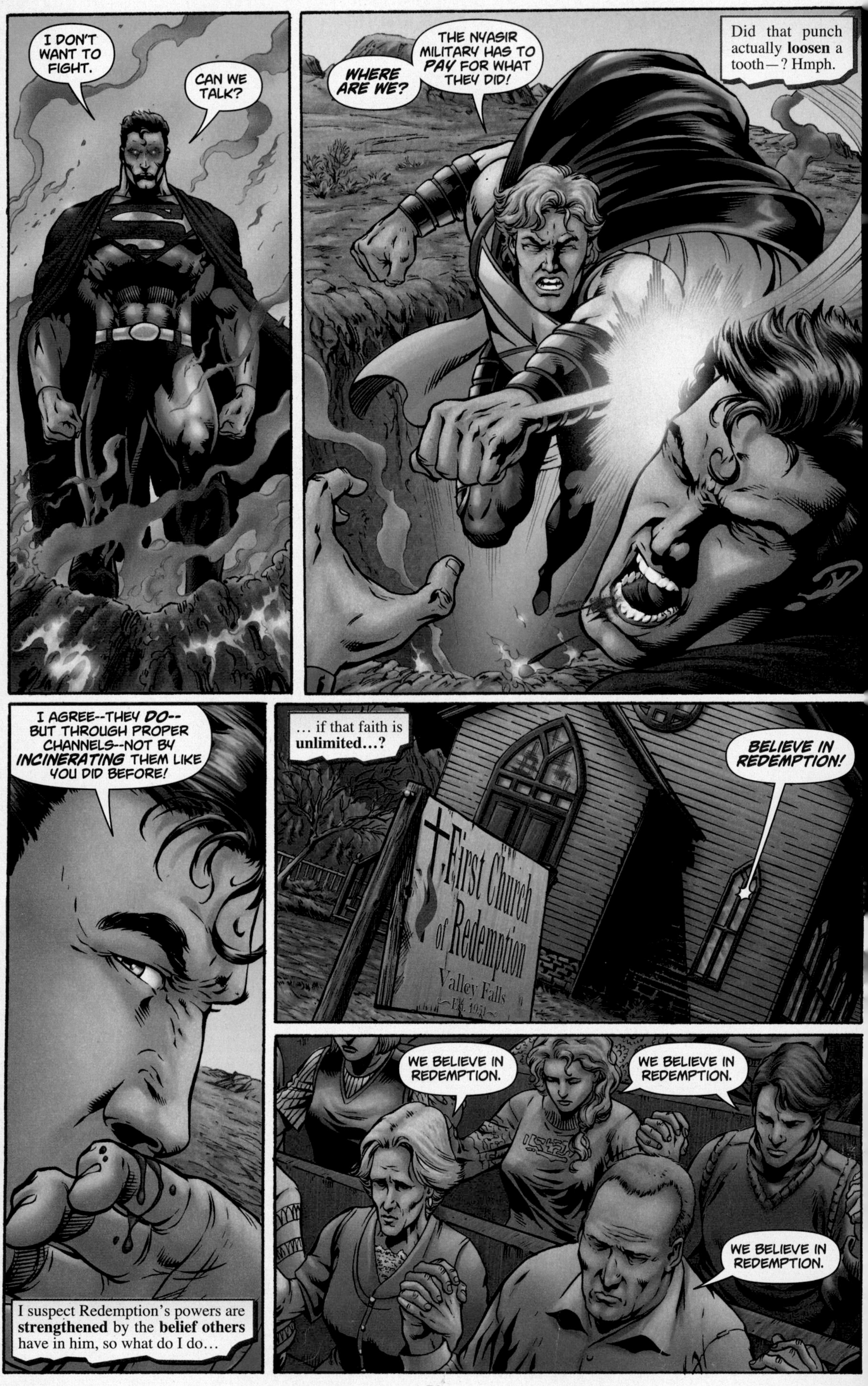

I DON'T WANT TO FIGHT.
CAN WE TALK?
WHERE ARE WE?
THE NYASIR MILITARY HAS TO PAY FOR WHAT THEY DID!
Did that punch actually loosen a tooth—? Hmph.
I AGREE--THEY DO--BUT THROUGH PROPER CHANNELS--NOT BY INCINERATING THEM LIKE YOU DID BEFORE!
I suspect Redemption's powers are strengthened by the belief others have in him, so what do I do…
… if that faith is unlimited…?
First Church of Redemption
Valley Falls
Est. 1951
BELIEVE IN REDEMPTION!
WE BELIEVE IN REDEMPTION.
WE BELIEVE IN REDEMPTION.
WE BELIEVE IN REDEMPTION.

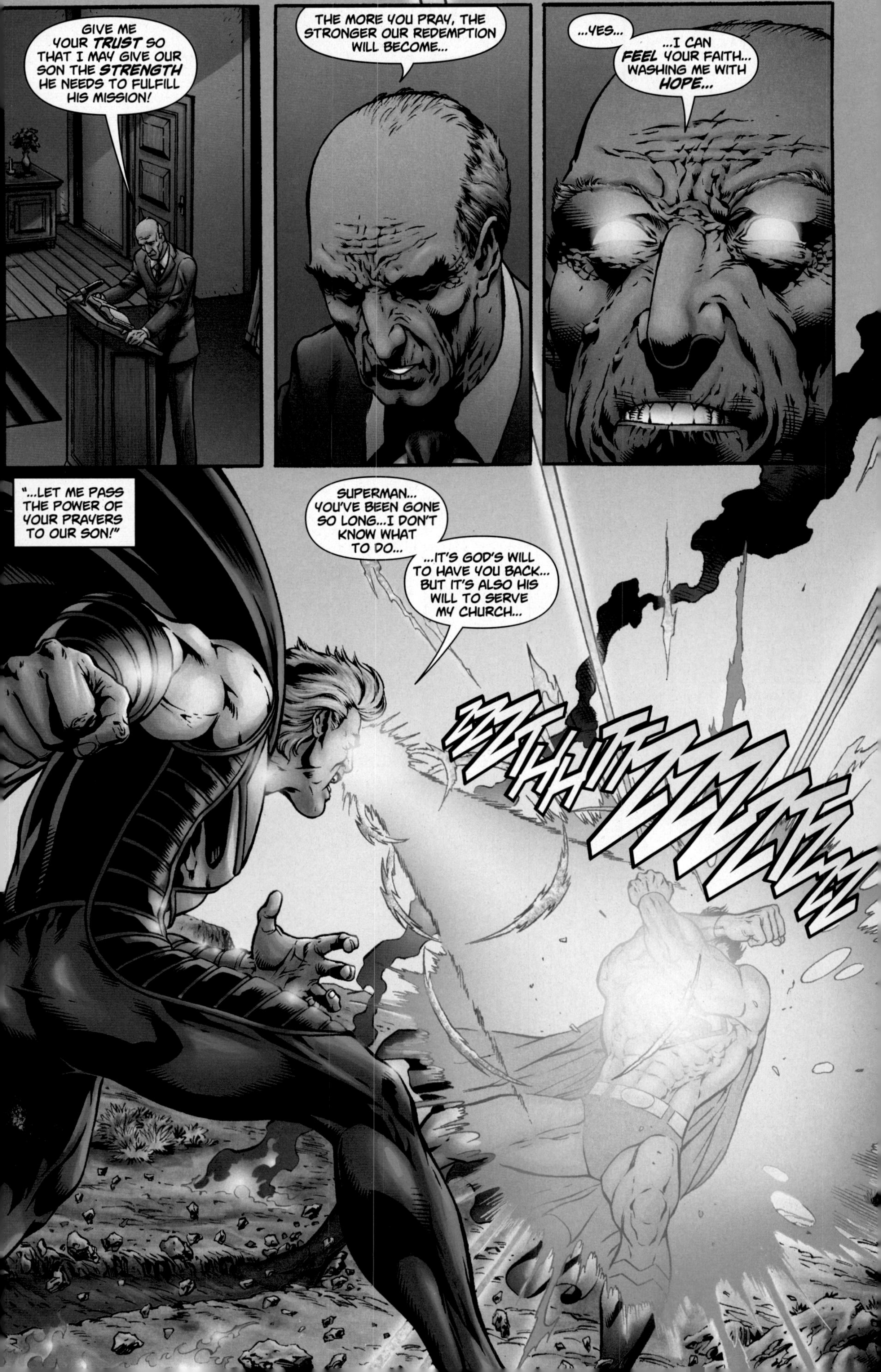

GIVE ME YOUR TRUST SO THAT I MAY GIVE OUR SON THE STRENGTH HE NEEDS TO FULFILL HIS MISSION!
THE MORE YOU PRAY, THE STRONGER OUR REDEMPTION WILL BECOME...
...YES...
...I CAN FEEL YOUR FAITH... WASHING ME WITH HOPE...
"...LET ME PASS THE POWER OF YOUR PRAYERS TO OUR SON!"
SUPERMAN... YOU'VE BEEN GONE SO LONG...I DON'T KNOW WHAT TO DO...
...IT'S GOD'S WILL TO HAVE YOU BACK... BUT IT'S ALSO HIS WILL TO SERVE MY CHURCH...
ZZZHHHTTTZZZZZZZZ

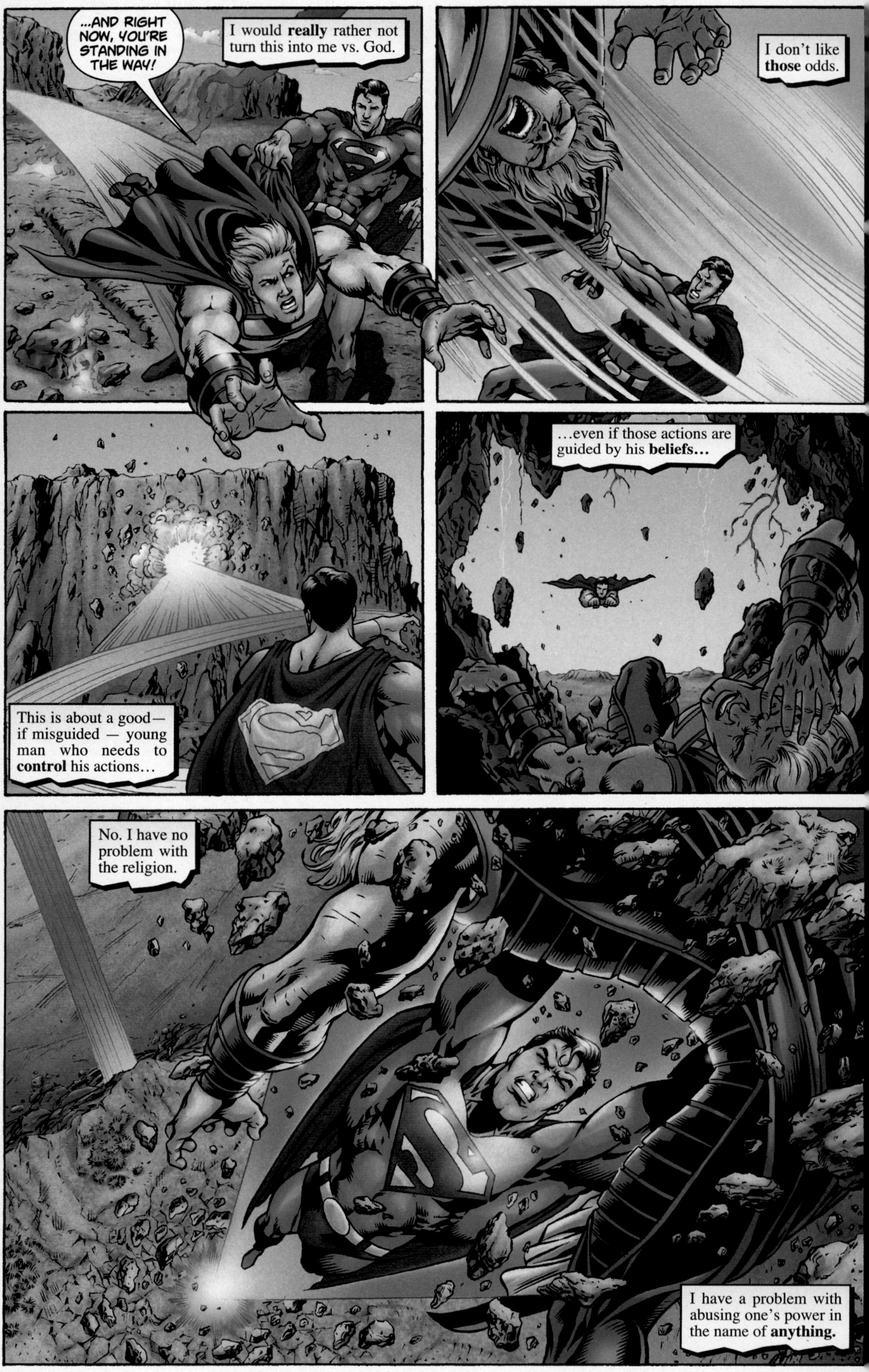

...AND RIGHT NOW, YOU'RE STANDING IN THE WAY!
I would **really** rather not turn this into me vs. God.
I don't like **those** odds.
This is about a good— if misguided — young man who needs to **control** his actions...
...even if those actions are guided by his **beliefs...**
No. I have no problem with the religion.
I have a problem with abusing one's power in the name of **anything.**

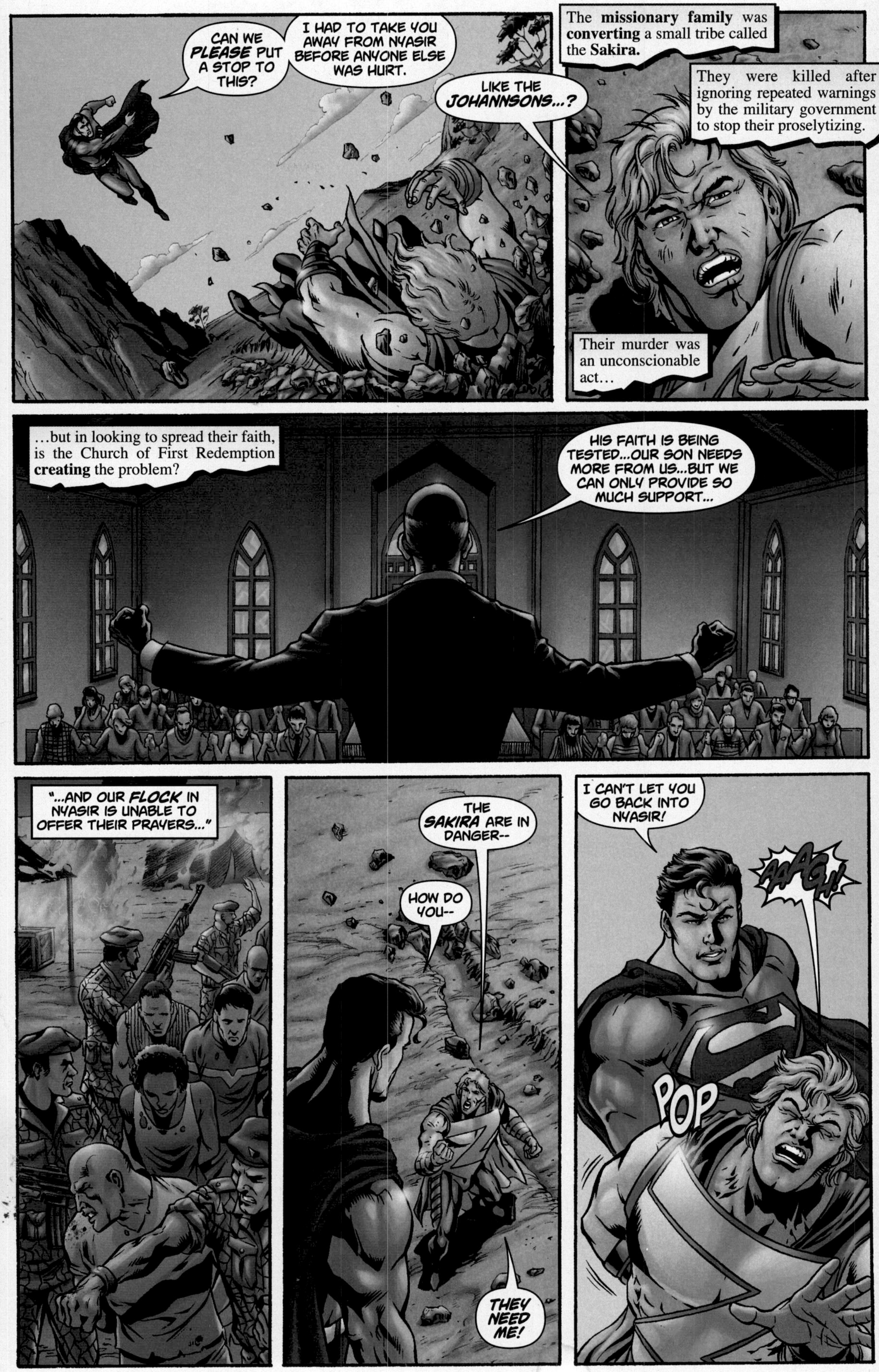

CAN WE PLEASE PUT A STOP TO THIS?
I HAD TO TAKE YOU AWAY FROM NYASIR BEFORE ANYONE ELSE WAS HURT.
LIKE THE JOHANNSONS...?
The missionary family was converting a small tribe called the Sakira.
They were killed after ignoring repeated warnings by the military government to stop their proselytizing.
Their murder was an unconscionable act…
…but in looking to spread their faith, is the Church of First Redemption creating the problem?
HIS FAITH IS BEING TESTED...OUR SON NEEDS MORE FROM US...BUT WE CAN ONLY PROVIDE SO MUCH SUPPORT...
"...AND OUR FLOCK IN NYASIR IS UNABLE TO OFFER THEIR PRAYERS..."
THE SAKIRA ARE IN DANGER--
HOW DO YOU--
THEY NEED ME!
I CAN'T LET YOU GO BACK INTO NYASIR!
AAAGH!
POP

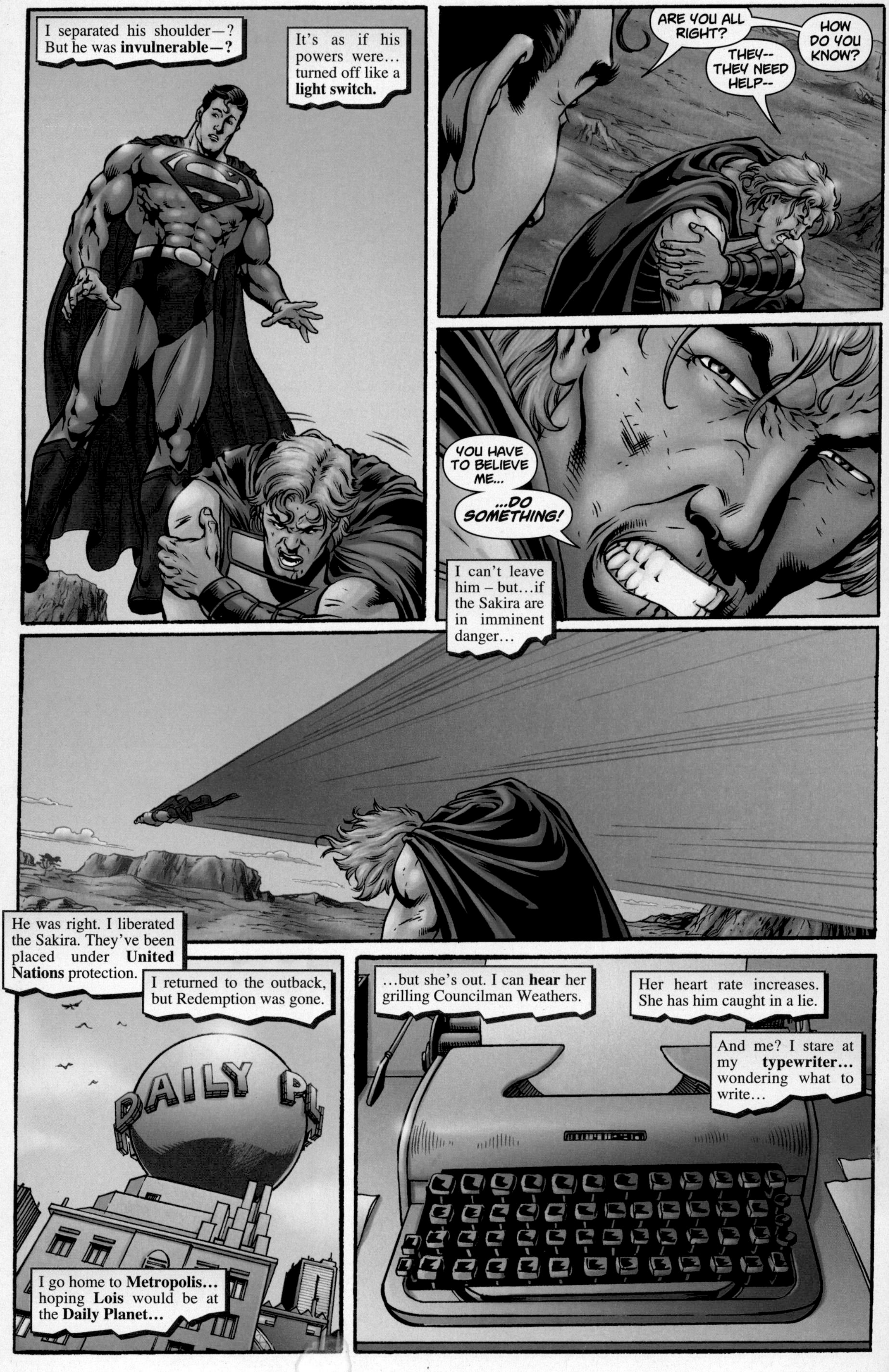

I separated his shoulder—? But he was **invulnerable—?**
It's as if his powers were… turned off like a **light switch.**
ARE YOU ALL RIGHT?
THEY-- THEY NEED HELP--
HOW DO YOU KNOW?
YOU HAVE TO BELIEVE ME...
...DO SOMETHING!
I can't leave him – but…if the Sakira are in imminent danger…
He was right. I liberated the Sakira. They've been placed under **United Nations** protection.
I returned to the outback, but Redemption was gone.
DAILY PL
I go home to **Metropolis…** hoping **Lois** would be at the **Daily Planet…**
…but she's out. I can **hear** her grilling Councilman Weathers.
Her heart rate increases. She has him caught in a lie.
And me? I stare at my **typewriter…** wondering what to write…

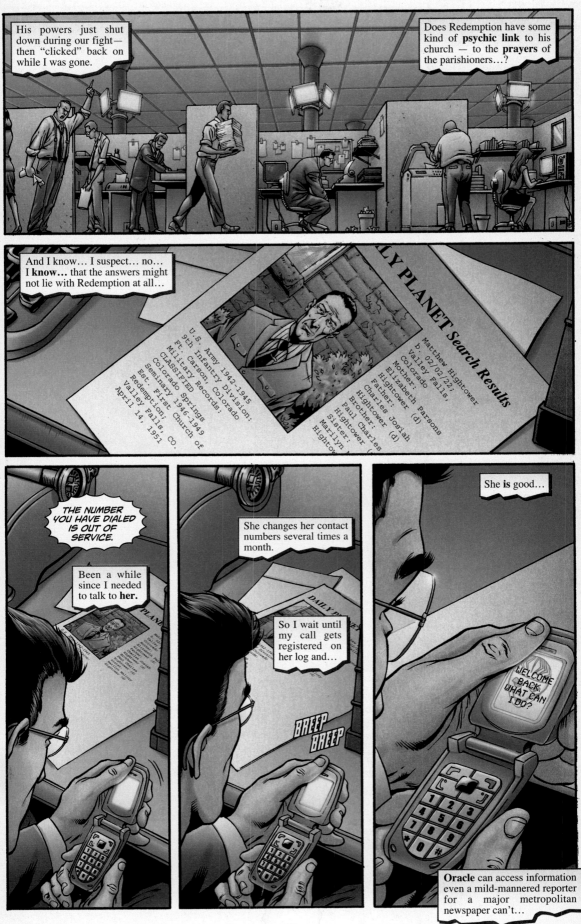

His powers just shut down during our fight— then "clicked" back on while I was gone.

Does Redemption have some kind of **psychic link** to his church — to the **prayers** of the parishioners...?

And I know... I suspect... no... I **know**... that the answers might not lie with Redemption at all...

DAILY PLANET Search Results

Matthew Hightower
b. 02/02/22;
Valley Falls,
Colorado
Mother:
Elizabeth Parsons
Hightower (d)
Father:
Charles Josiah
Hightower (d)
Brother:
Paul Charles
Hightower (
Sister:
Marilyn
Hightow

U.S. Army 1942-1945
9th Infantry Division
Ft. Carson, Colorado
Military Records:
CLASSIFIED
Colorado Springs
Seminary 1946-1949
Est. First Church of
Redemption,
Valley Falls, CO.
April 14, 1951

THE NUMBER YOU HAVE DIALED IS OUT OF SERVICE.

Been a while since I needed to talk to **her.**

She changes her contact numbers several times a month.

So I wait until my call gets registered on her log and...

BREEP BREEP

She **is** good...

WELCOME BACK. WHAT CAN I DO?

Oracle can access information even a mild-mannered reporter for a major metropolitan newspaper can't...

59

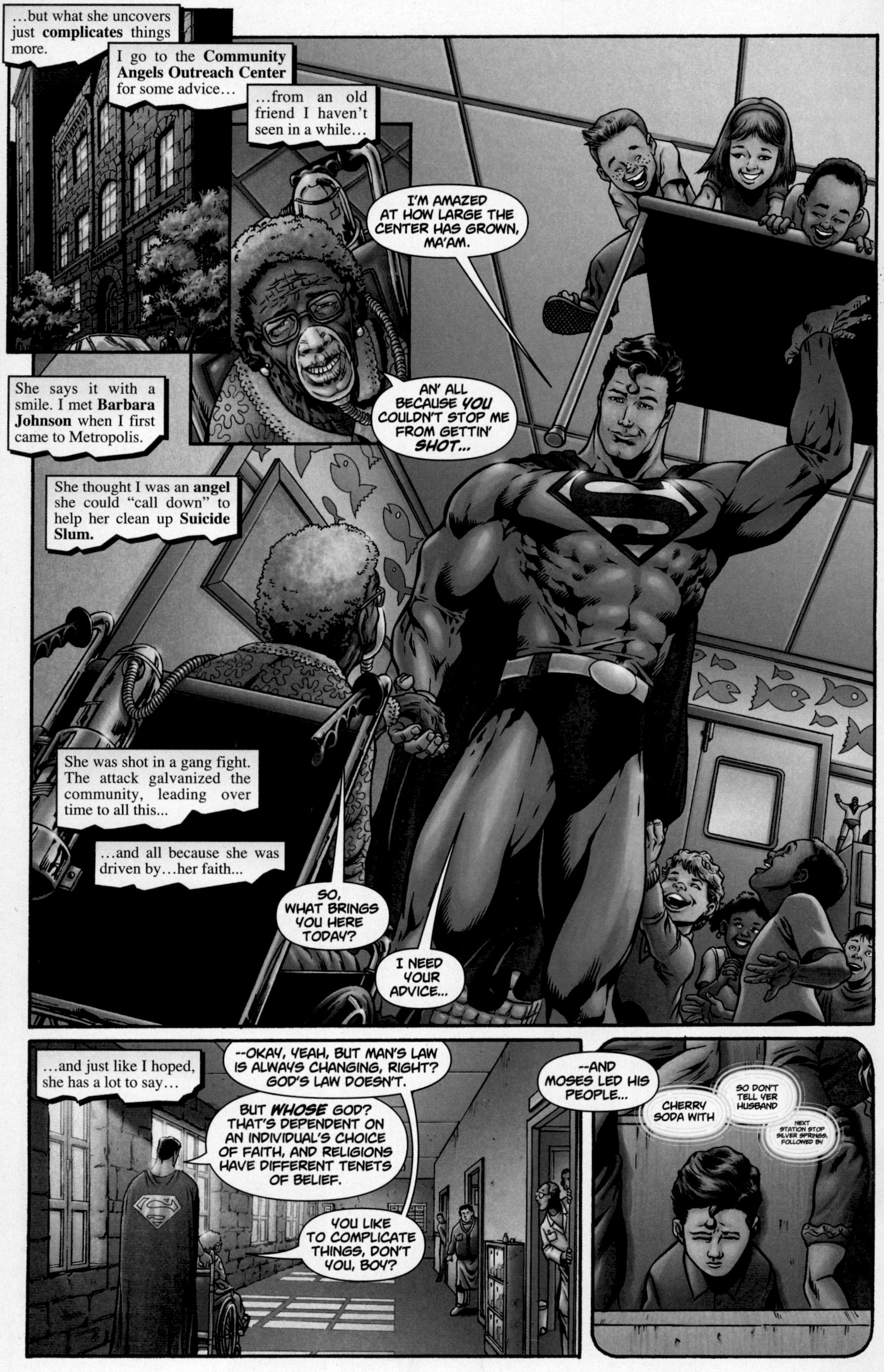
…but what she uncovers just complicates things more.
I go to the Community Angels Outreach Center for some advice…
…from an old friend I haven't seen in a while…
I'M AMAZED AT HOW LARGE THE CENTER HAS GROWN, MA'AM.
AN' ALL BECAUSE YOU COULDN'T STOP ME FROM GETTIN' SHOT…
She says it with a smile. I met Barbara Johnson when I first came to Metropolis.
She thought I was an angel she could "call down" to help her clean up Suicide Slum.
She was shot in a gang fight. The attack galvanized the community, leading over time to all this...
…and all because she was driven by…her faith...
SO, WHAT BRINGS YOU HERE TODAY?
I NEED YOUR ADVICE...
…and just like I hoped, she has a lot to say…
--OKAY, YEAH, BUT MAN'S LAW IS ALWAYS CHANGING, RIGHT? GOD'S LAW DOESN'T.
BUT WHOSE GOD? THAT'S DEPENDENT ON AN INDIVIDUAL'S CHOICE OF FAITH, AND RELIGIONS HAVE DIFFERENT TENETS OF BELIEF.
YOU LIKE TO COMPLICATE THINGS, DON'T YOU, BOY?
--AND MOSES LED HIS PEOPLE…
CHERRY SODA WITH
SO DON'T TELL YER HUSBAND
NEXT STATION STOP SILVER SPRINGS, FOLLOWED BY

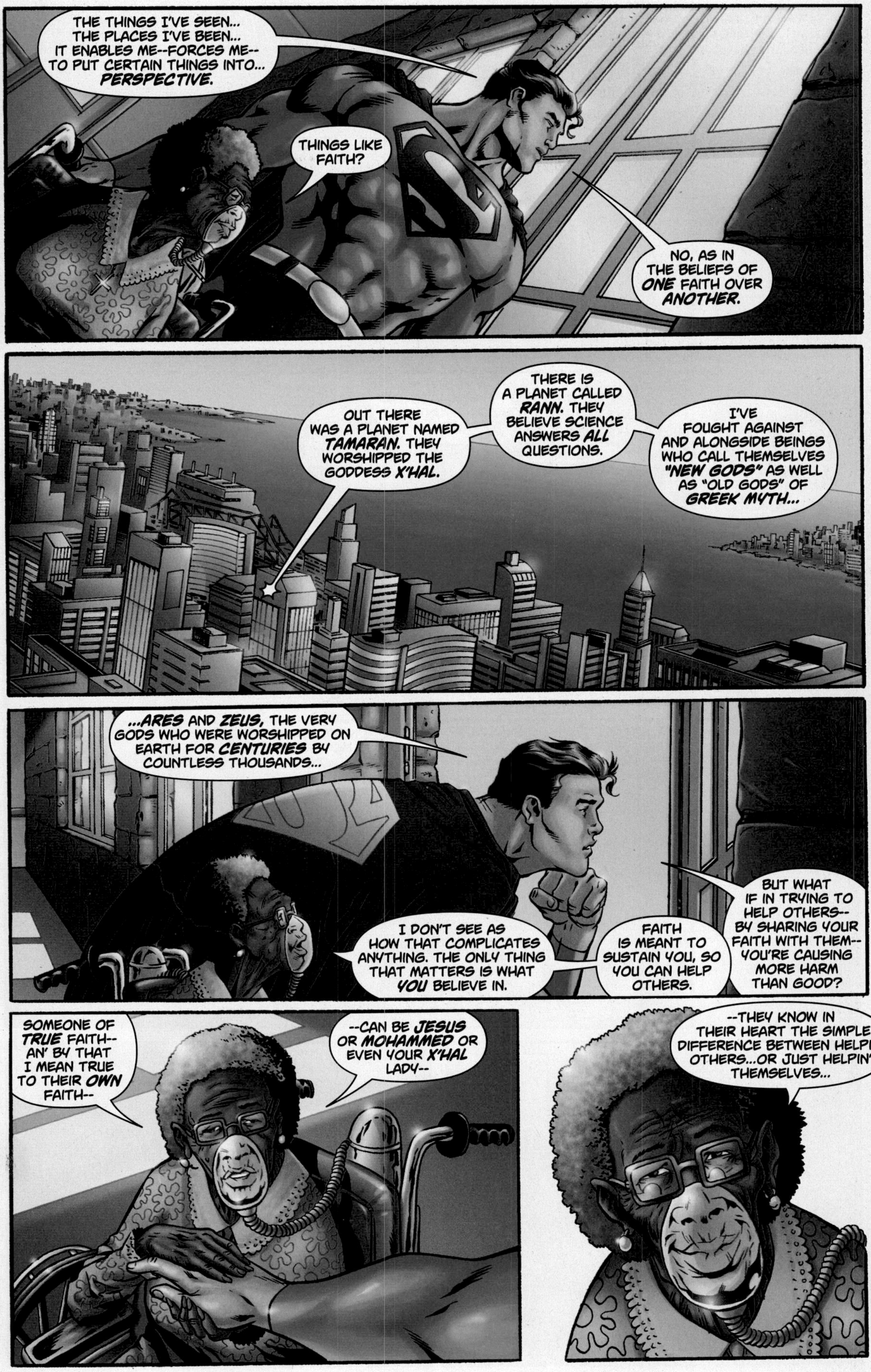
THE THINGS I'VE SEEN... THE PLACES I'VE BEEN... IT ENABLES ME--FORCES ME-- TO PUT CERTAIN THINGS INTO... PERSPECTIVE.
THINGS LIKE FAITH?
NO, AS IN THE BELIEFS OF ONE FAITH OVER ANOTHER.
OUT THERE WAS A PLANET NAMED TAMARAN. THEY WORSHIPPED THE GODDESS X'HAL.
THERE IS A PLANET CALLED RANN. THEY BELIEVE SCIENCE ANSWERS ALL QUESTIONS.
I'VE FOUGHT AGAINST AND ALONGSIDE BEINGS WHO CALL THEMSELVES "NEW GODS" AS WELL AS "OLD GODS" OF GREEK MYTH...
...ARES AND ZEUS, THE VERY GODS WHO WERE WORSHIPPED ON EARTH FOR CENTURIES BY COUNTLESS THOUSANDS...
BUT WHAT IF IN TRYING TO HELP OTHERS-- BY SHARING YOUR FAITH WITH THEM-- YOU'RE CAUSING MORE HARM THAN GOOD?
I DON'T SEE AS HOW THAT COMPLICATES ANYTHING. THE ONLY THING THAT MATTERS IS WHAT YOU BELIEVE IN.
FAITH IS MEANT TO SUSTAIN YOU, SO YOU CAN HELP OTHERS.
SOMEONE OF TRUE FAITH-- AN' BY THAT I MEAN TRUE TO THEIR OWN FAITH--
--CAN BE JESUS OR MOHAMMED OR EVEN YOUR X'HAL LADY--
--THEY KNOW IN THEIR HEART THE SIMPLE DIFFERENCE BETWEEN HELPIN' OTHERS...OR JUST HELPIN' THEMSELVES...

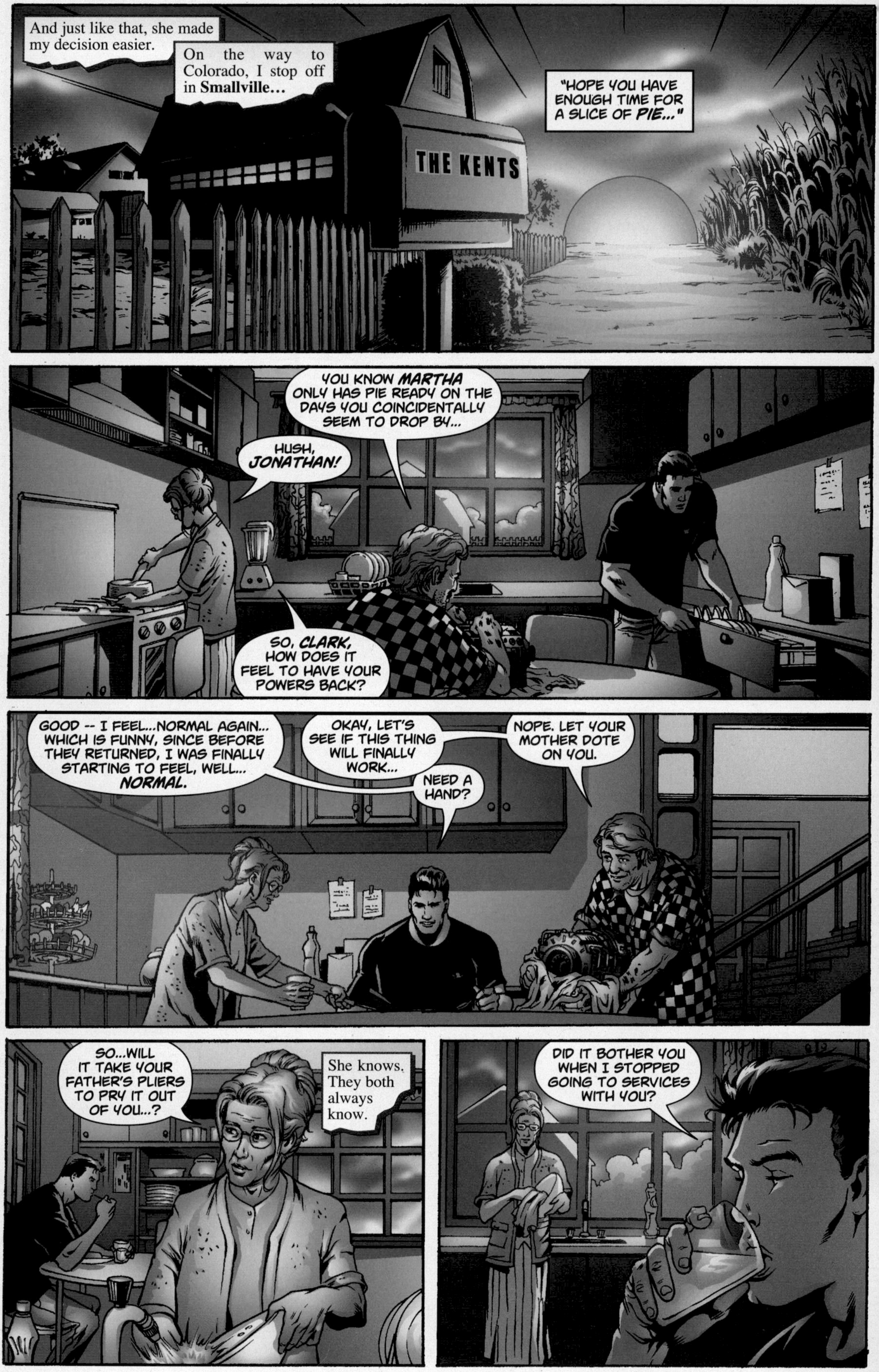
And just like that, she made my decision easier.
On the way to Colorado, I stop off in **Smallville...**
"HOPE YOU HAVE ENOUGH TIME FOR A SLICE OF *PIE...*"
THE KENTS
YOU KNOW *MARTHA* ONLY HAS PIE READY ON THE DAYS YOU COINCIDENTALLY SEEM TO DROP BY...
HUSH, *JONATHAN!*
SO, *CLARK,* HOW DOES IT FEEL TO HAVE YOUR POWERS BACK?
GOOD -- I FEEL...NORMAL AGAIN... WHICH IS FUNNY, SINCE BEFORE THEY RETURNED, I WAS FINALLY STARTING TO FEEL, WELL... *NORMAL.*
OKAY, LET'S SEE IF THIS THING WILL FINALLY WORK...
NEED A HAND?
NOPE. LET YOUR MOTHER DOTE ON YOU.
SO...WILL IT TAKE YOUR FATHER'S PLIERS TO PRY IT OUT OF YOU...?
She knows. They both always know.
DID IT BOTHER YOU WHEN I STOPPED GOING TO SERVICES WITH YOU?

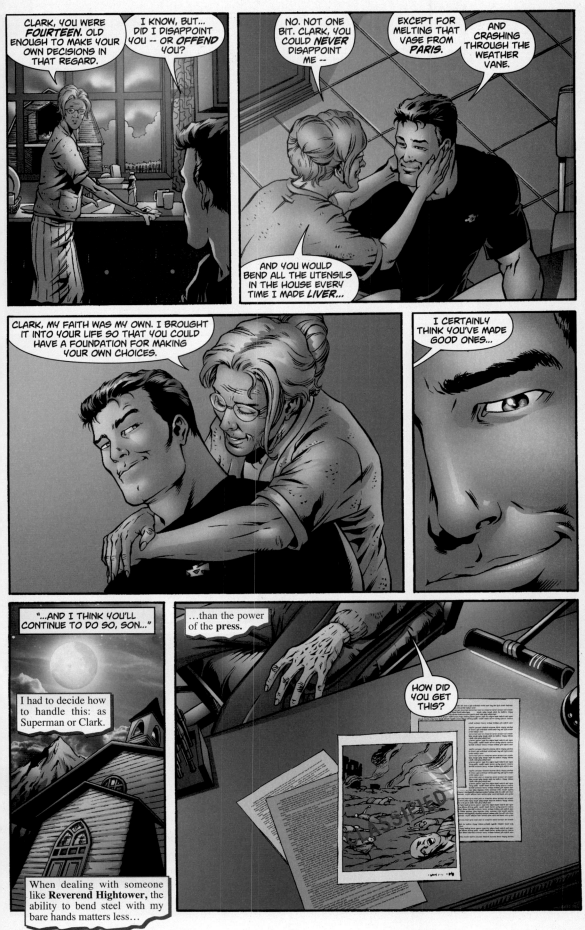

CLARK, YOU WERE **FOURTEEN.** OLD ENOUGH TO MAKE YOUR OWN DECISIONS IN THAT REGARD.

I KNOW, BUT... DID I DISAPPOINT YOU -- OR **OFFEND** YOU?

NO. NOT ONE BIT. CLARK, YOU COULD **NEVER** DISAPPOINT ME --

EXCEPT FOR MELTING THAT VASE FROM **PARIS.**

AND CRASHING THROUGH THE WEATHER VANE.

AND YOU WOULD BEND ALL THE UTENSILS IN THE HOUSE EVERY TIME I MADE **LIVER**...

CLARK, MY FAITH WAS MY OWN. I BROUGHT IT INTO YOUR LIFE SO THAT YOU COULD HAVE A FOUNDATION FOR MAKING YOUR OWN CHOICES.

I CERTAINLY THINK YOU'VE MADE GOOD ONES...

"...AND I THINK YOU'LL CONTINUE TO DO SO, SON..."

I had to decide how to handle this: as Superman or Clark.

When dealing with someone like **Reverend Hightower,** the ability to bend steel with my bare hands matters less...

...than the power of the **press.**

HOW DID YOU GET THIS?

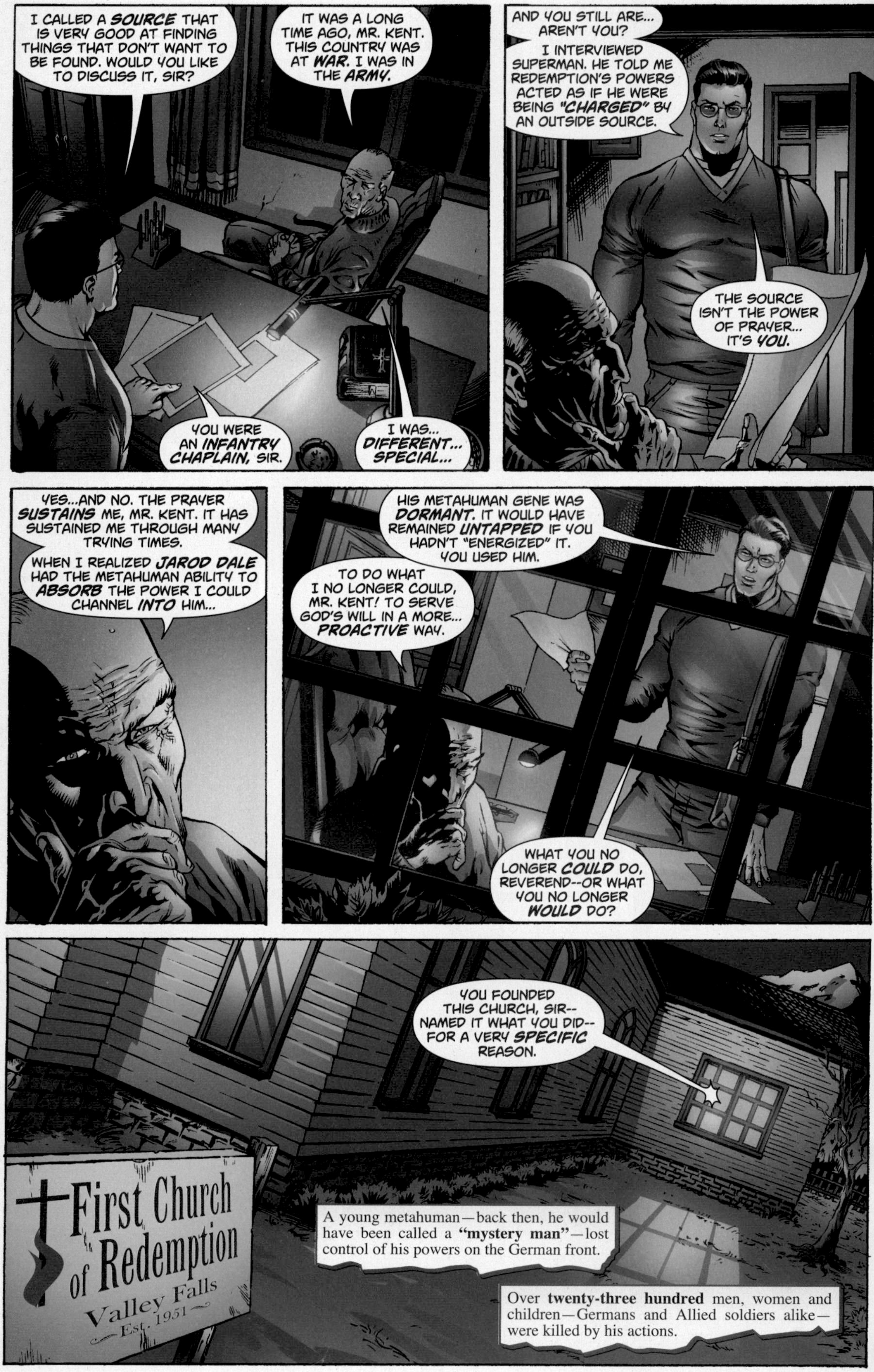
I CALLED A SOURCE THAT IS VERY GOOD AT FINDING THINGS THAT DON'T WANT TO BE FOUND. WOULD YOU LIKE TO DISCUSS IT, SIR?
IT WAS A LONG TIME AGO, MR. KENT. THIS COUNTRY WAS AT WAR. I WAS IN THE ARMY.
YOU WERE AN INFANTRY CHAPLAIN, SIR.
I WAS... DIFFERENT... SPECIAL...
AND YOU STILL ARE... AREN'T YOU?
I INTERVIEWED SUPERMAN. HE TOLD ME REDEMPTION'S POWERS ACTED AS IF HE WERE BEING "CHARGED" BY AN OUTSIDE SOURCE.
THE SOURCE ISN'T THE POWER OF PRAYER... IT'S YOU.
YES...AND NO. THE PRAYER SUSTAINS ME, MR. KENT. IT HAS SUSTAINED ME THROUGH MANY TRYING TIMES.
WHEN I REALIZED JAROD DALE HAD THE METAHUMAN ABILITY TO ABSORB THE POWER I COULD CHANNEL INTO HIM...
HIS METAHUMAN GENE WAS DORMANT. IT WOULD HAVE REMAINED UNTAPPED IF YOU HADN'T "ENERGIZED" IT. YOU USED HIM.
TO DO WHAT I NO LONGER COULD, MR. KENT! TO SERVE GOD'S WILL IN A MORE... PROACTIVE WAY.
WHAT YOU NO LONGER COULD DO, REVEREND--OR WHAT YOU NO LONGER WOULD DO?
YOU FOUNDED THIS CHURCH, SIR-- NAMED IT WHAT YOU DID-- FOR A VERY SPECIFIC REASON.
First Church of Redemption
Valley Falls
Est. 1951
A young metahuman—back then, he would have been called a **"mystery man"**—lost control of his powers on the German front.
Over **twenty-three hundred** men, women and children—Germans and Allied soldiers alike—were killed by his actions.

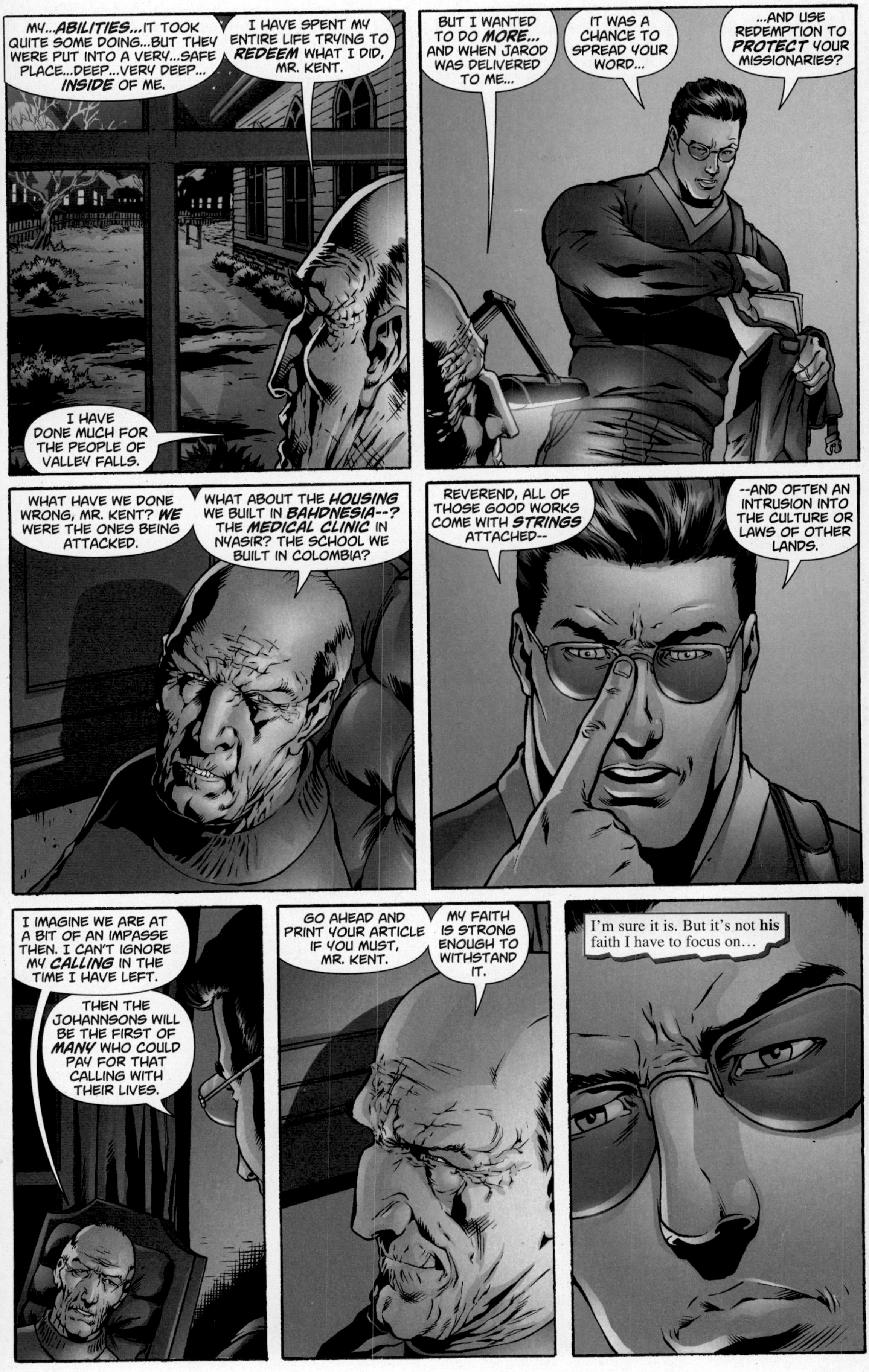
MY...ABILITIES...IT TOOK QUITE SOME DOING...BUT THEY WERE PUT INTO A VERY...SAFE PLACE...DEEP...VERY DEEP... INSIDE OF ME.
I HAVE SPENT MY ENTIRE LIFE TRYING TO REDEEM WHAT I DID, MR. KENT.
I HAVE DONE MUCH FOR THE PEOPLE OF VALLEY FALLS.
BUT I WANTED TO DO MORE... AND WHEN JAROD WAS DELIVERED TO ME...
IT WAS A CHANCE TO SPREAD YOUR WORD...
...AND USE REDEMPTION TO PROTECT YOUR MISSIONARIES?
WHAT HAVE WE DONE WRONG, MR. KENT? WE WERE THE ONES BEING ATTACKED.
WHAT ABOUT THE HOUSING WE BUILT IN BAHDNESIA--? THE MEDICAL CLINIC IN NYASIR? THE SCHOOL WE BUILT IN COLOMBIA?
REVEREND, ALL OF THOSE GOOD WORKS COME WITH STRINGS ATTACHED--
--AND OFTEN AN INTRUSION INTO THE CULTURE OR LAWS OF OTHER LANDS.
I IMAGINE WE ARE AT A BIT OF AN IMPASSE THEN. I CAN'T IGNORE MY CALLING IN THE TIME I HAVE LEFT.
THEN THE JOHANNSONS WILL BE THE FIRST OF MANY WHO COULD PAY FOR THAT CALLING WITH THEIR LIVES.
GO AHEAD AND PRINT YOUR ARTICLE IF YOU MUST, MR. KENT.
MY FAITH IS STRONG ENOUGH TO WITHSTAND IT.
I'm sure it is. But it's not his faith I have to focus on…

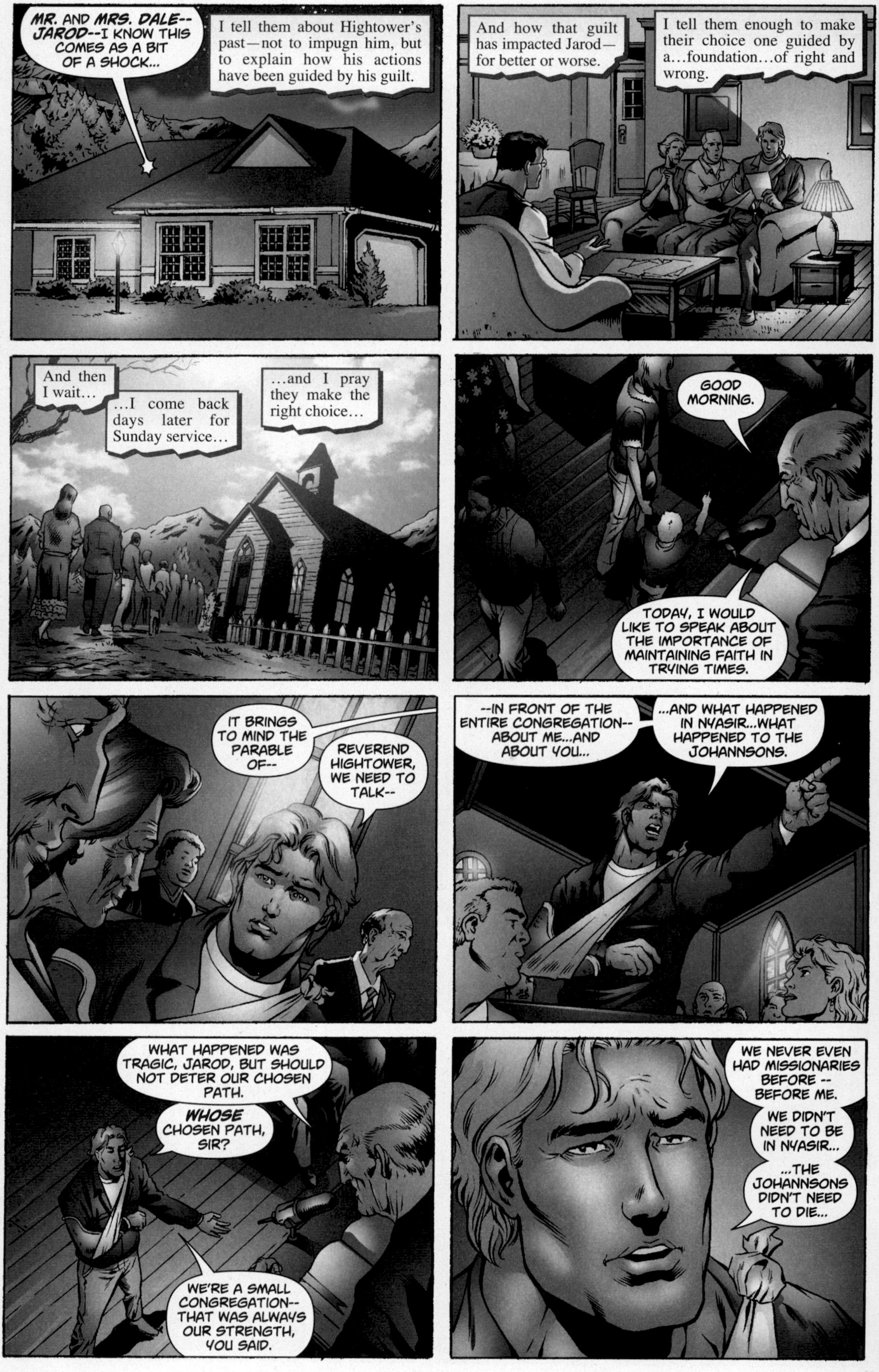
MR. AND MRS. DALE--JAROD--I KNOW THIS COMES AS A BIT OF A SHOCK...
I tell them about Hightower's past—not to impugn him, but to explain how his actions have been guided by his guilt.
And how that guilt has impacted Jarod—for better or worse.
I tell them enough to make their choice one guided by a…foundation…of right and wrong.
And then I wait…
…I come back days later for Sunday service…
…and I pray they make the right choice…
GOOD MORNING.
TODAY, I WOULD LIKE TO SPEAK ABOUT THE IMPORTANCE OF MAINTAINING FAITH IN TRYING TIMES.
IT BRINGS TO MIND THE PARABLE OF--
REVEREND HIGHTOWER, WE NEED TO TALK--
--IN FRONT OF THE ENTIRE CONGREGATION--ABOUT ME...AND ABOUT YOU...
...AND WHAT HAPPENED IN NYASIR...WHAT HAPPENED TO THE JOHANNSONS.
WHAT HAPPENED WAS TRAGIC, JAROD, BUT SHOULD NOT DETER OUR CHOSEN PATH.
WHOSE CHOSEN PATH, SIR?
WE'RE A SMALL CONGREGATION--THAT WAS ALWAYS OUR STRENGTH, YOU SAID.
WE NEVER EVEN HAD MISSIONARIES BEFORE -- BEFORE ME.
WE DIDN'T NEED TO BE IN NYASIR...
...THE JOHANNSONS DIDN'T NEED TO DIE...

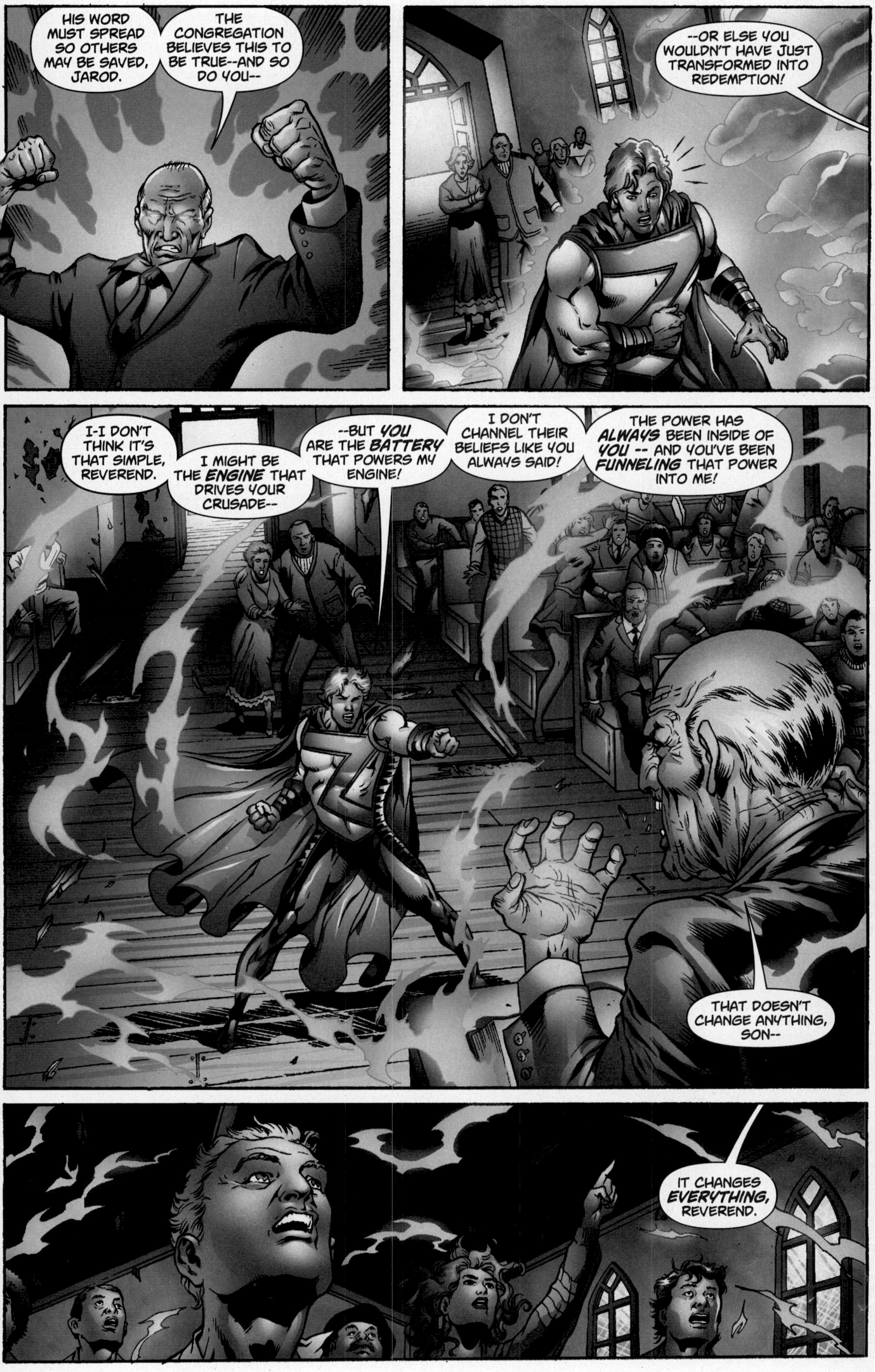
HIS WORD MUST SPREAD SO OTHERS MAY BE SAVED, JAROD.
THE CONGREGATION BELIEVES THIS TO BE TRUE--AND SO DO YOU--
--OR ELSE YOU WOULDN'T HAVE JUST TRANSFORMED INTO REDEMPTION!
I-I DON'T THINK IT'S THAT SIMPLE, REVEREND.
I MIGHT BE THE ENGINE THAT DRIVES YOUR CRUSADE--
--BUT YOU ARE THE BATTERY THAT POWERS MY ENGINE!
I DON'T CHANNEL THEIR BELIEFS LIKE YOU ALWAYS SAID!
THE POWER HAS ALWAYS BEEN INSIDE OF YOU -- AND YOU'VE BEEN FUNNELING THAT POWER INTO ME!
THAT DOESN'T CHANGE ANYTHING, SON--
IT CHANGES EVERYTHING, REVEREND.

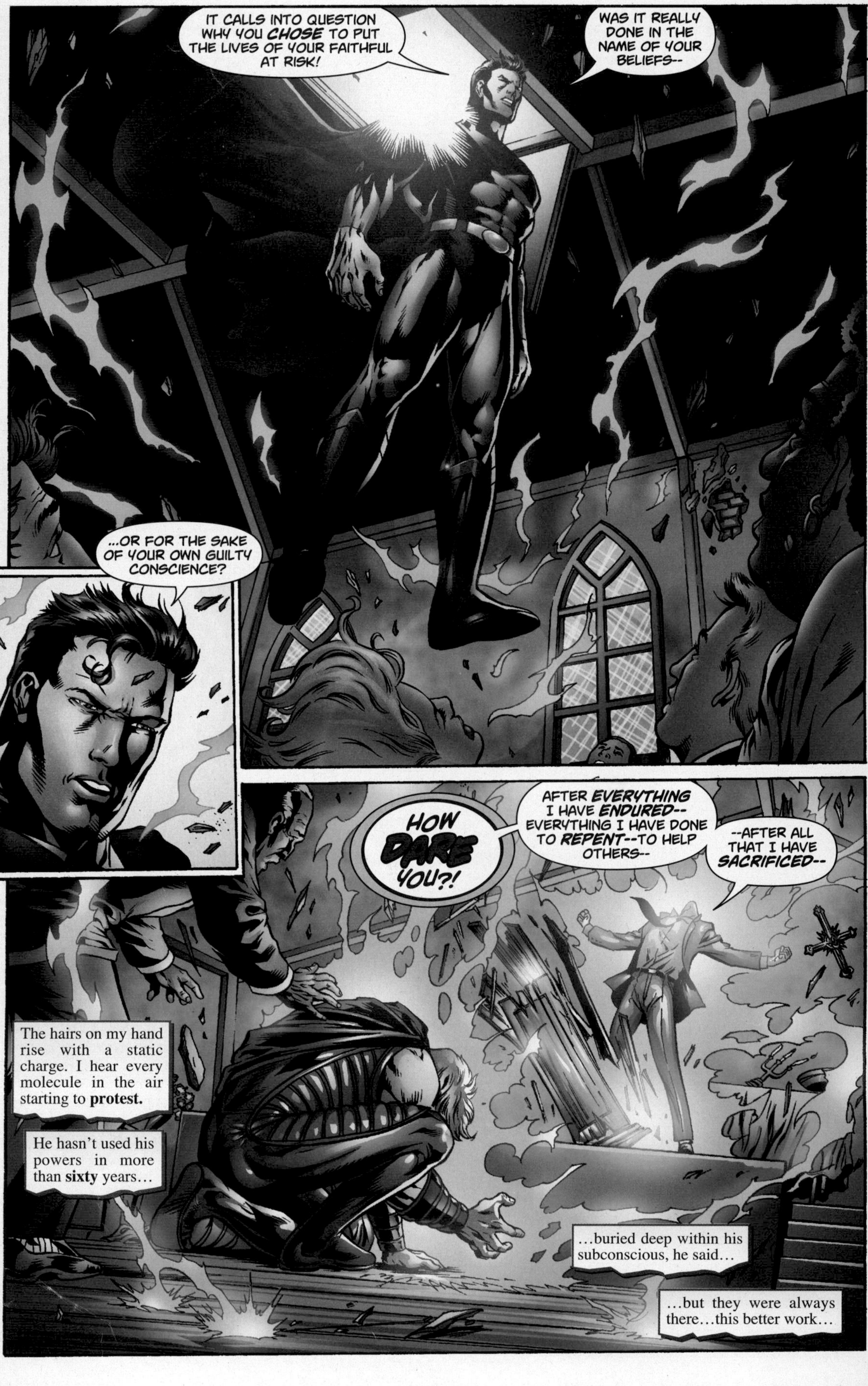
IT CALLS INTO QUESTION WHY YOU CHOSE TO PUT THE LIVES OF YOUR FAITHFUL AT RISK!
WAS IT REALLY DONE IN THE NAME OF YOUR BELIEFS--
...OR FOR THE SAKE OF YOUR OWN GUILTY CONSCIENCE?
HOW DARE YOU?!
AFTER EVERYTHING I HAVE ENDURED-- EVERYTHING I HAVE DONE TO REPENT--TO HELP OTHERS--
--AFTER ALL THAT I HAVE SACRIFICED--
The hairs on my hand rise with a static charge. I hear every molecule in the air starting to protest.
He hasn't used his powers in more than sixty years...
...buried deep within his subconscious, he said...
...but they were always there...this better work...

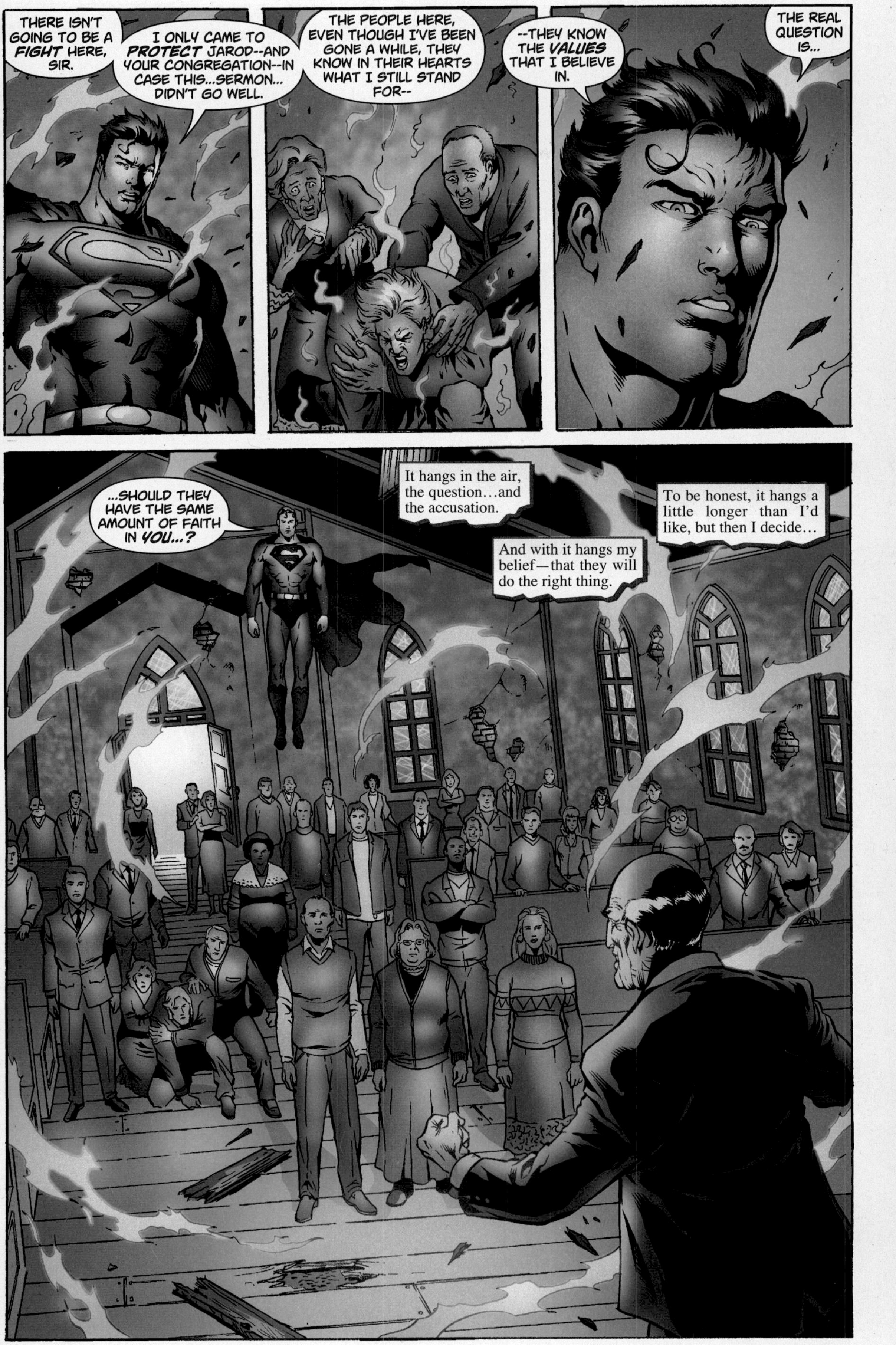
THERE ISN'T GOING TO BE A FIGHT HERE, SIR.
I ONLY CAME TO PROTECT JAROD--AND YOUR CONGREGATION--IN CASE THIS...SERMON... DIDN'T GO WELL.
THE PEOPLE HERE, EVEN THOUGH I'VE BEEN GONE A WHILE, THEY KNOW IN THEIR HEARTS WHAT I STILL STAND FOR--
--THEY KNOW THE VALUES THAT I BELIEVE IN.
THE REAL QUESTION IS...
...SHOULD THEY HAVE THE SAME AMOUNT OF FAITH IN YOU...?
It hangs in the air, the question…and the accusation.
And with it hangs my belief—that they will do the right thing.
To be honest, it hangs a little longer than I'd like, but then I decide…

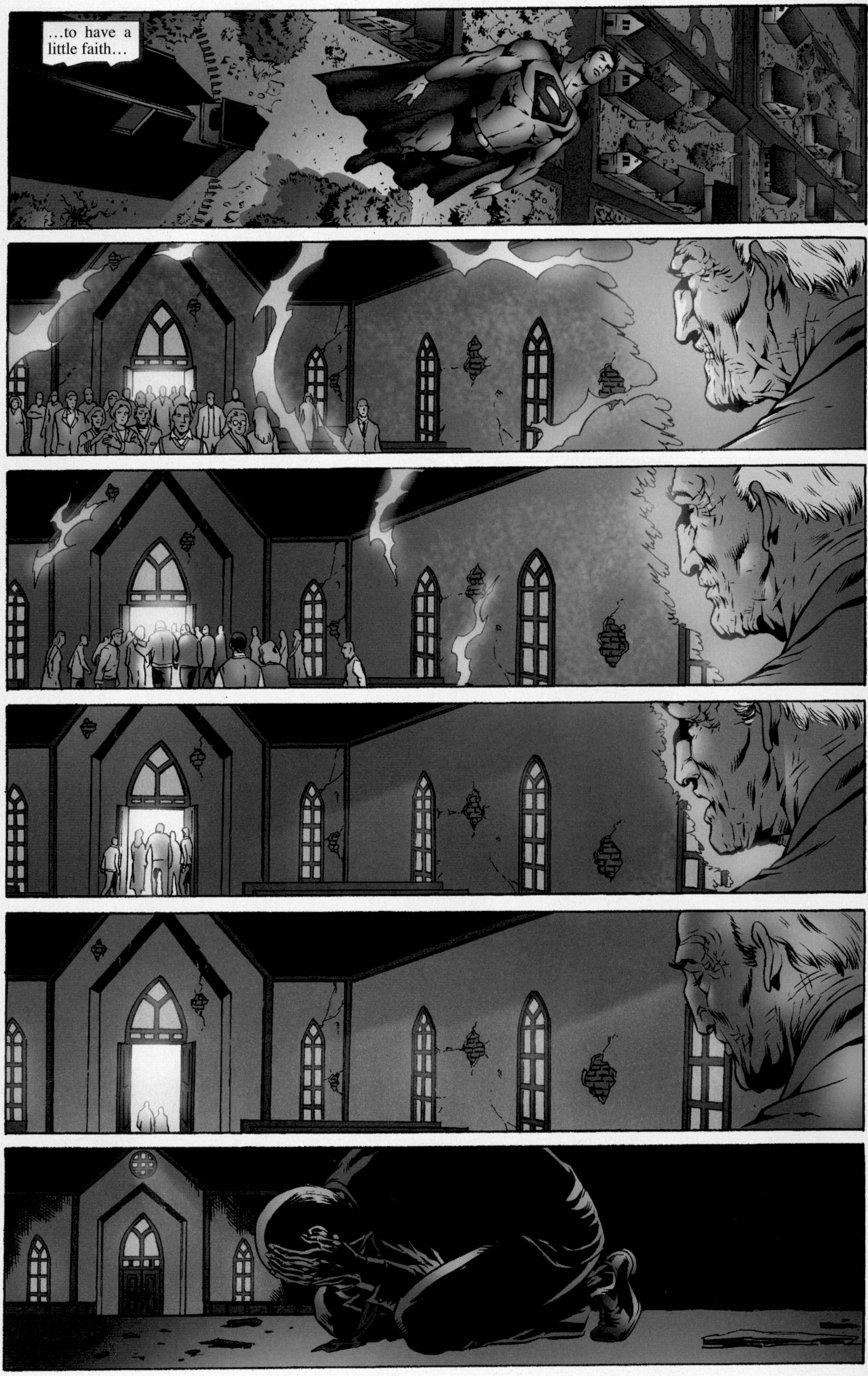
...to have a little faith...

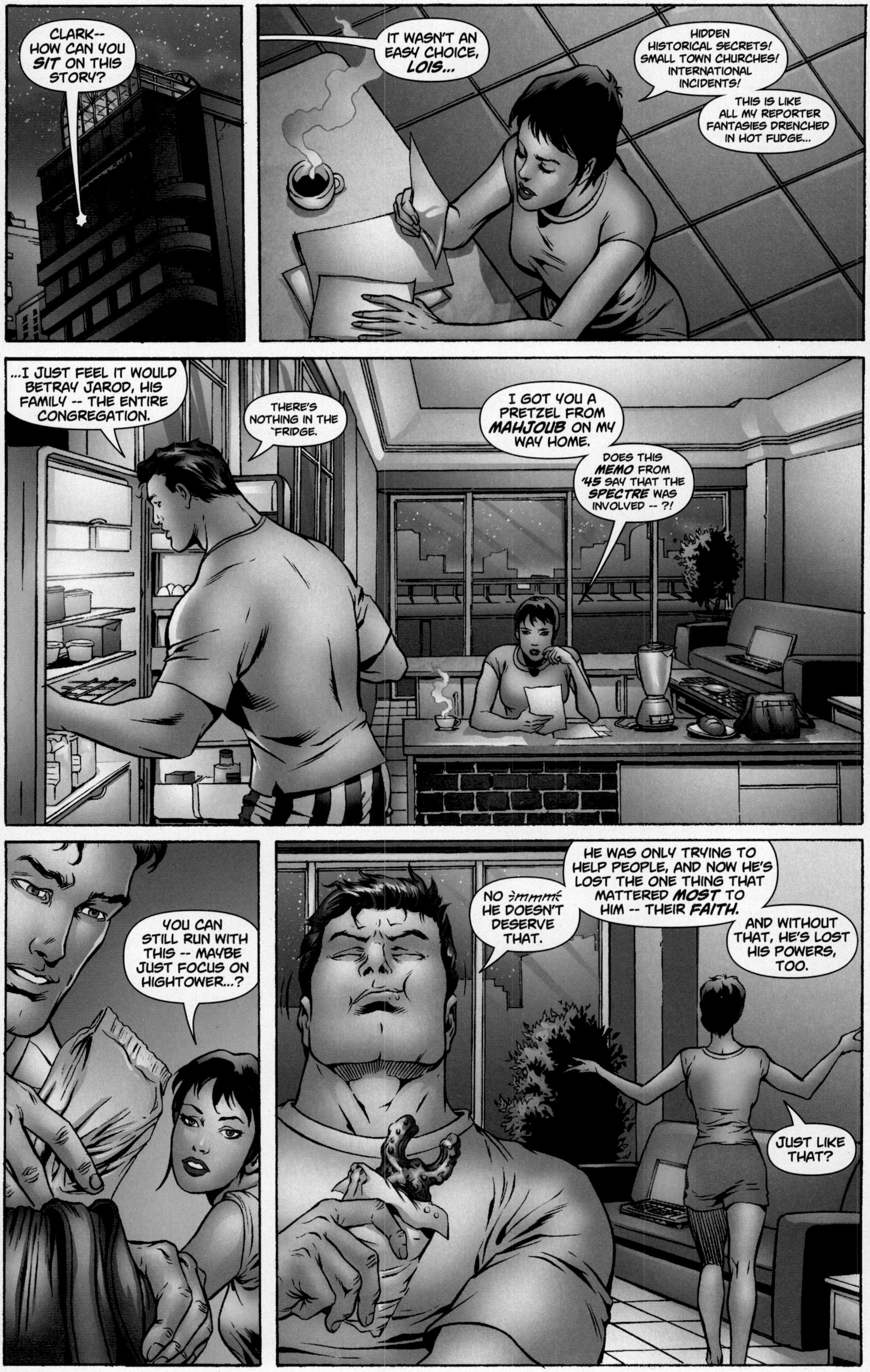
CLARK-- HOW CAN YOU SIT ON THIS STORY?
IT WASN'T AN EASY CHOICE, LOIS...
HIDDEN HISTORICAL SECRETS! SMALL TOWN CHURCHES! INTERNATIONAL INCIDENTS!
THIS IS LIKE ALL MY REPORTER FANTASIES DRENCHED IN HOT FUDGE...
...I JUST FEEL IT WOULD BETRAY JAROD, HIS FAMILY -- THE ENTIRE CONGREGATION.
THERE'S NOTHING IN THE 'FRIDGE.
I GOT YOU A PRETZEL FROM MAHJOUB ON MY WAY HOME.
DOES THIS MEMO FROM '45 SAY THAT THE SPECTRE WAS INVOLVED -- ?!
YOU CAN STILL RUN WITH THIS -- MAYBE JUST FOCUS ON HIGHTOWER...?
NO mmm HE DOESN'T DESERVE THAT.
HE WAS ONLY TRYING TO HELP PEOPLE, AND NOW HE'S LOST THE ONE THING THAT MATTERED MOST TO HIM -- THEIR FAITH.
AND WITHOUT THAT, HE'S LOST HIS POWERS, TOO.
JUST LIKE THAT?

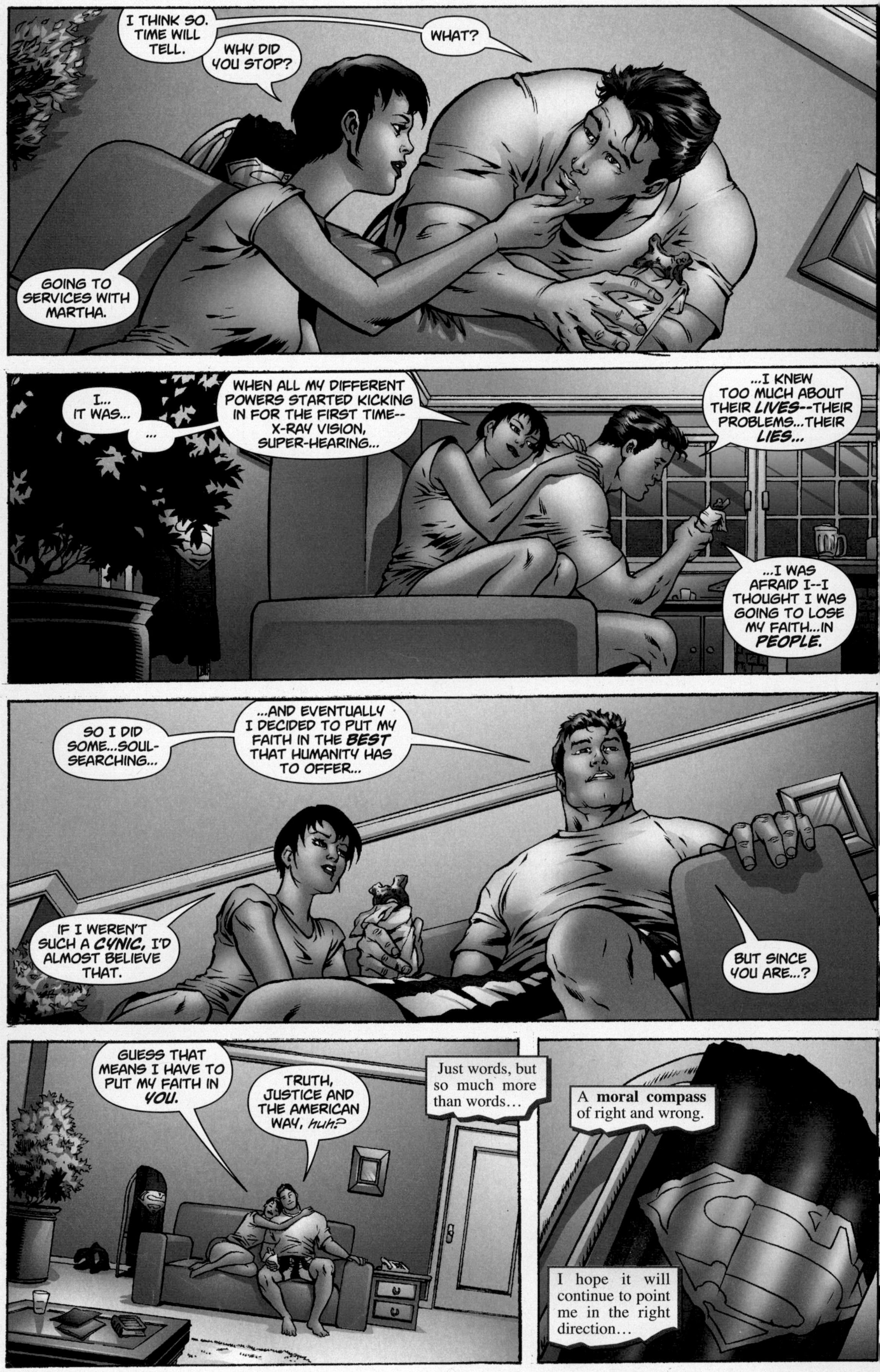
I THINK SO. TIME WILL TELL.
WHAT?
WHY DID YOU STOP?
GOING TO SERVICES WITH MARTHA.
I... IT WAS...
...
WHEN ALL MY DIFFERENT POWERS STARTED KICKING IN FOR THE FIRST TIME-- X-RAY VISION, SUPER-HEARING...
...I KNEW TOO MUCH ABOUT THEIR LIVES--THEIR PROBLEMS...THEIR LIES...
...I WAS AFRAID I--I THOUGHT I WAS GOING TO LOSE MY FAITH...IN PEOPLE.
SO I DID SOME...SOUL-SEARCHING...
...AND EVENTUALLY I DECIDED TO PUT MY FAITH IN THE BEST THAT HUMANITY HAS TO OFFER...
IF I WEREN'T SUCH A CYNIC, I'D ALMOST BELIEVE THAT.
BUT SINCE YOU ARE...?
GUESS THAT MEANS I HAVE TO PUT MY FAITH IN YOU.
TRUTH, JUSTICE AND THE AMERICAN WAY, huh?
Just words, but so much more than words...
A moral compass of right and wrong.
I hope it will continue to point me in the right direction...

The Beast from Krypton Cover to Superman 686 by Walter Simonson

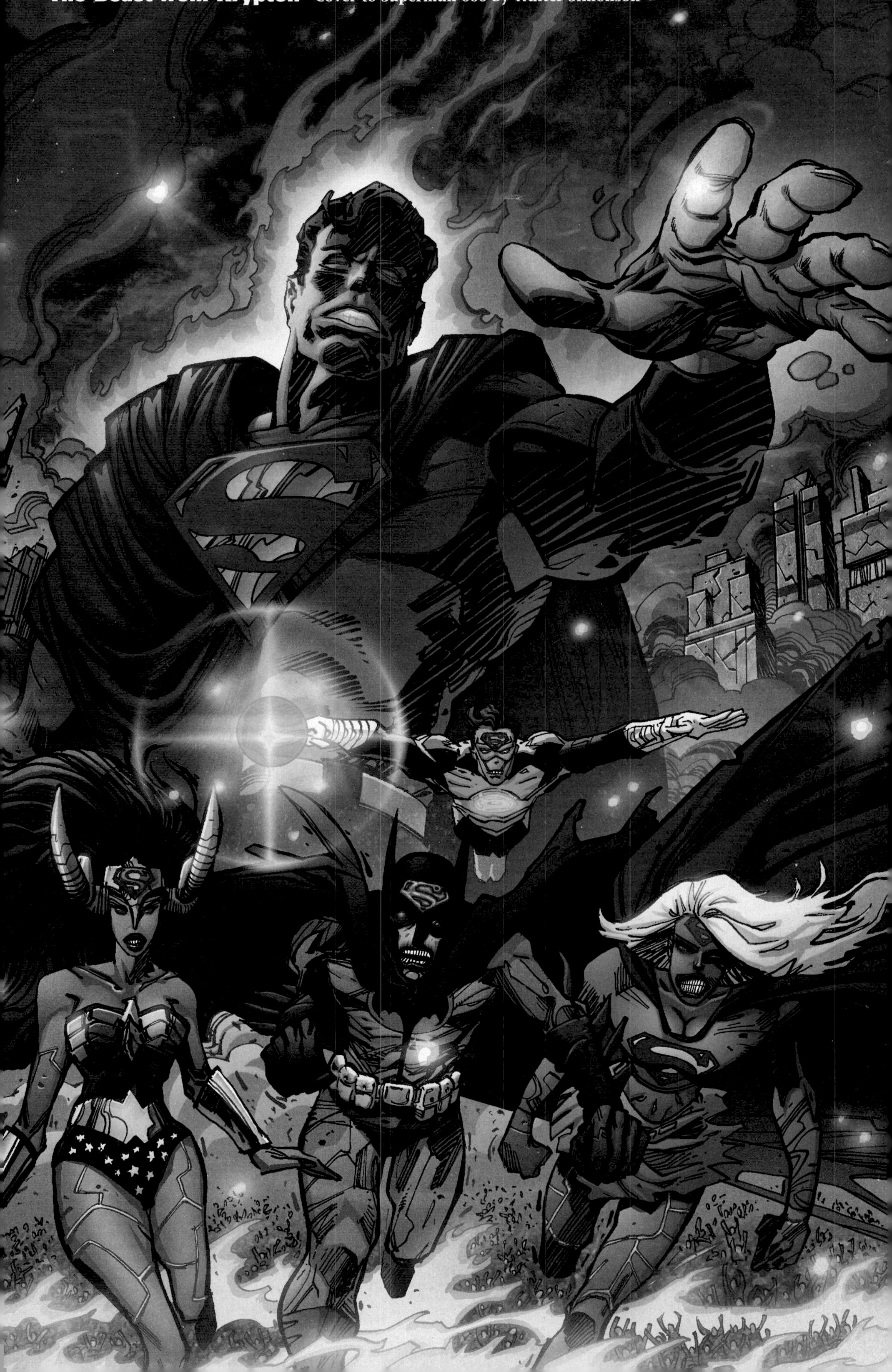

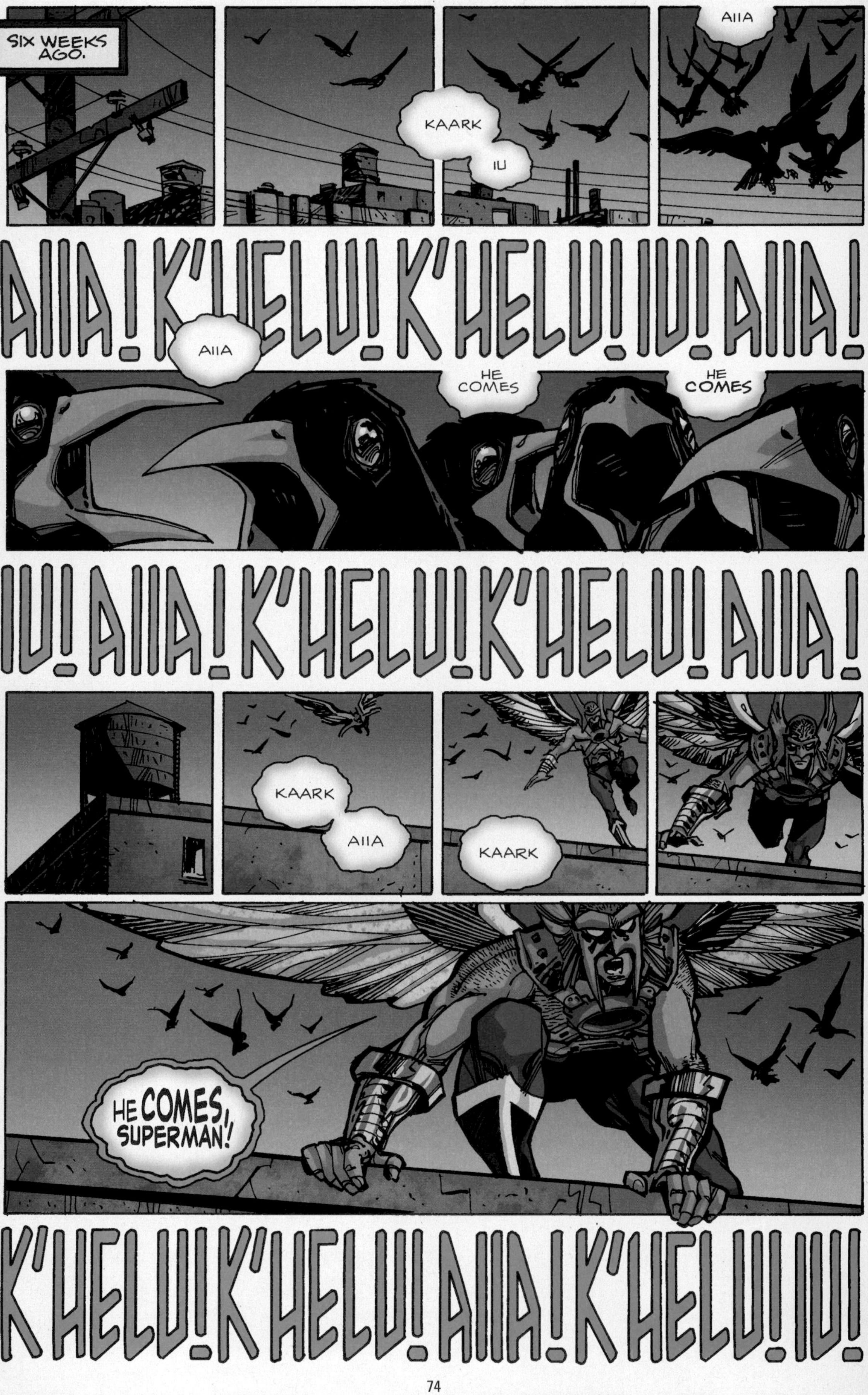
SIX WEEKS AGO.
KAARK
IU
AIIA
AIIA! K'HELU! K'HELU! IU! AIIA!
AIIA
HE COMES
HE COMES
IU! AIIA! K'HELU! K'HELU! AIIA!
KAARK
AIIA
KAARK
HE COMES, SUPERMAN!
K'HELU! K'HELU! AIIA! K'HELU! IU!

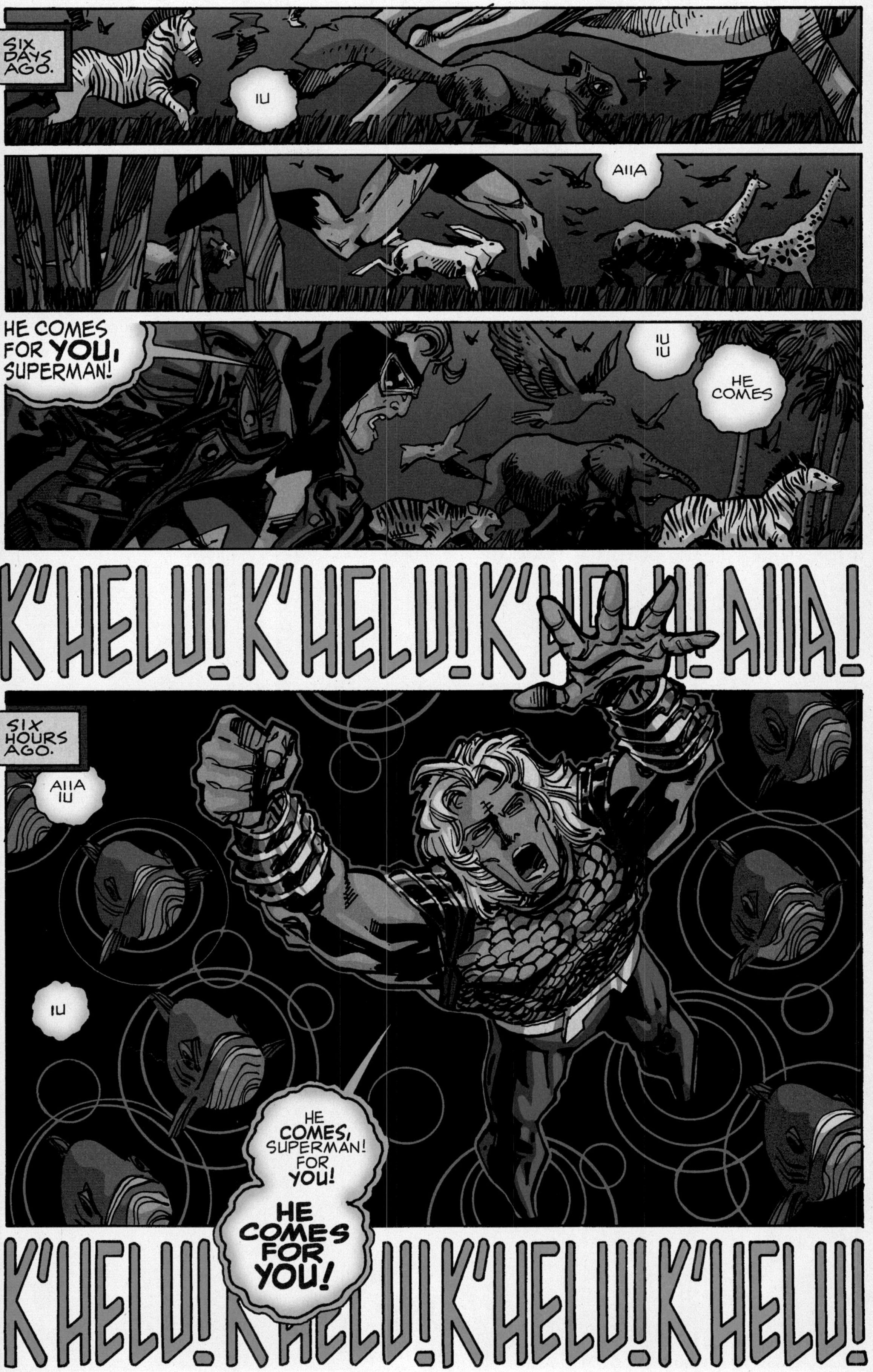
SIX DAYS AGO.
IU
AIIA
HE COMES FOR YOU, SUPERMAN!
IU IU
HE COMES
K'HELU! K'HELU! K'HELU! AIIA!
SIX HOURS AGO.
AIIA IU
IU
HE COMES, SUPERMAN! FOR YOU!
HE COMES FOR YOU!
K'HELU! K'HELU! K'HELU! K'HELU!

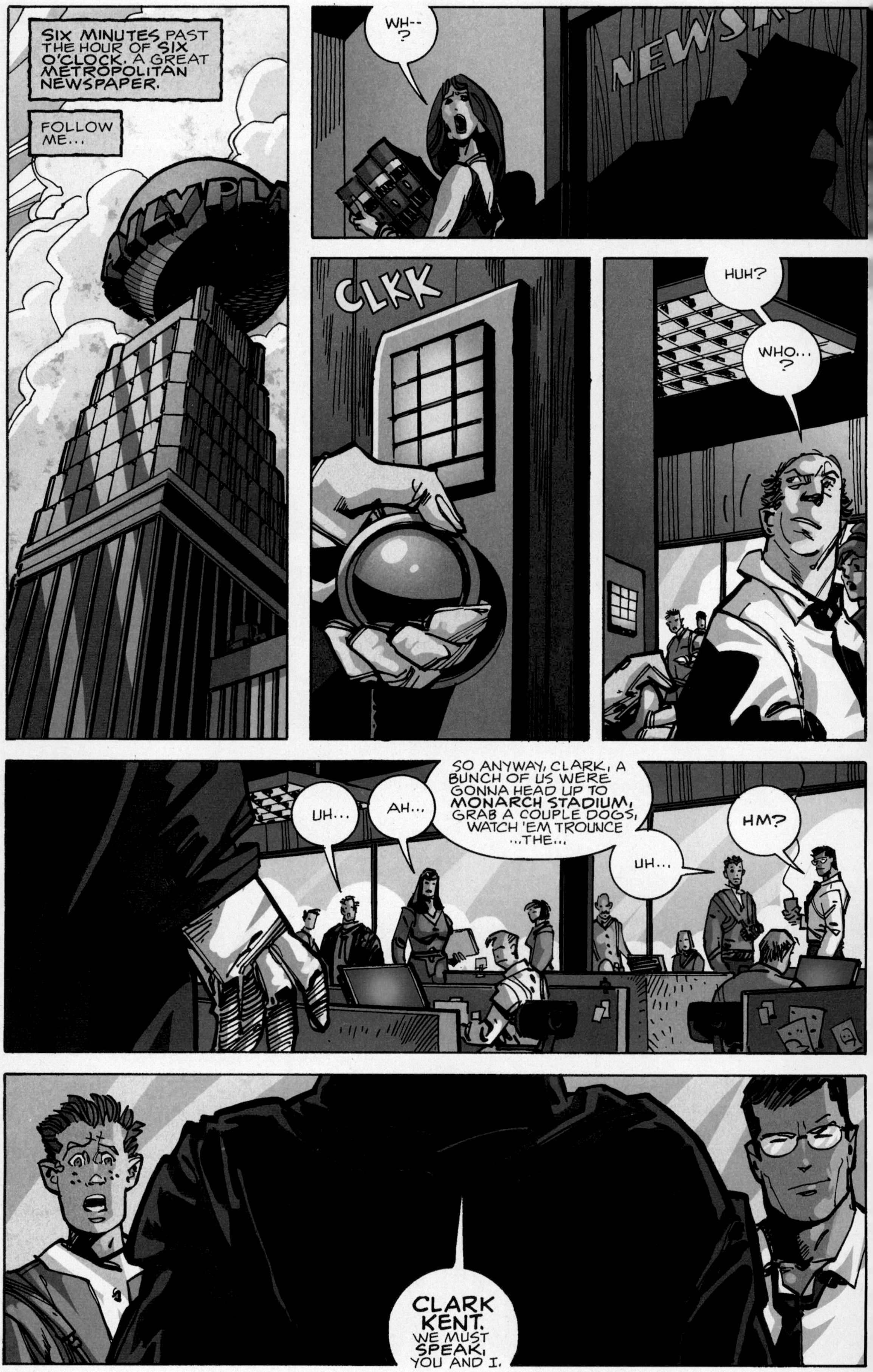

SIX MINUTES PAST THE HOUR OF SIX O'CLOCK. A GREAT METROPOLITAN NEWSPAPER.
FOLLOW ME...
WH-- ?
CLKK
HUH?
WHO... ?
UH...
AH...
SO ANYWAY, CLARK, A BUNCH OF US WERE GONNA HEAD UP TO MONARCH STADIUM, GRAB A COUPLE DOGS, WATCH 'EM TROUNCE ...THE...
UH...
HM?
CLARK KENT. WE MUST SPEAK, YOU AND I.

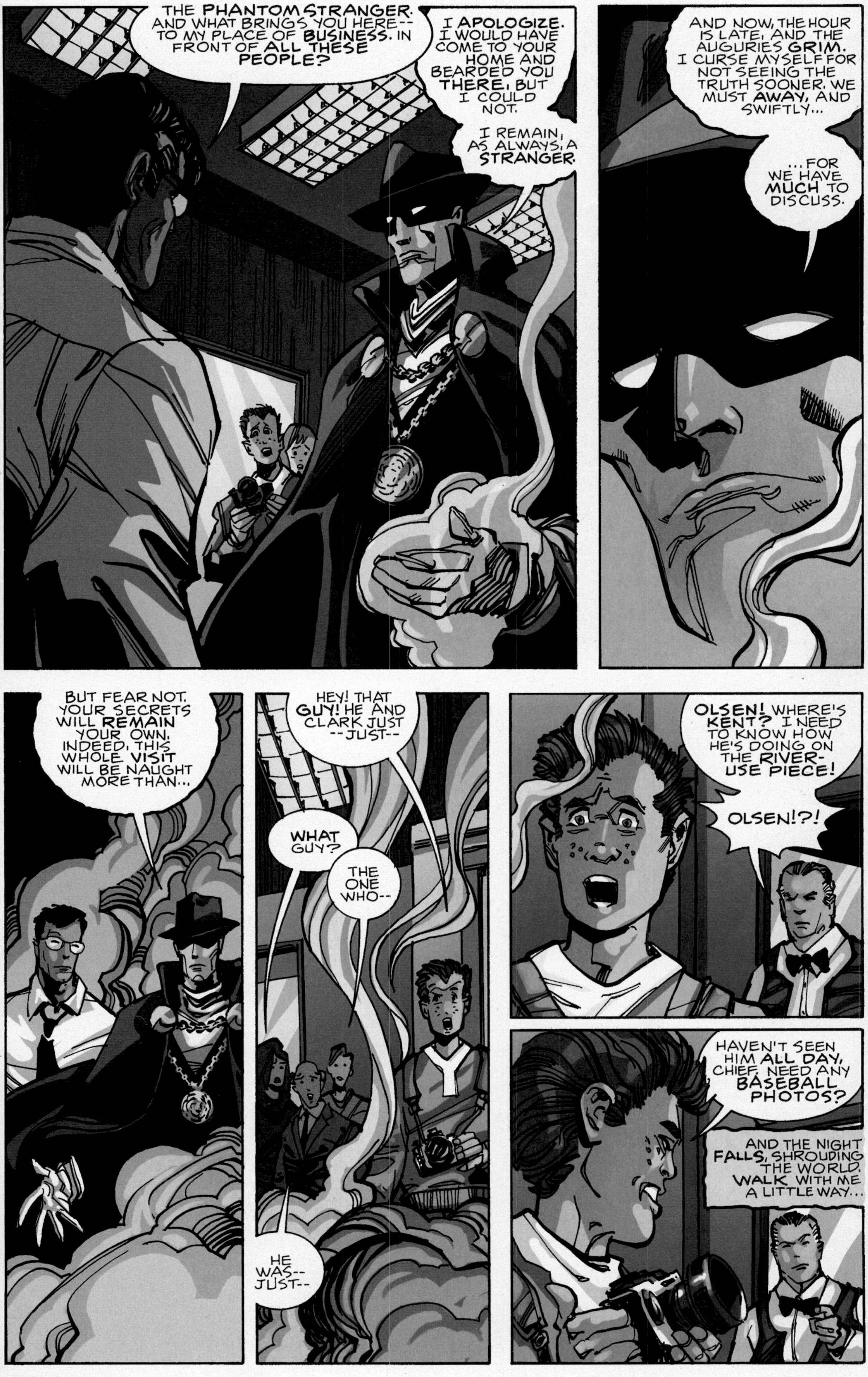

THE PHANTOM STRANGER. AND WHAT BRINGS YOU HERE-- TO MY PLACE OF BUSINESS. IN FRONT OF ALL THESE PEOPLE?
I APOLOGIZE. I WOULD HAVE COME TO YOUR HOME AND BEARDED YOU THERE, BUT I COULD NOT.
I REMAIN, AS ALWAYS, A STRANGER.
AND NOW, THE HOUR IS LATE, AND THE AUGURIES GRIM. I CURSE MYSELF FOR NOT SEEING THE TRUTH SOONER. WE MUST AWAY, AND SWIFTLY...
...FOR WE HAVE MUCH TO DISCUSS.
BUT FEAR NOT. YOUR SECRETS WILL REMAIN YOUR OWN. INDEED, THIS WHOLE VISIT WILL BE NAUGHT MORE THAN...
HEY! THAT GUY! HE AND CLARK JUST --JUST--
WHAT GUY?
THE ONE WHO--
HE WAS-- JUST--
OLSEN! WHERE'S KENT? I NEED TO KNOW HOW HE'S DOING ON THE RIVER-USE PIECE!
OLSEN!?!
HAVEN'T SEEN HIM ALL DAY, CHIEF. NEED ANY BASEBALL PHOTOS?
AND THE NIGHT FALLS, SHROUDING THE WORLD. WALK WITH ME A LITTLE WAY...

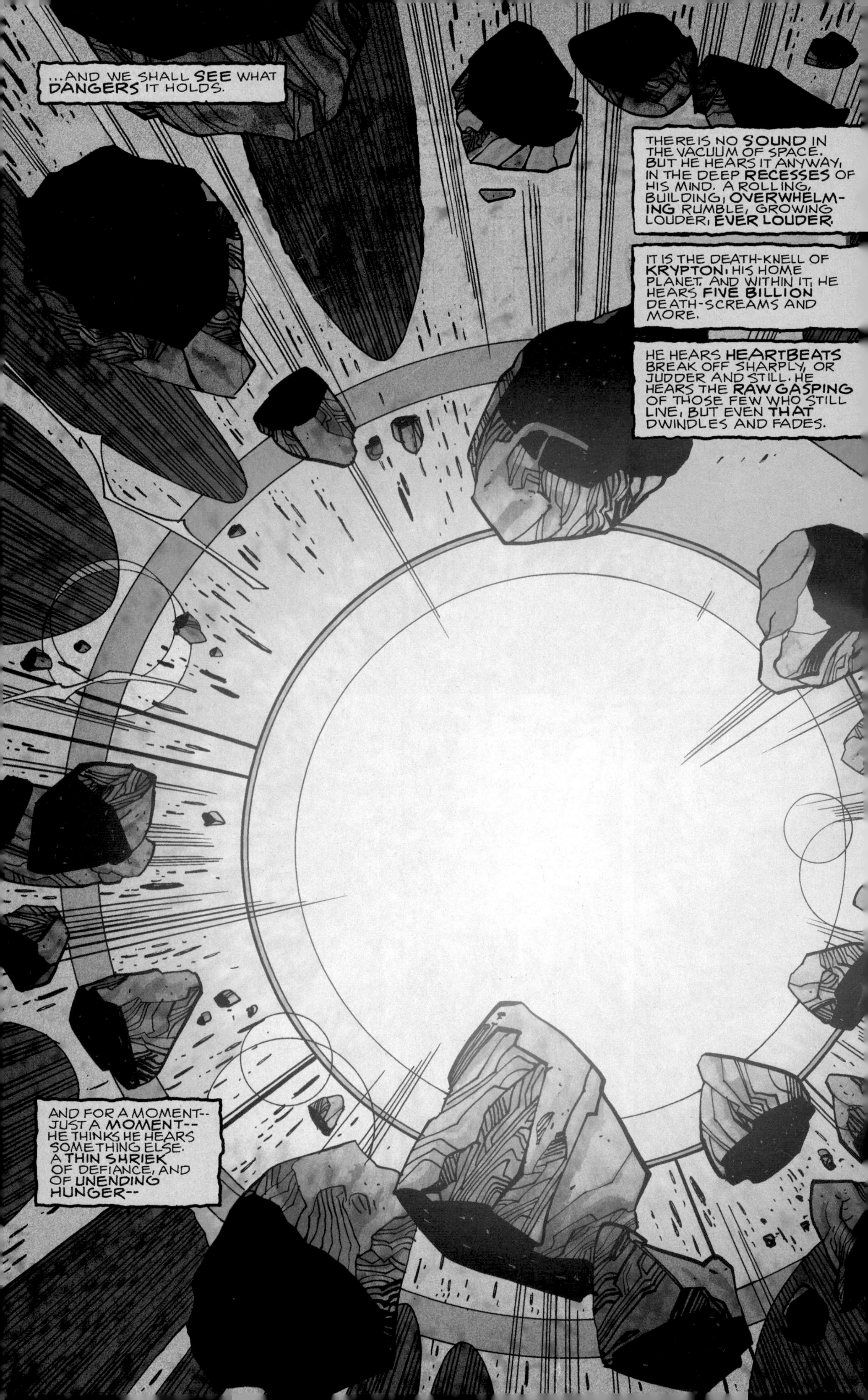
...AND WE SHALL SEE WHAT DANGERS IT HOLDS.
THERE IS NO SOUND IN THE VACUUM OF SPACE. BUT HE HEARS IT ANYWAY, IN THE DEEP RECESSES OF HIS MIND. A ROLLING, BUILDING, OVERWHELMING RUMBLE, GROWING LOUDER, EVER LOUDER.
IT IS THE DEATH-KNELL OF KRYPTON, HIS HOME PLANET. AND WITHIN IT, HE HEARS FIVE BILLION DEATH-SCREAMS AND MORE.
HE HEARS HEARTBEATS BREAK OFF SHARPLY, OR JUDDER AND STILL. HE HEARS THE RAW GASPING OF THOSE FEW WHO STILL LIVE, BUT EVEN THAT DWINDLES AND FADES.
AND FOR A MOMENT-- JUST A MOMENT-- HE THINKS HE HEARS SOMETHING ELSE. A THIN SHRIEK OF DEFIANCE, AND OF UNENDING HUNGER--

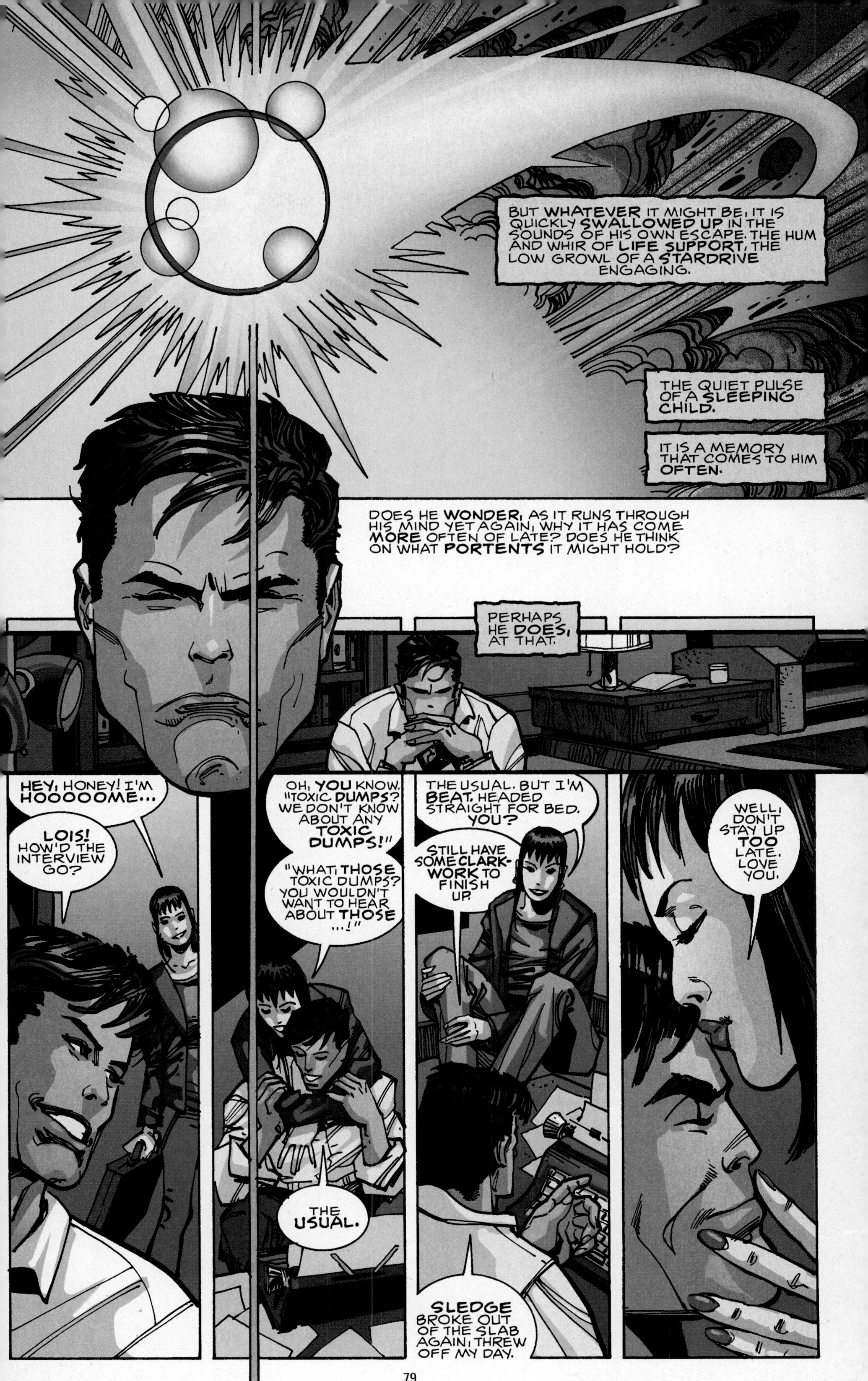

BUT WHATEVER IT MIGHT BE, IT IS QUICKLY SWALLOWED UP IN THE SOUNDS OF HIS OWN ESCAPE. THE HUM AND WHIR OF LIFE SUPPORT, THE LOW GROWL OF A STARDRIVE ENGAGING.
THE QUIET PULSE OF A SLEEPING CHILD.
IT IS A MEMORY THAT COMES TO HIM OFTEN.
DOES HE WONDER, AS IT RUNS THROUGH HIS MIND YET AGAIN, WHY IT HAS COME MORE OFTEN OF LATE? DOES HE THINK ON WHAT PORTENTS IT MIGHT HOLD?
PERHAPS HE DOES, AT THAT.
HEY, HONEY! I'M HOOOOOME...
LOIS! HOW'D THE INTERVIEW GO?
THE USUAL.
OH, YOU KNOW. "TOXIC DUMPS? WE DON'T KNOW ABOUT ANY TOXIC DUMPS!"
"WHAT, THOSE TOXIC DUMPS? YOU WOULDN'T WANT TO HEAR ABOUT THOSE ...!"
THE USUAL. BUT I'M BEAT. HEADED STRAIGHT FOR BED. YOU?
STILL HAVE SOME CLARK-WORK TO FINISH UP.
SLEDGE BROKE OUT OF THE SLAB AGAIN, THREW OFF MY DAY.
WELL, DON'T STAY UP TOO LATE. LOVE YOU.

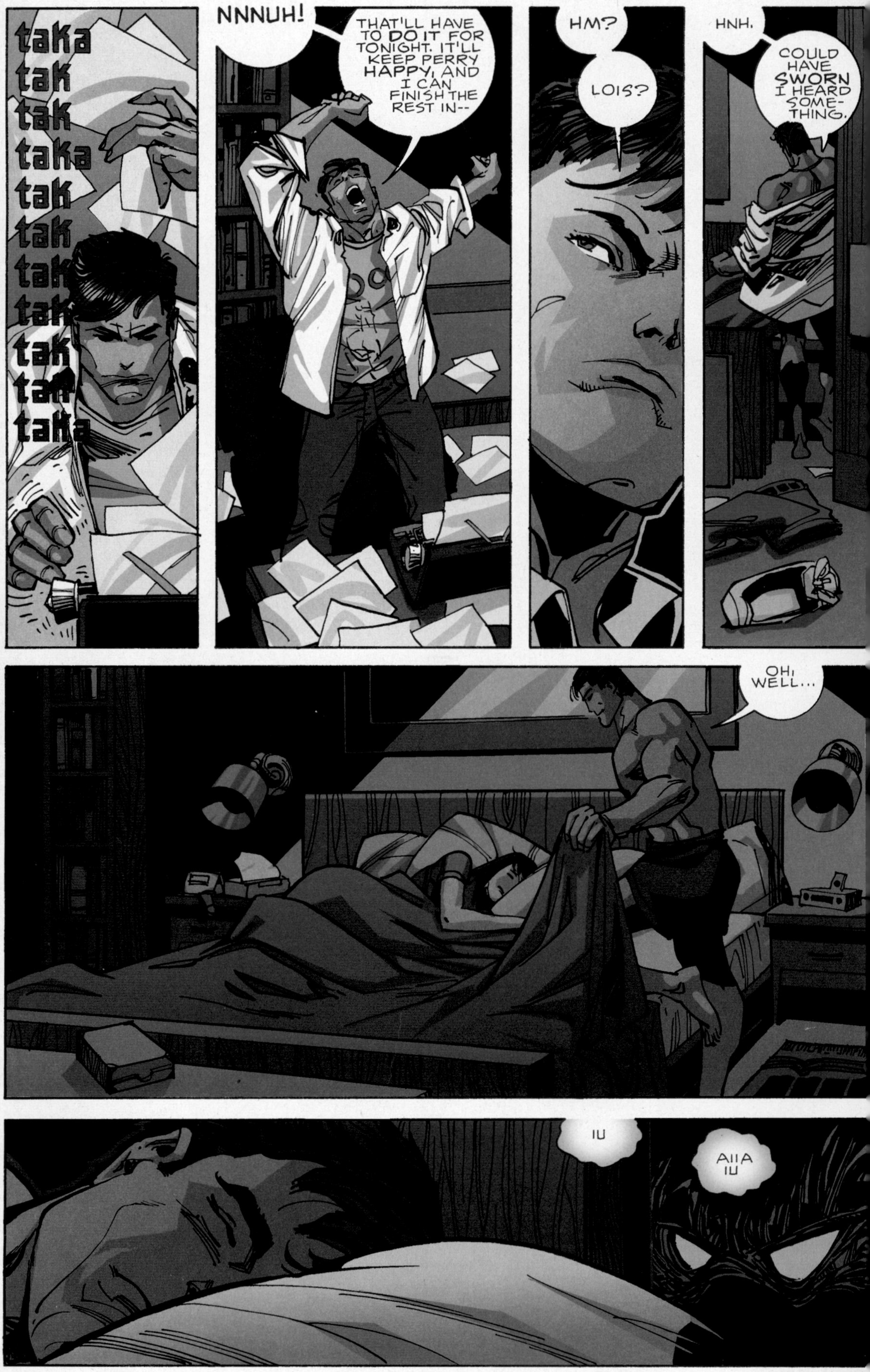
taka
tak
tak
taka
tak
tak
tak
tak
tak
tak
taka
NNNUH!
THAT'LL HAVE TO DO IT FOR TONIGHT. IT'LL KEEP PERRY HAPPY, AND I CAN FINISH THE REST IN--
HM?
LOIS?
HNH.
COULD HAVE SWORN I HEARD SOME-THING.
OH, WELL...
IU
AIIA IU

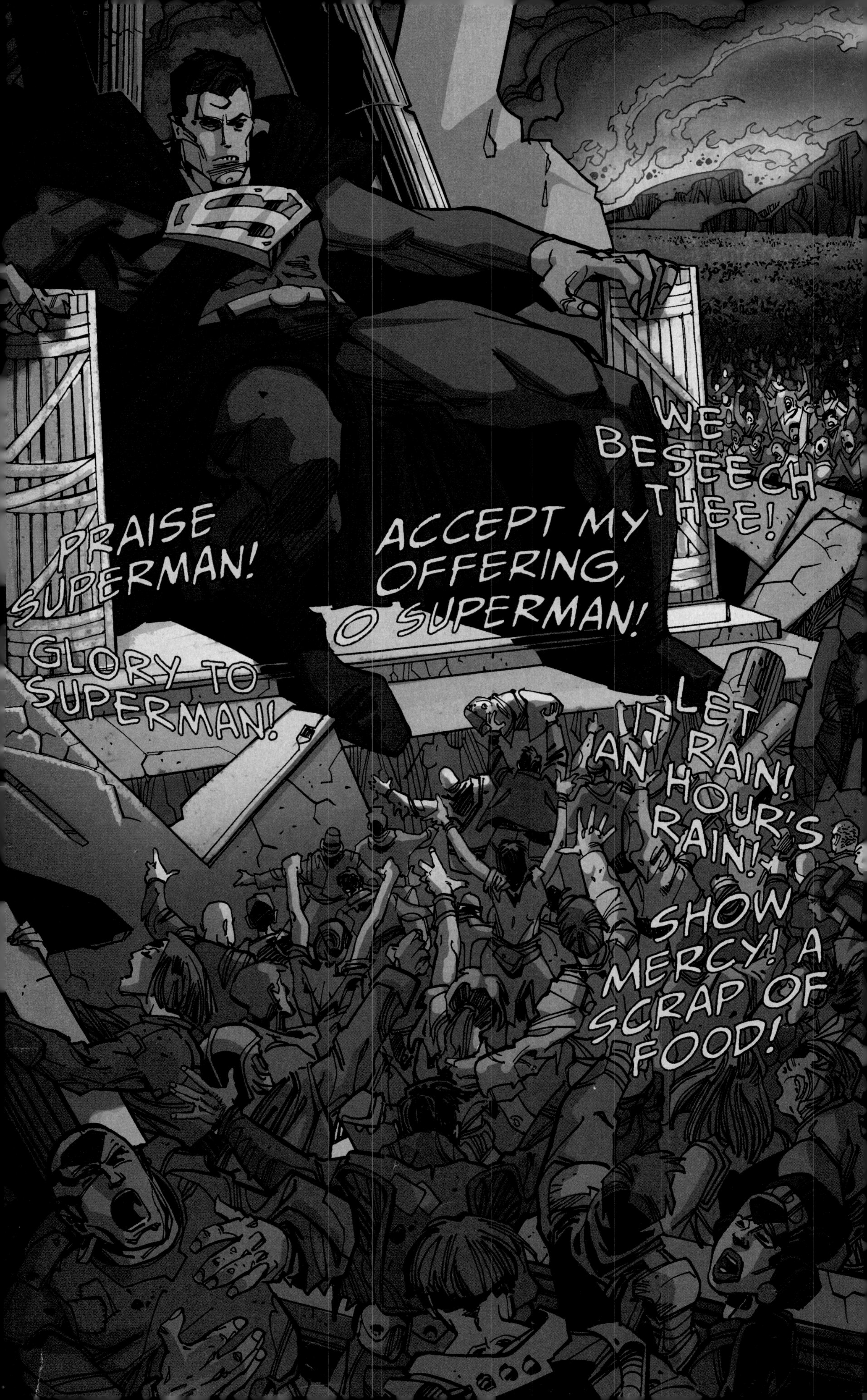
PRAISE SUPERMAN!
GLORY TO SUPERMAN!
ACCEPT MY OFFERING, O SUPERMAN!
WE BESEECH THEE!
LET IT RAIN! AN HOUR'S RAIN!
SHOW MERCY! A SCRAP OF FOOD!

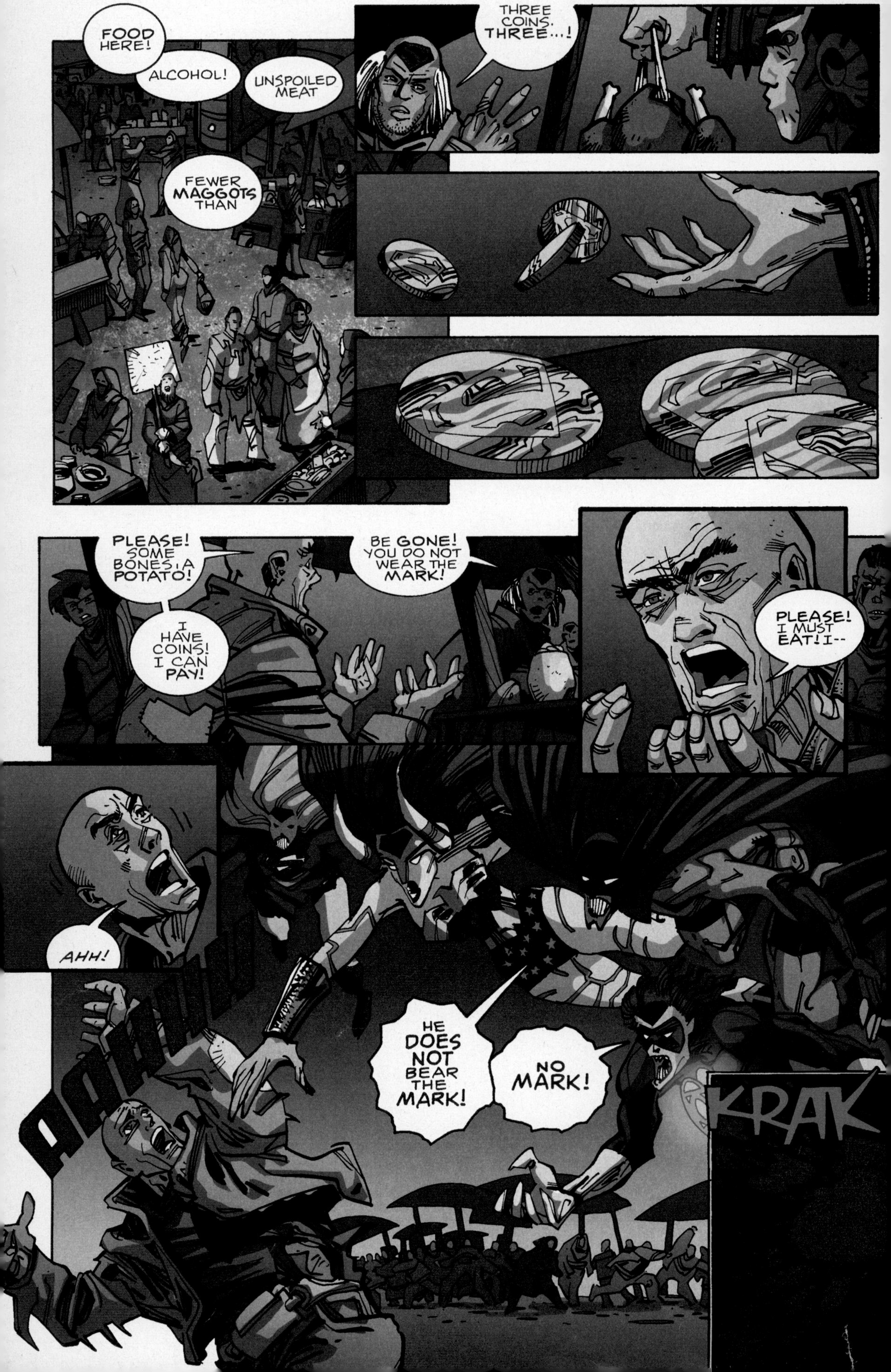
FOOD HERE!
ALCOHOL!
UNSPOILED MEAT
FEWER MAGGOTS THAN
THREE COINS. THREE...!
PLEASE! SOME BONES, A POTATO!
I HAVE COINS! I CAN PAY!
BE GONE! YOU DO NOT WEAR THE MARK!
PLEASE! I MUST EAT! I--
AHH!
HE DOES NOT BEAR THE MARK!
NO MARK!
KRAK

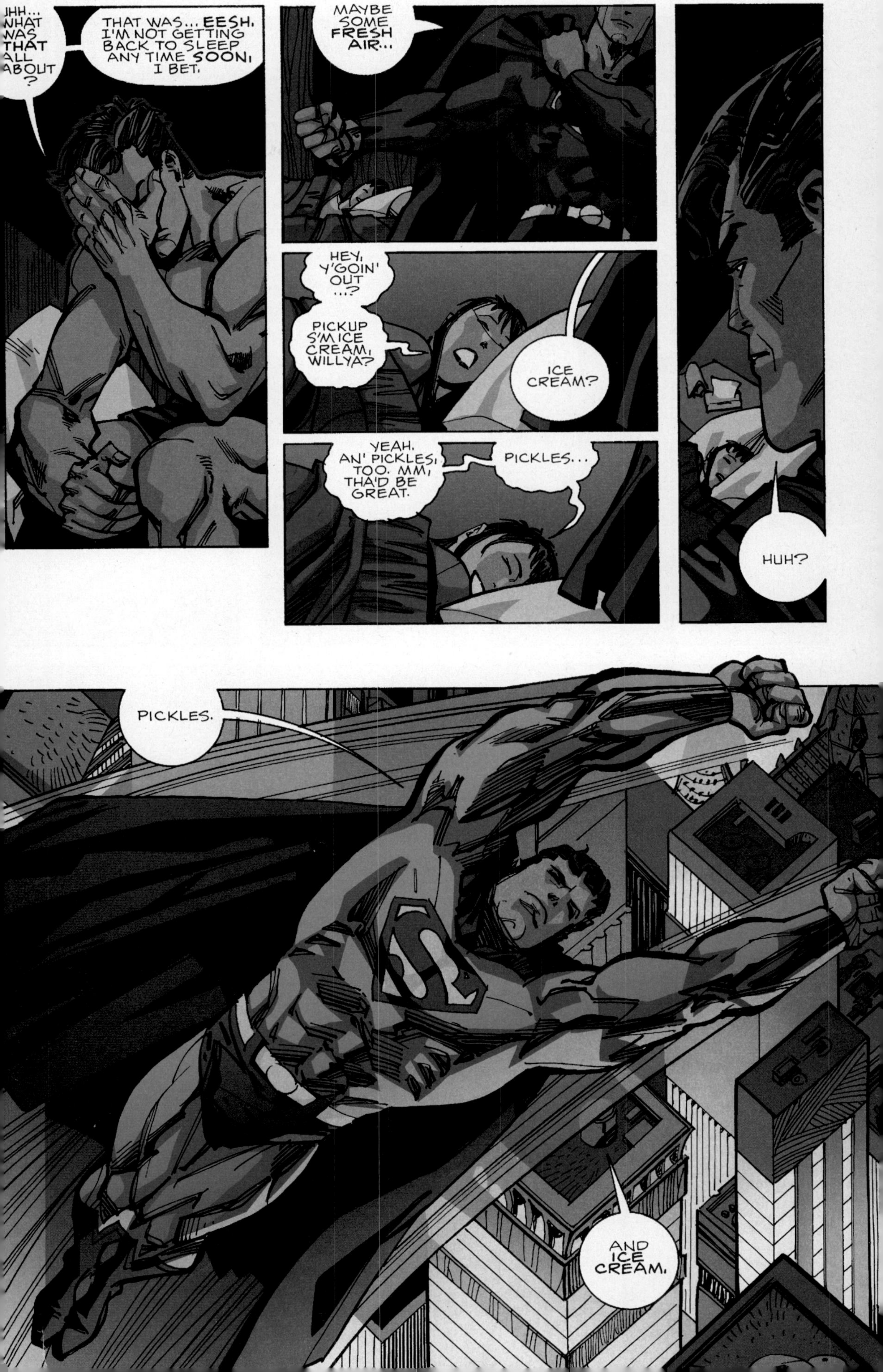
UHH... WHAT WAS THAT ALL ABOUT?
THAT WAS... EESH. I'M NOT GETTING BACK TO SLEEP ANY TIME SOON, I BET.
MAYBE SOME FRESH AIR...
HEY, Y'GOIN' OUT ...?
PICKUP S'M ICE CREAM, WILLYA?
ICE CREAM?
YEAH. AN' PICKLES, TOO. MM, THA'D BE GREAT.
PICKLES...
HUH?
PICKLES.
AND ICE CREAM.

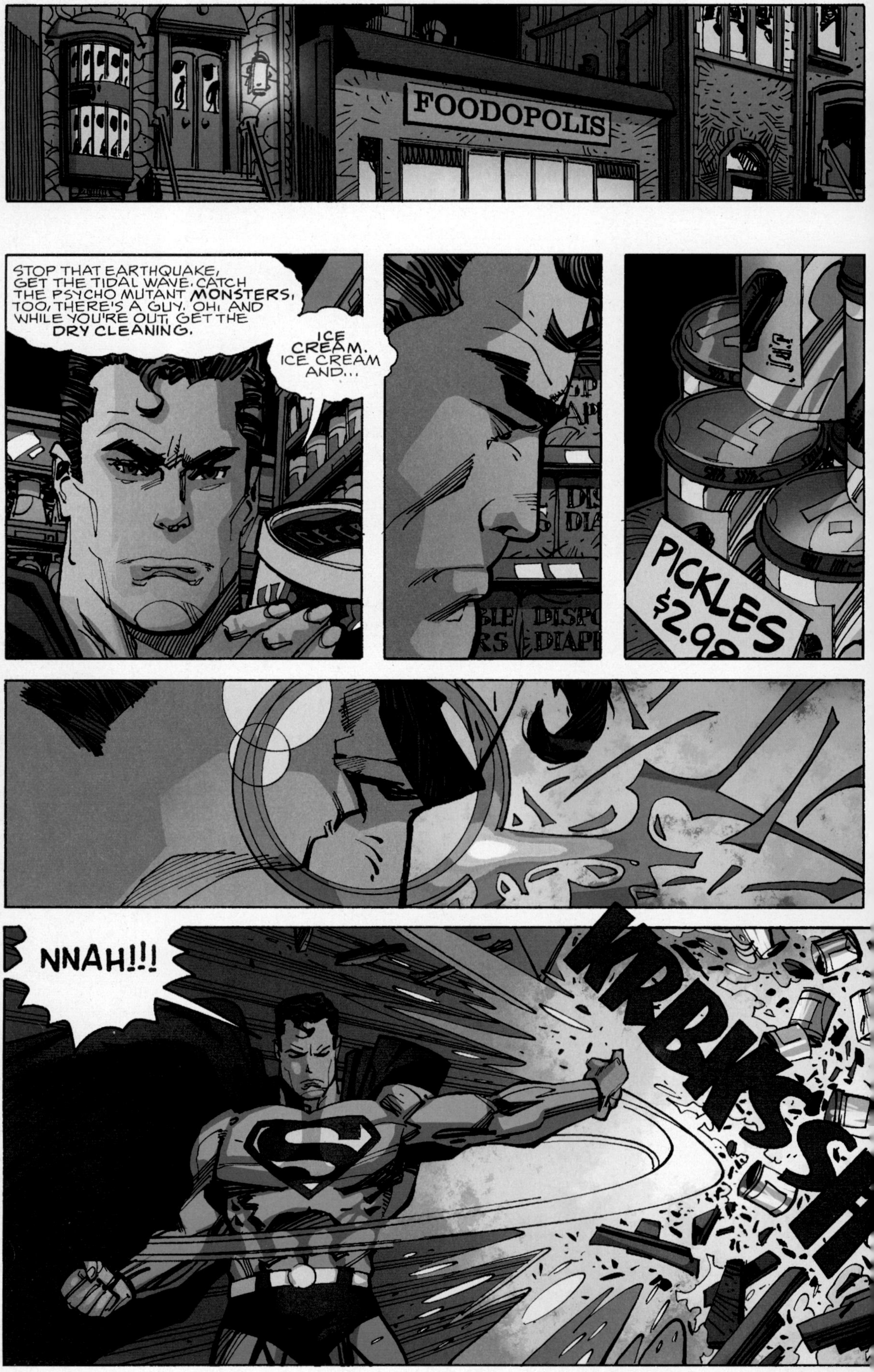
FOODOPOLIS
STOP THAT EARTHQUAKE, GET THE TIDAL WAVE. CATCH THE PSYCHO MUTANT MONSTERS, TOO, THERE'S A GUY. OH! AND WHILE YOU'RE OUT, GET THE DRY CLEANING.
ICE CREAM. ICE CREAM AND...
PICKLES $2.98
NNAH!!!

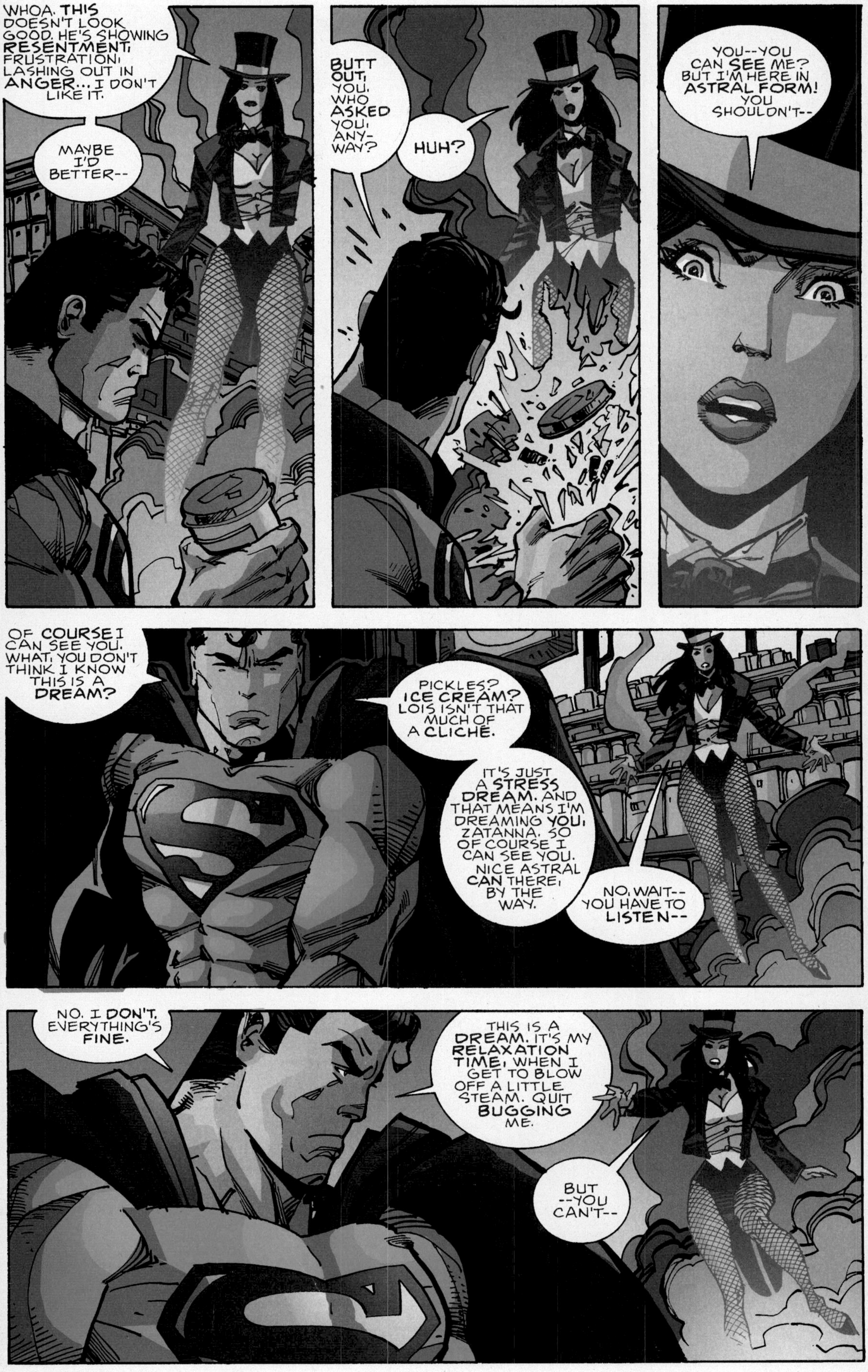

WHOA. THIS DOESN'T LOOK GOOD. HE'S SHOWING RESENTMENT, FRUSTRATION, LASHING OUT IN ANGER... I DON'T LIKE IT.
MAYBE I'D BETTER--
BUTT OUT, YOU. WHO ASKED YOU, ANYWAY?
HUH?
YOU--YOU CAN SEE ME? BUT I'M HERE IN ASTRAL FORM! YOU SHOULDN'T--
OF COURSE I CAN SEE YOU. WHAT, YOU DON'T THINK I KNOW THIS IS A DREAM?
PICKLES? ICE CREAM? LOIS ISN'T THAT MUCH OF A CLICHÉ.
IT'S JUST A STRESS DREAM. AND THAT MEANS I'M DREAMING YOU, ZATANNA. SO OF COURSE I CAN SEE YOU. NICE ASTRAL CAN THERE, BY THE WAY.
NO, WAIT-- YOU HAVE TO LISTEN--
NO. I DON'T. EVERYTHING'S FINE.
THIS IS A DREAM. IT'S MY RELAXATION TIME, WHEN I GET TO BLOW OFF A LITTLE STEAM. QUIT BUGGING ME.
BUT --YOU CAN'T--

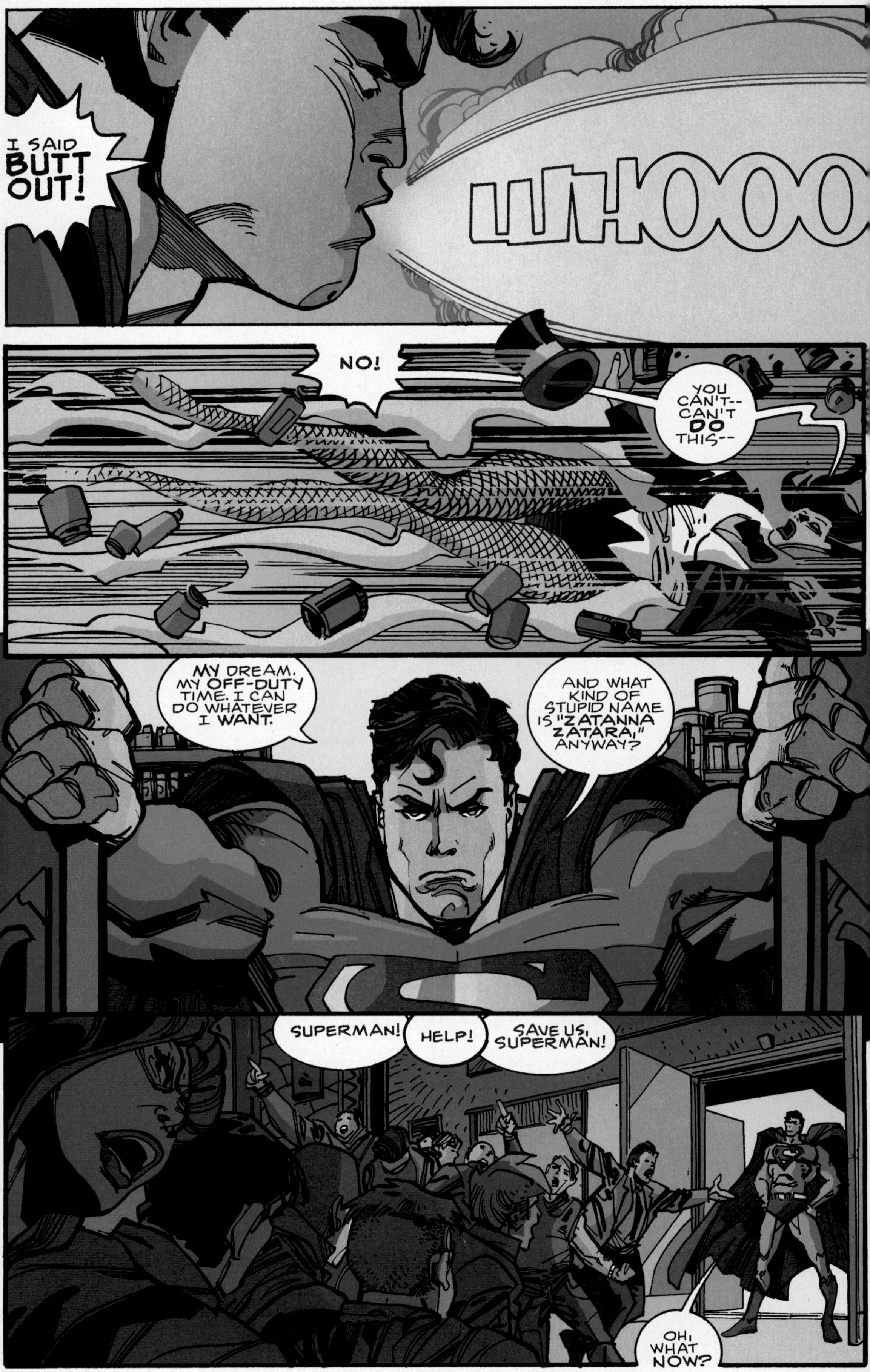
I SAID BUTT OUT!
WHOOOO
NO!
YOU CAN'T-- CAN'T DO THIS--
MY DREAM. MY OFF-DUTY TIME. I CAN DO WHATEVER I WANT.
AND WHAT KIND OF STUPID NAME IS "ZATANNA ZATARA," ANYWAY?
SUPERMAN!
HELP!
SAVE US, SUPERMAN!
OH, WHAT NOW?

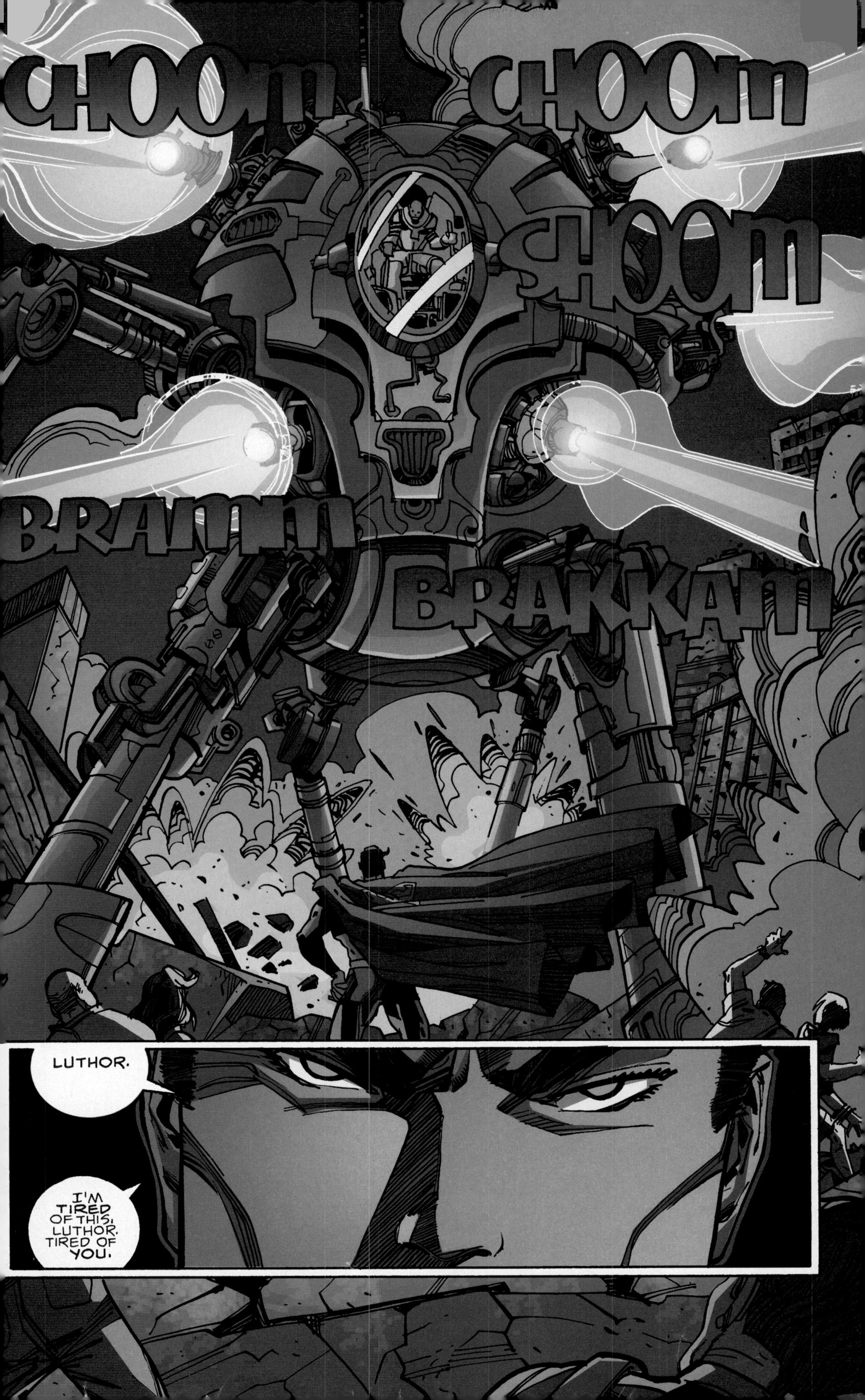
CHOOM
CHOOM
CHOOM
BRAMM
BRAKKAM
LUTHOR.
I'M TIRED OF THIS, LUTHOR. TIRED OF YOU.

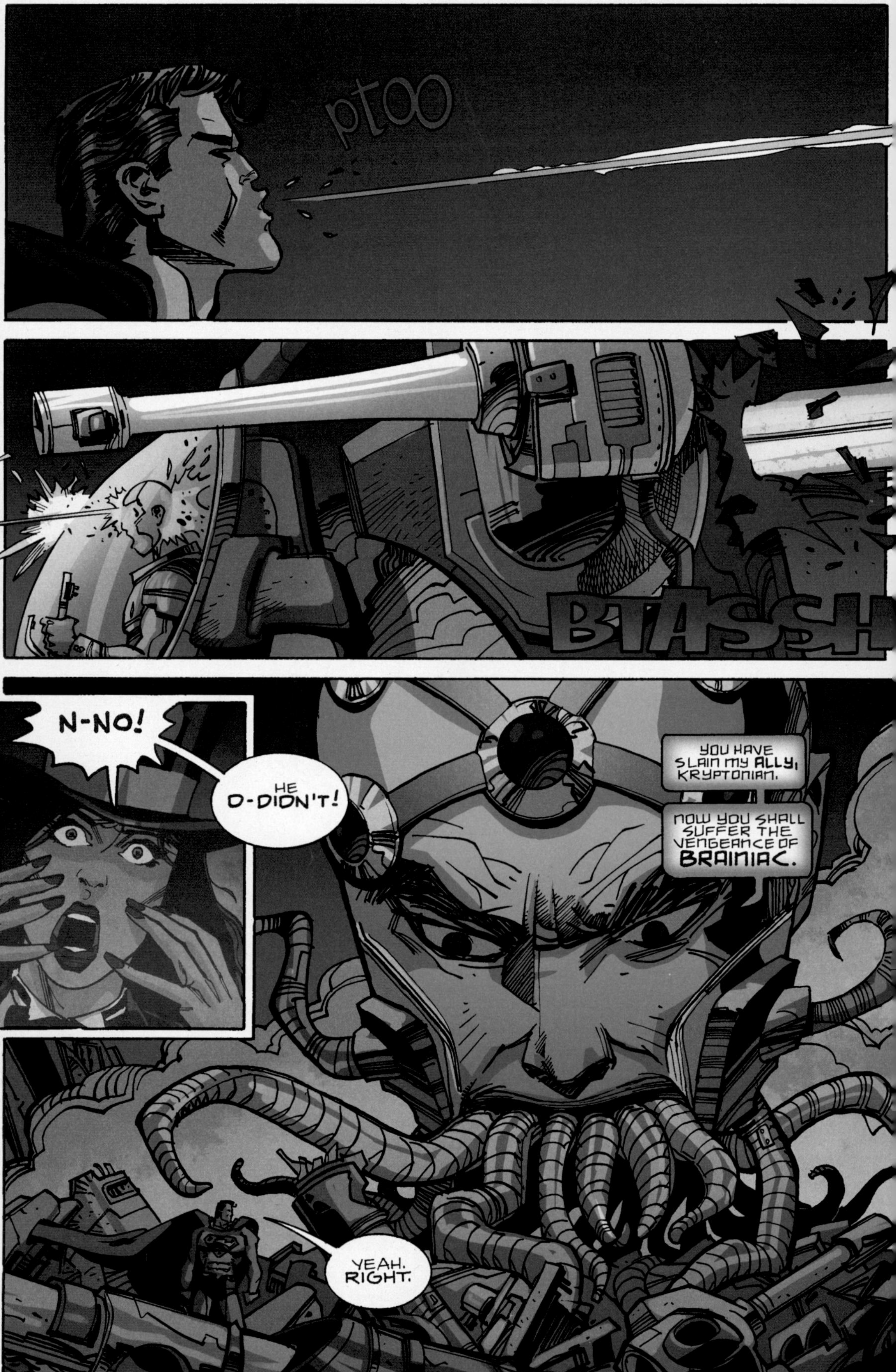
ptoo
BTASSH
N-NO!
HE D-DIDN'T!
YOU HAVE SLAIN MY ALLY, KRYPTONIAN.
NOW YOU SHALL SUFFER THE VENGEANCE OF BRAINIAC.
YEAH. RIGHT.

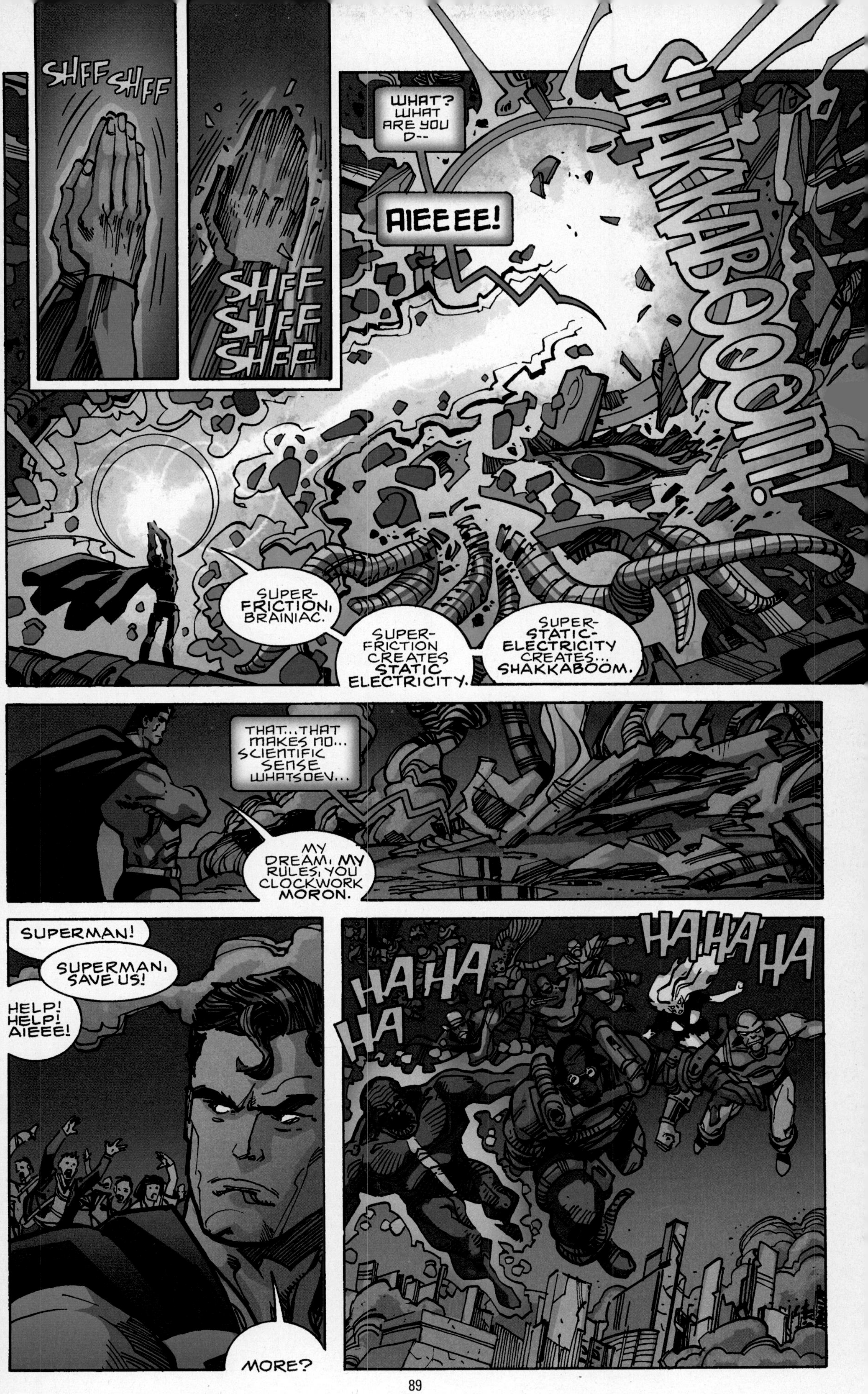
SHFF SHFF
SHFF SHFF SHFF
WHAT? WHAT ARE YOU D--
AIEEEE!
SHAKKABOOOM!!
SUPER-FRICTION, BRAINIAC.
SUPER-FRICTION CREATES STATIC ELECTRICITY.
SUPER-STATIC-ELECTRICITY CREATES... SHAKKABOOM.
THAT...THAT MAKES NO... SCIENTIFIC SENSE WHATSOEV...
MY DREAM, MY RULES, YOU CLOCKWORK MORON.
SUPERMAN!
SUPERMAN, SAVE US!
HELP! HELP! AIEEE!
MORE?
HA HA HA HA
HA HA HA

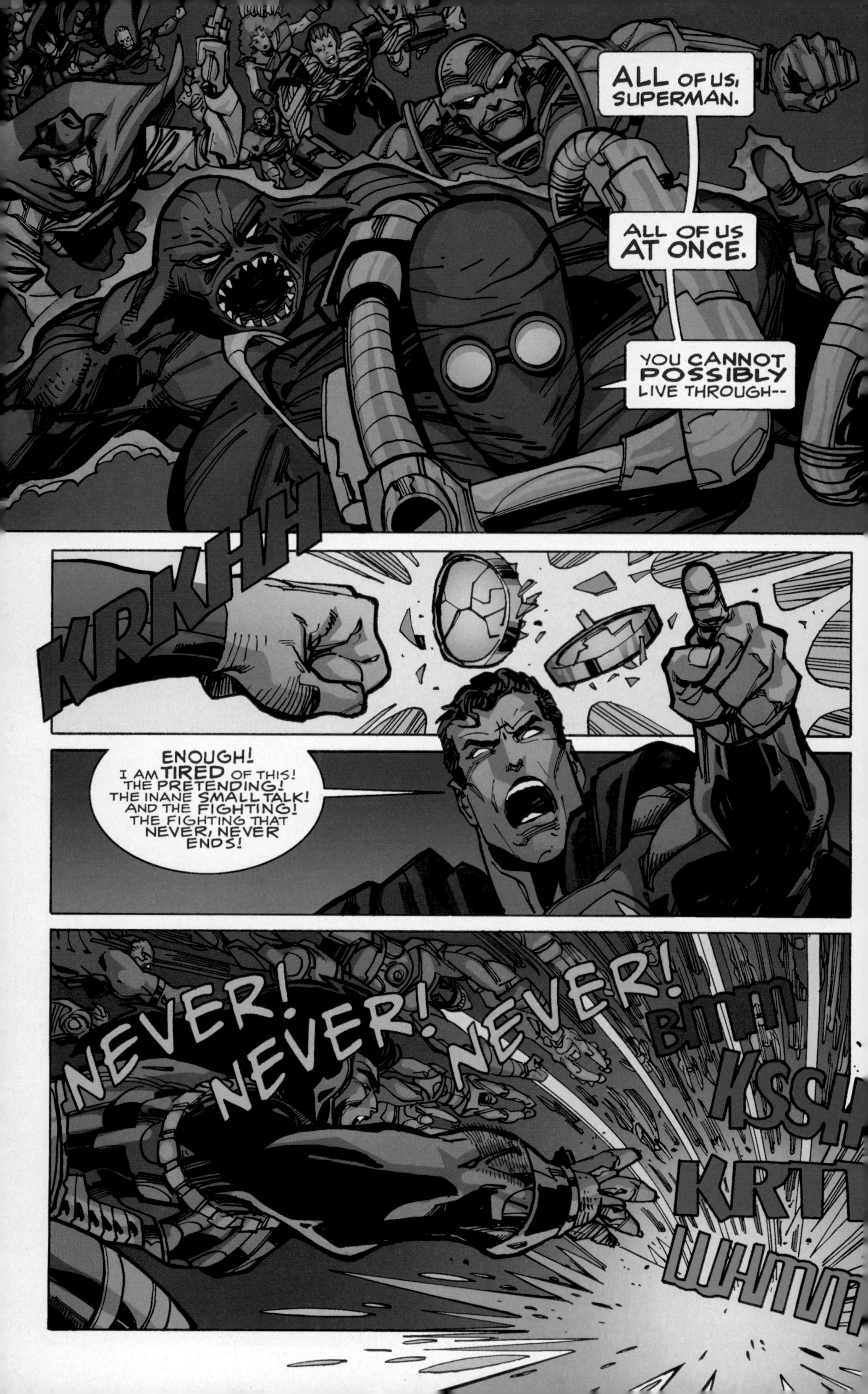
ALL OF US, SUPERMAN.
ALL OF US AT ONCE.
YOU CANNOT POSSIBLY LIVE THROUGH--
KRKHH
ENOUGH! I AM TIRED OF THIS! THE PRETENDING! THE INANE SMALL TALK! AND THE FIGHTING! THE FIGHTING THAT NEVER, NEVER ENDS!
NEVER! NEVER! NEVER!

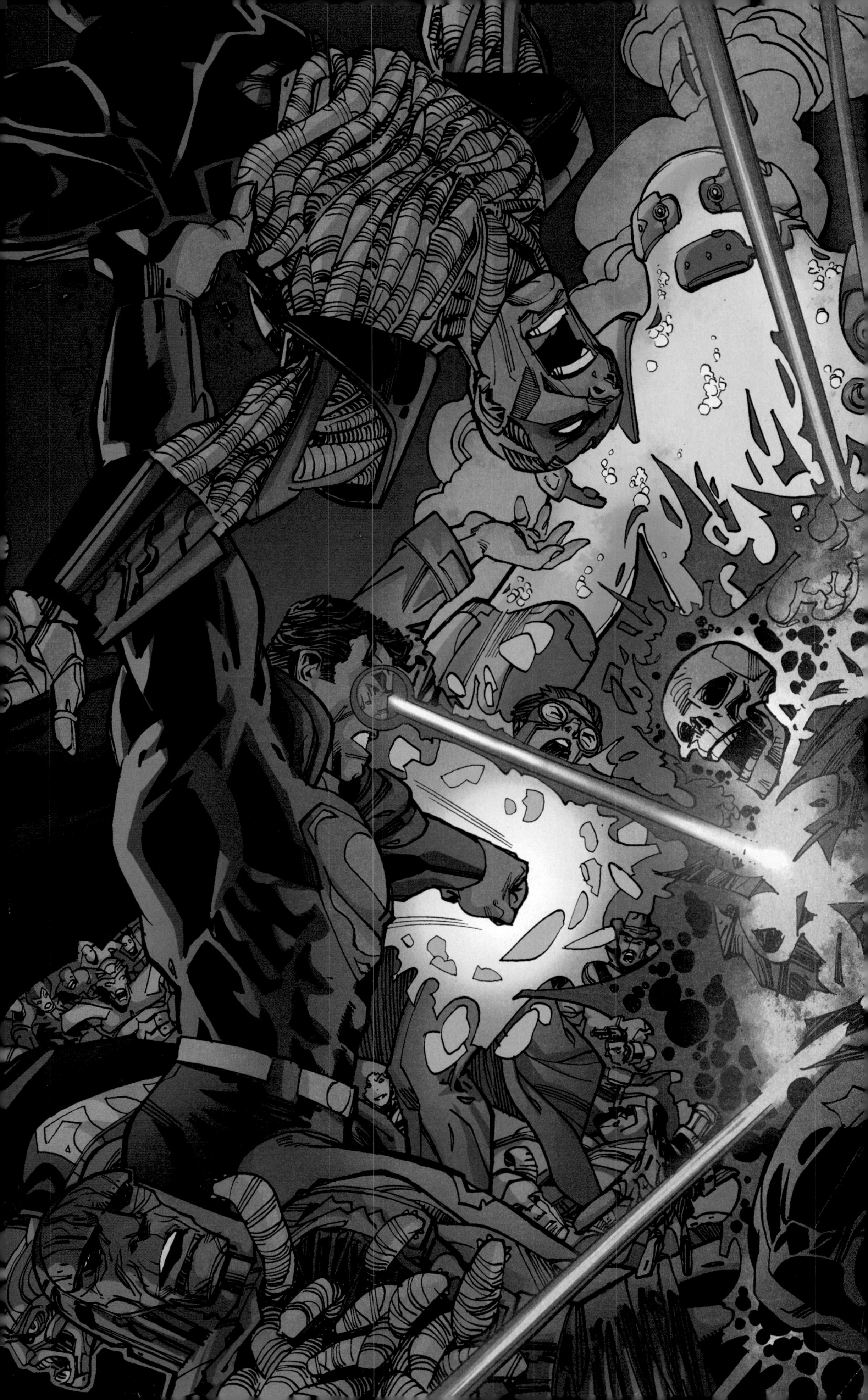

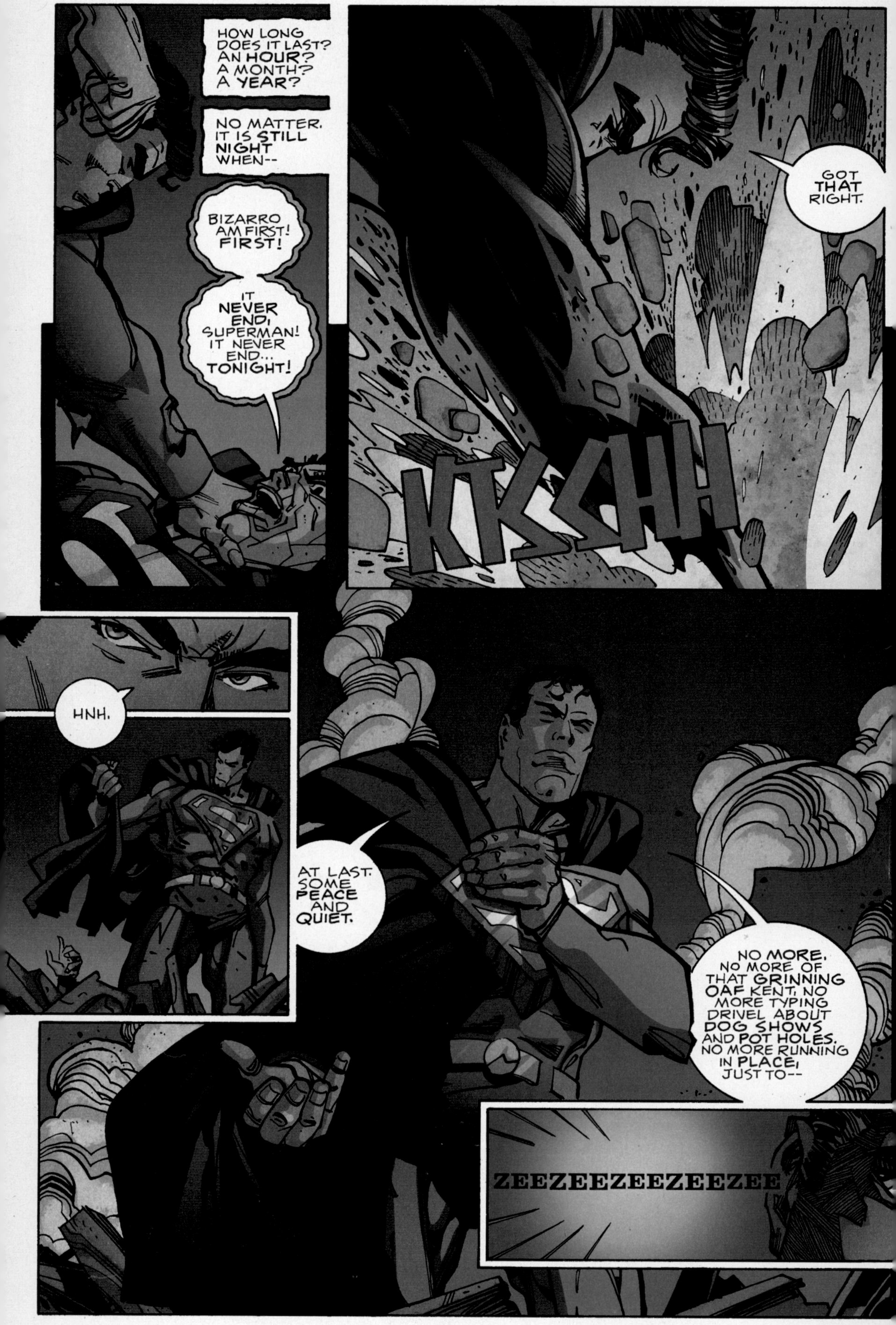
HOW LONG DOES IT LAST? AN HOUR? A MONTH? A YEAR?
NO MATTER. IT IS STILL NIGHT WHEN--
BIZARRO AM FIRST! FIRST!
IT NEVER END, SUPERMAN! IT NEVER END... TONIGHT!
GOT THAT RIGHT.
KKSSHH
HNH.
AT LAST. SOME PEACE AND QUIET.
NO MORE. NO MORE OF THAT GRINNING OAF KENT. NO MORE TYPING DRIVEL ABOUT DOG SHOWS AND POT HOLES. NO MORE RUNNING IN PLACE, JUST TO--
ZEEZEEZEEZEEZEE

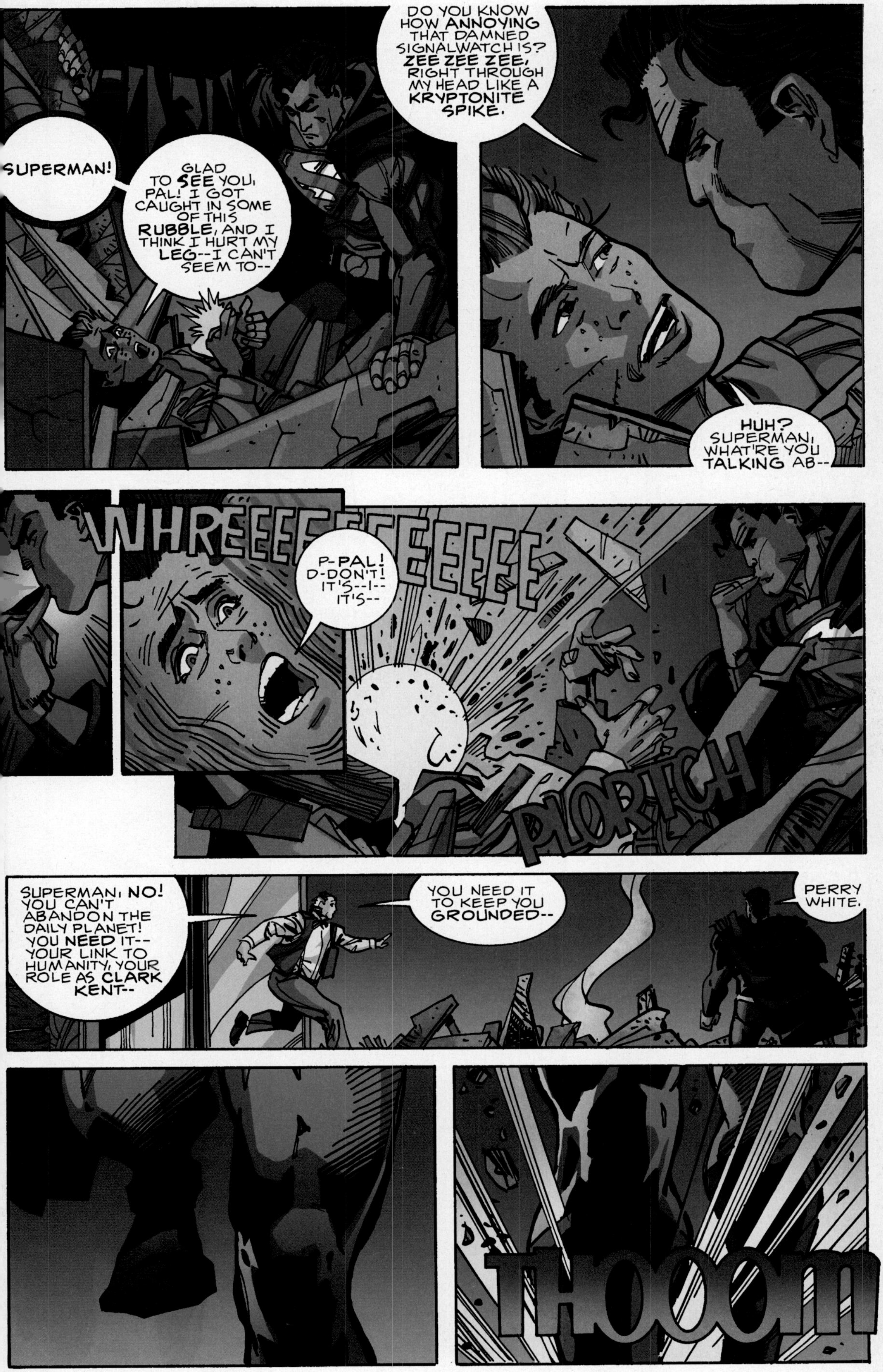
SUPERMAN!
GLAD TO SEE YOU, PAL! I GOT CAUGHT IN SOME OF THIS RUBBLE, AND I THINK I HURT MY LEG--I CAN'T SEEM TO--
DO YOU KNOW HOW ANNOYING THAT DAMNED SIGNALWATCH IS? ZEE ZEE ZEE, RIGHT THROUGH MY HEAD LIKE A KRYPTONITE SPIKE.
HUH? SUPERMAN, WHAT'RE YOU TALKING AB--
WHREEEEEEEEEEE
P-PAL! D-DON'T! IT'S--I-- IT'S--
PLORTCH
SUPERMAN, NO! YOU CAN'T ABANDON THE DAILY PLANET! YOU NEED IT--YOUR LINK TO HUMANITY, YOUR ROLE AS CLARK KENT--
YOU NEED IT TO KEEP YOU GROUNDED--
PERRY WHITE.
THOOOM

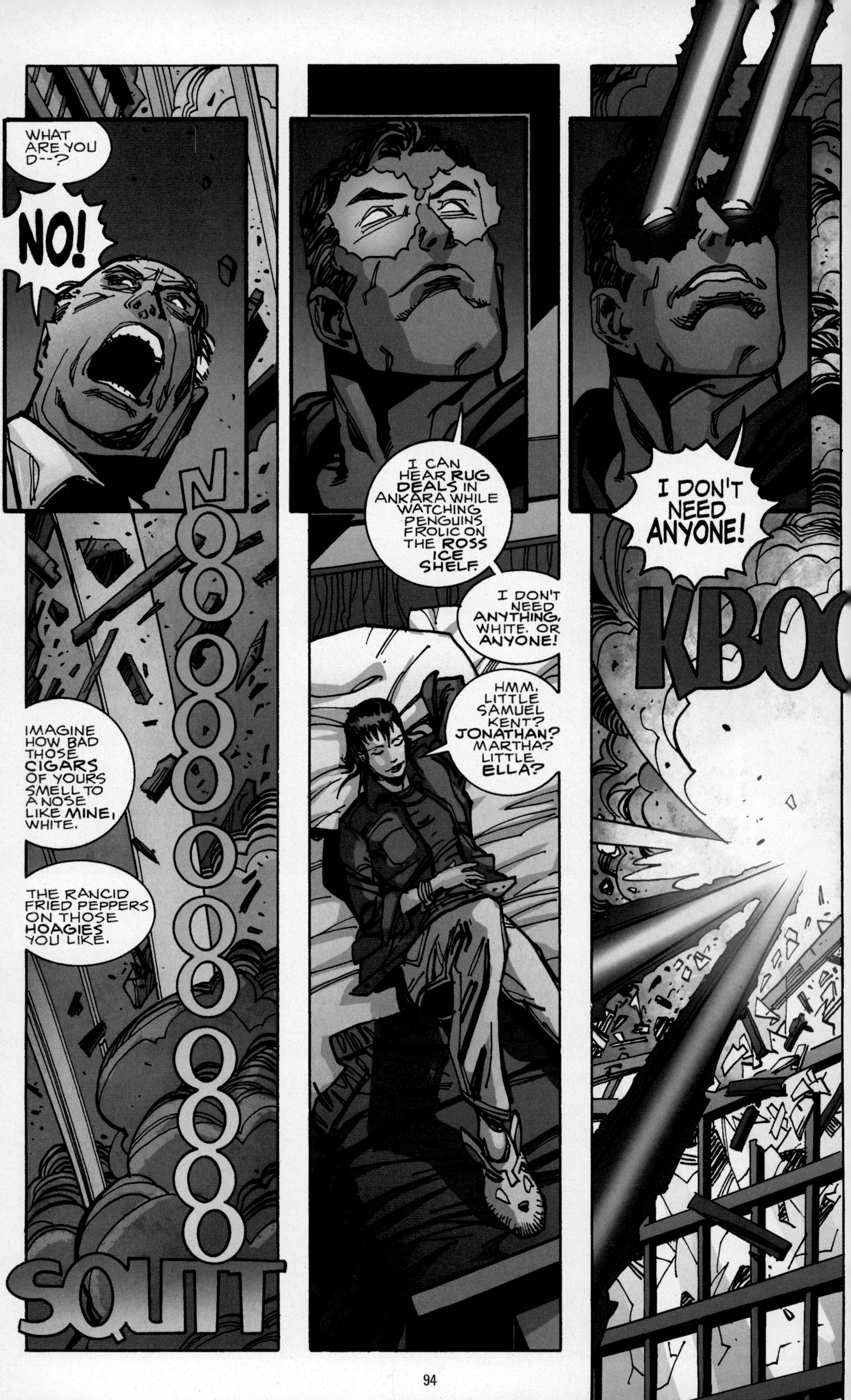
WHAT ARE YOU D--?
NO!
NOOOOOOOOOOO
IMAGINE HOW BAD THOSE CIGARS OF YOURS SMELL TO A NOSE LIKE MINE, WHITE.
THE RANCID FRIED PEPPERS ON THOSE HOAGIES YOU LIKE.
SQUIT
I CAN HEAR RUG DEALS IN ANKARA WHILE WATCHING PENGUINS FROLIC ON THE ROSS ICE SHELF.
I DON'T NEED ANYTHING, WHITE. OR ANYONE!
HMM. LITTLE SAMUEL KENT? JONATHAN? MARTHA? LITTLE ELLA?
I DON'T NEED ANYONE!
KBOO

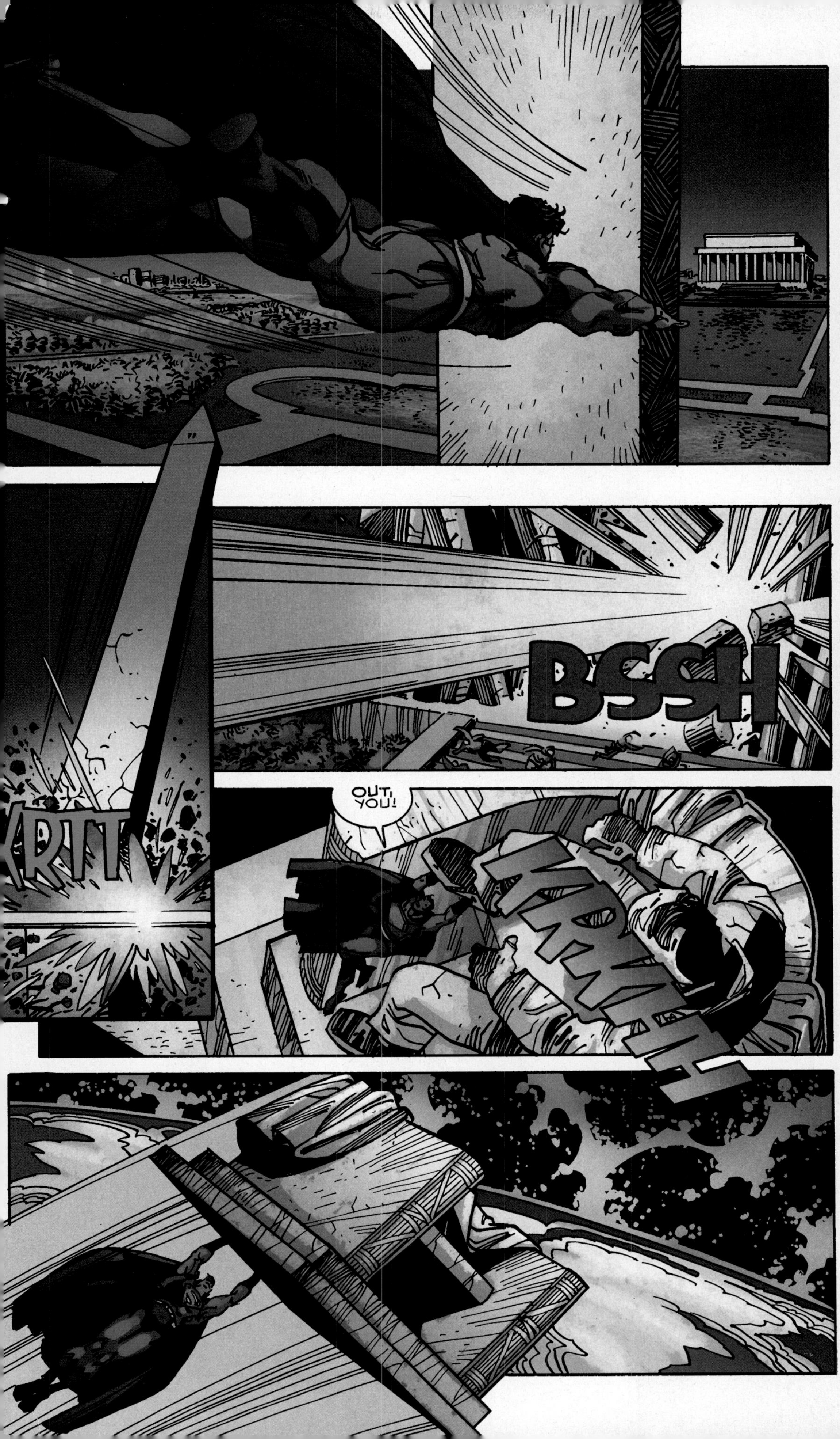
KRTT
BSSH
OUT, YOU!
KRAAHH

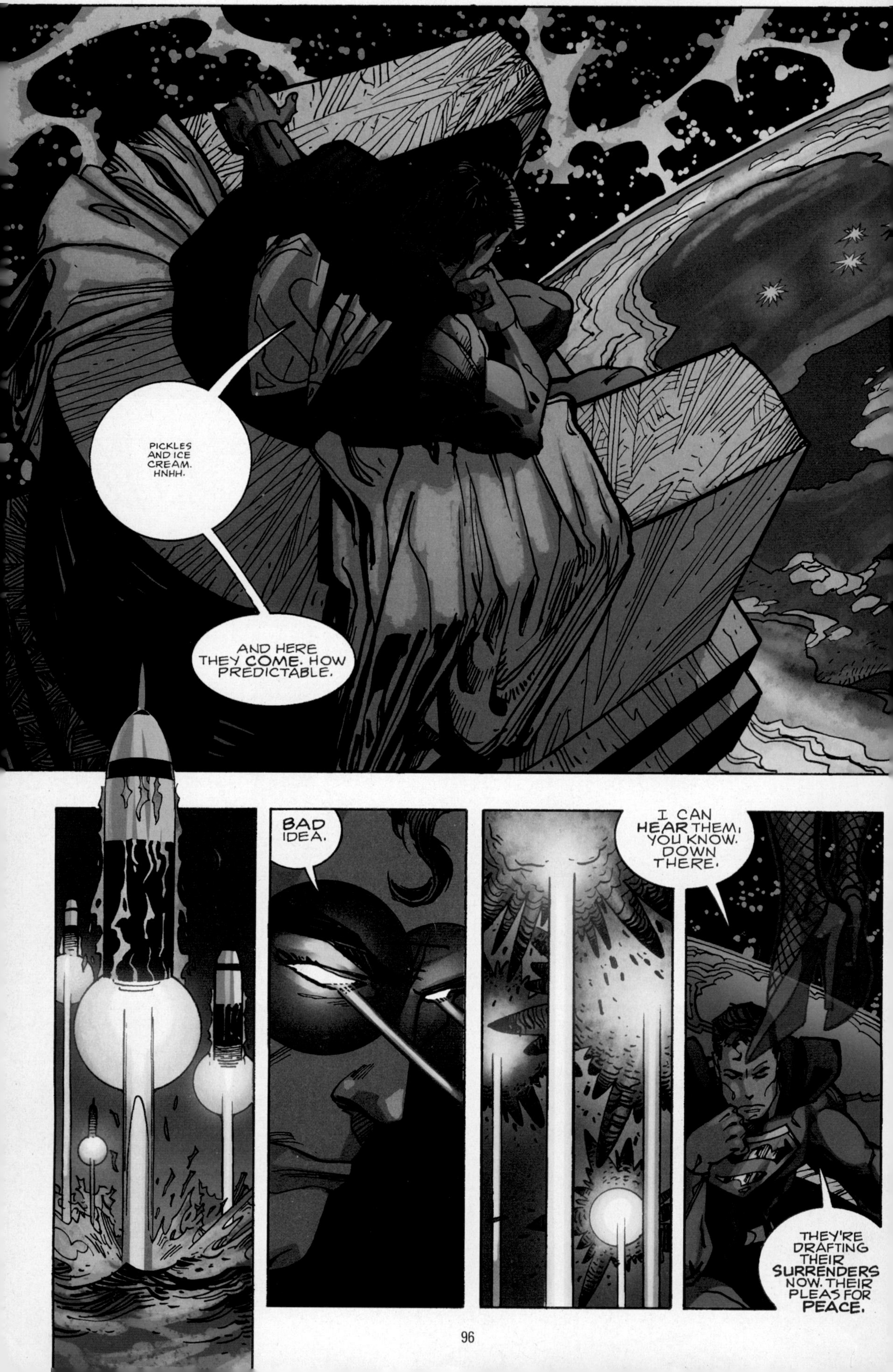
PICKLES AND ICE CREAM. HNHH.
AND HERE THEY COME. HOW PREDICTABLE.
BAD IDEA.
I CAN HEAR THEM, YOU KNOW. DOWN THERE.
THEY'RE DRAFTING THEIR SURRENDERS NOW. THEIR PLEAS FOR PEACE.

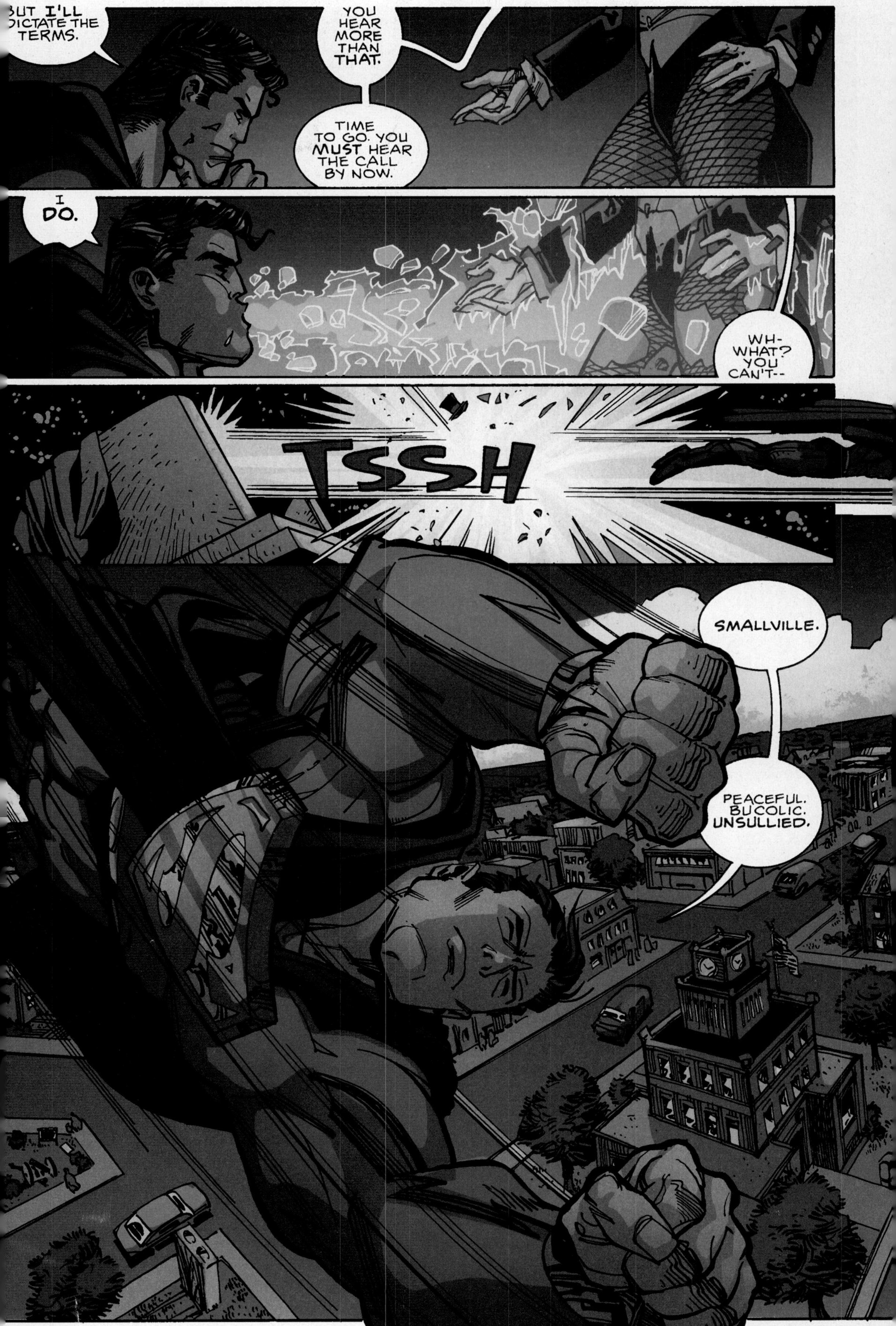
BUT I'LL DICTATE THE TERMS.
YOU HEAR MORE THAN THAT.
TIME TO GO. YOU MUST HEAR THE CALL BY NOW.
I DO.
WH-WHAT? YOU CAN'T--
TSSH
SMALLVILLE.
PEACEFUL. BUCOLIC. UNSULLIED.

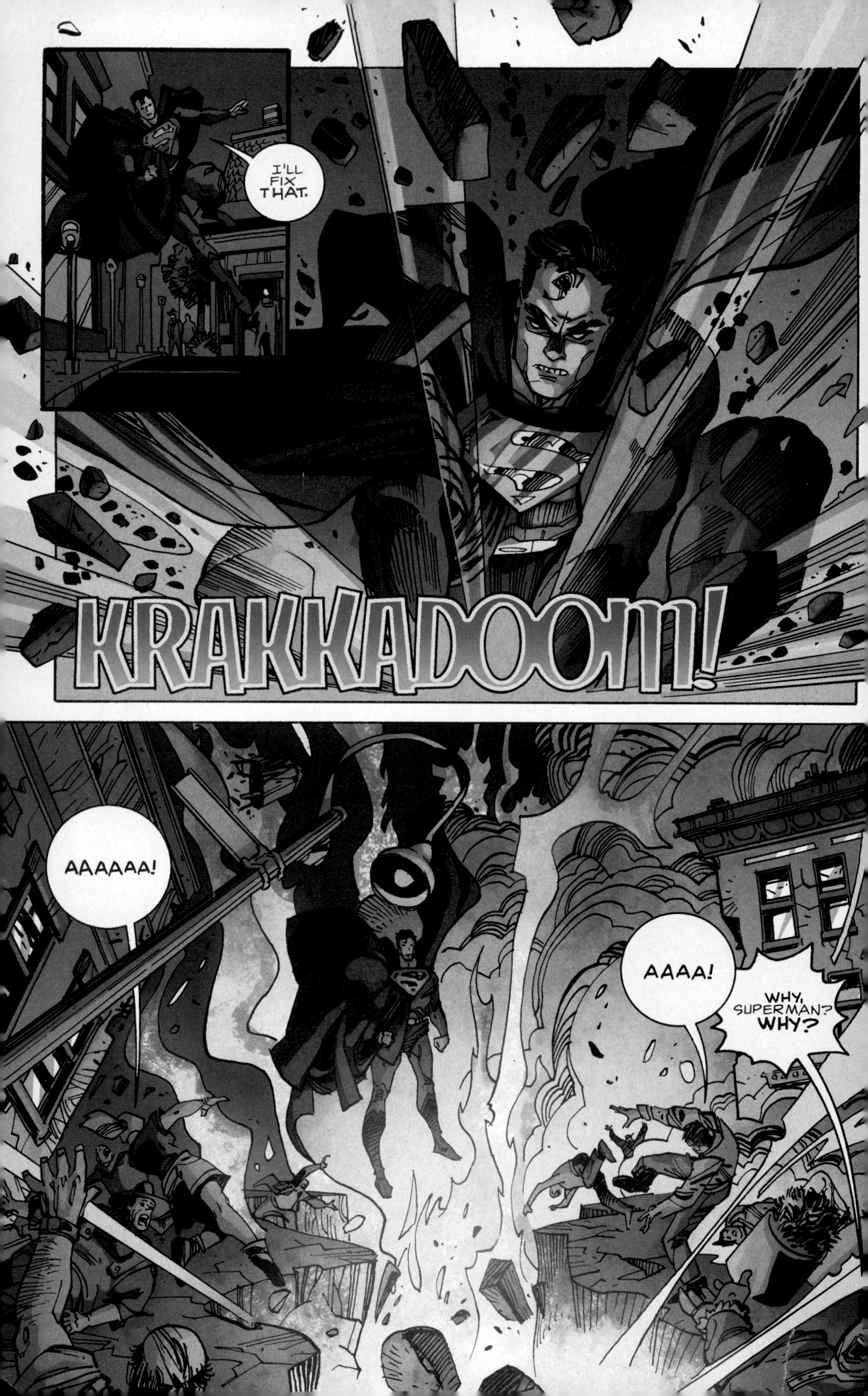
I'LL FIX THAT.
KRAKKADOOM!
AAAAAA!
AAAA!
WHY, SUPERMAN? WHY?

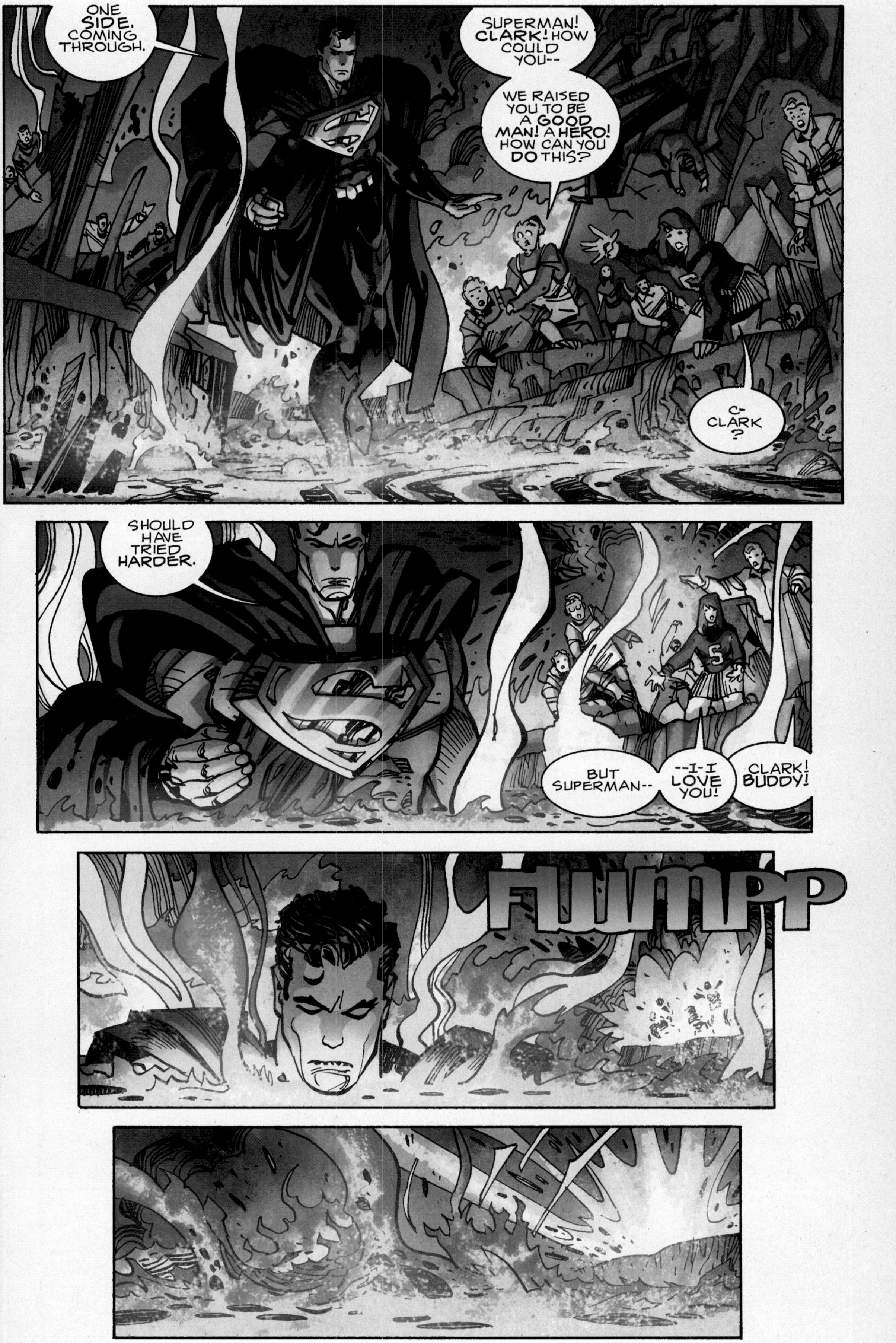
ONE SIDE. COMING THROUGH.
SUPERMAN! CLARK! HOW COULD YOU--
WE RAISED YOU TO BE A GOOD MAN! A HERO! HOW CAN YOU DO THIS?
C-CLARK?
SHOULD HAVE TRIED HARDER.
BUT SUPERMAN--
--I-I LOVE YOU!
CLARK! BUDDY!
FWUMPP

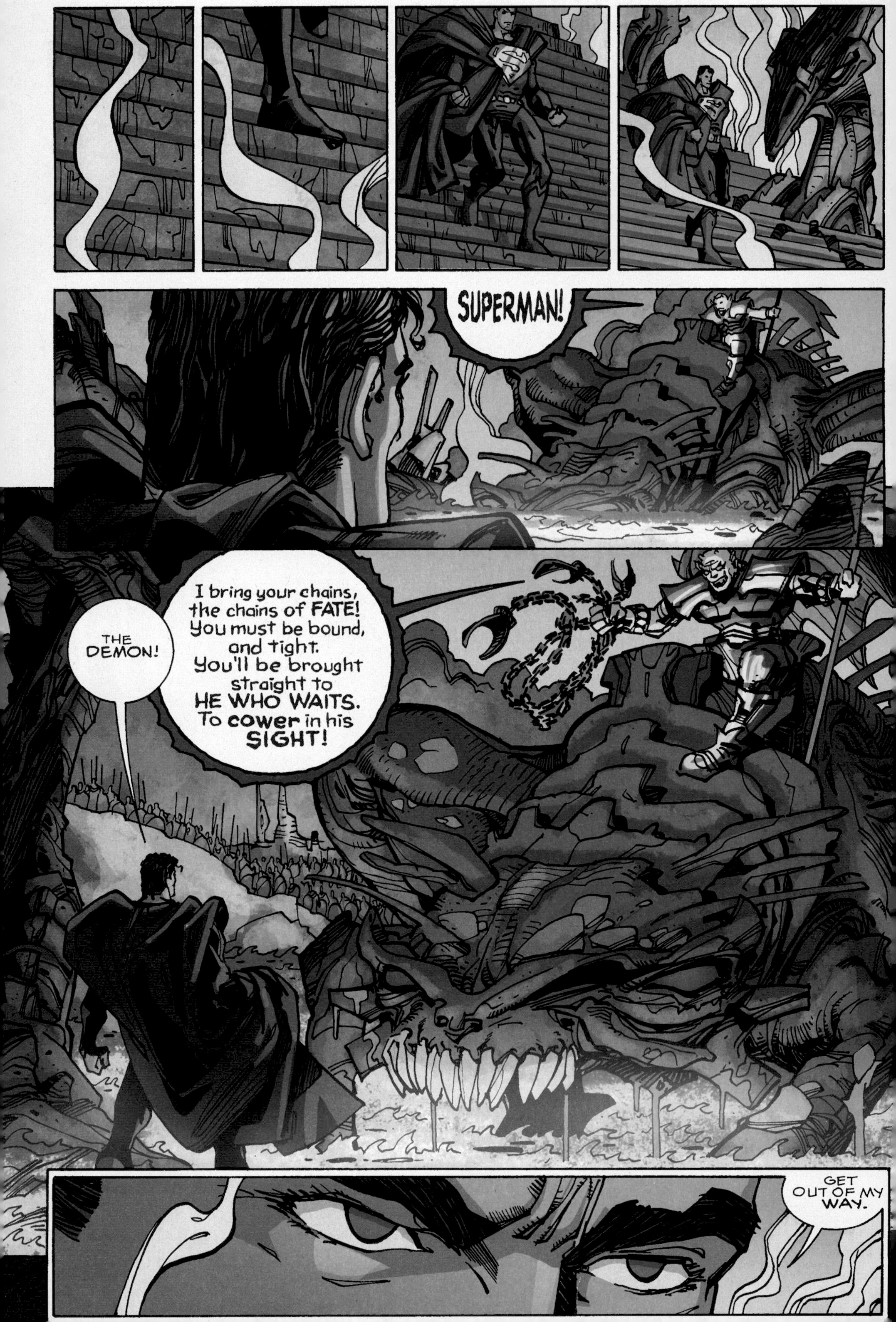
SUPERMAN!
I bring your chains, the chains of FATE! You must be bound, and tight. You'll be brought straight to HE WHO WAITS. To cower in his SIGHT!
THE DEMON!
GET OUT OF MY WAY.

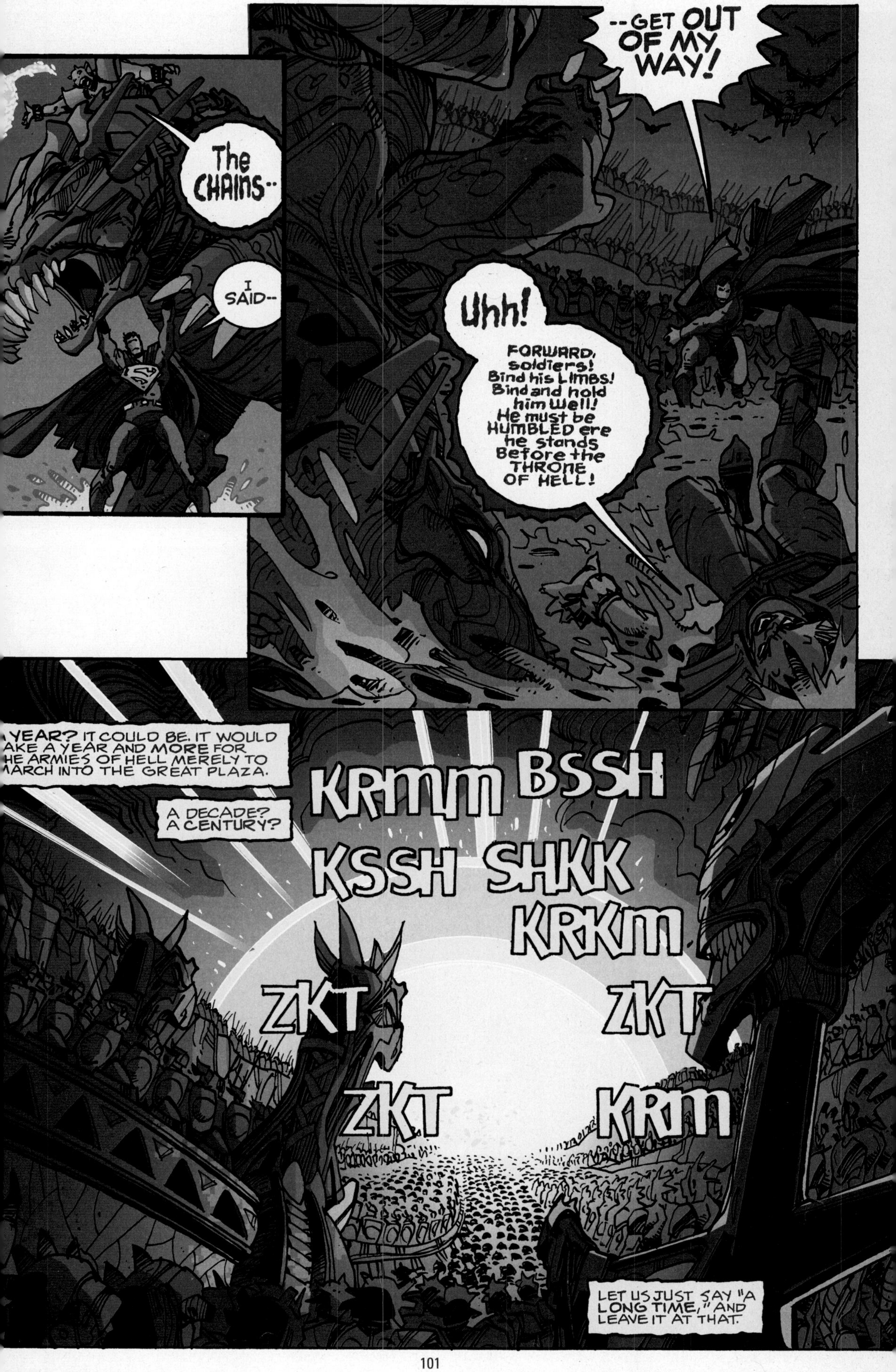
The CHAINS--
I SAID--
--GET OUT OF MY WAY!
Uhh!
FORWARD, soldiers! Bind his LIMBS! Bind and hold him well! He must be HUMBLED ere he stands before the THRONE OF HELL!
YEAR? IT COULD BE. IT WOULD AKE A YEAR AND MORE FOR HE ARMIES OF HELL MERELY TO ARCH INTO THE GREAT PLAZA.
A DECADE? A CENTURY?
KRMM BSSH
KSSH SHKK
KRKM
ZKT
ZKT
ZKT
KRM
LET US JUST SAY "A LONG TIME," AND LEAVE IT AT THAT.

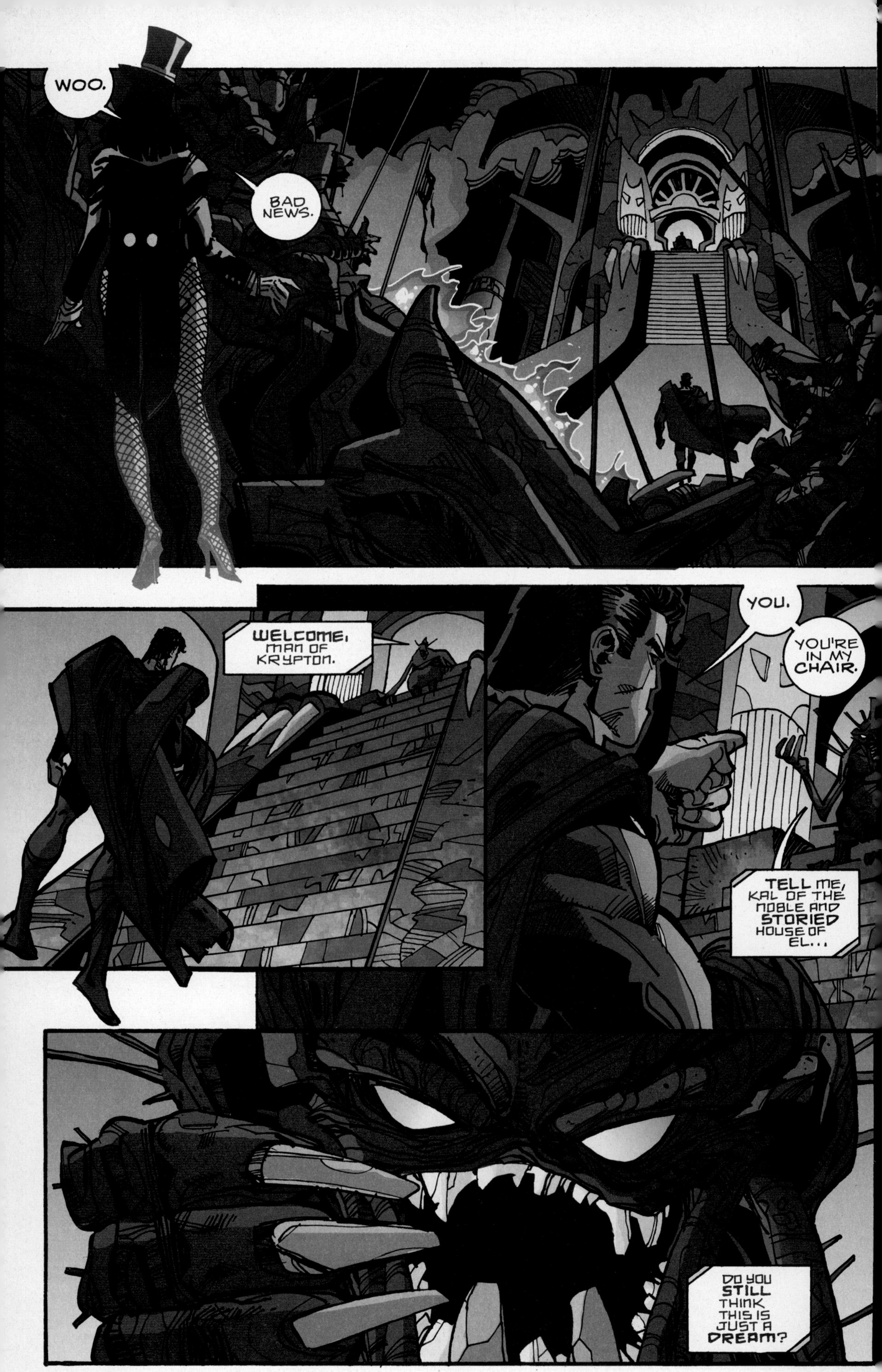
WOO.
BAD NEWS.
WELCOME, MAN OF KRYPTON.
YOU.
YOU'RE IN MY CHAIR.
TELL ME, KAL OF THE NOBLE AND STORIED HOUSE OF EL...
DO YOU STILL THINK THIS IS JUST A DREAM?

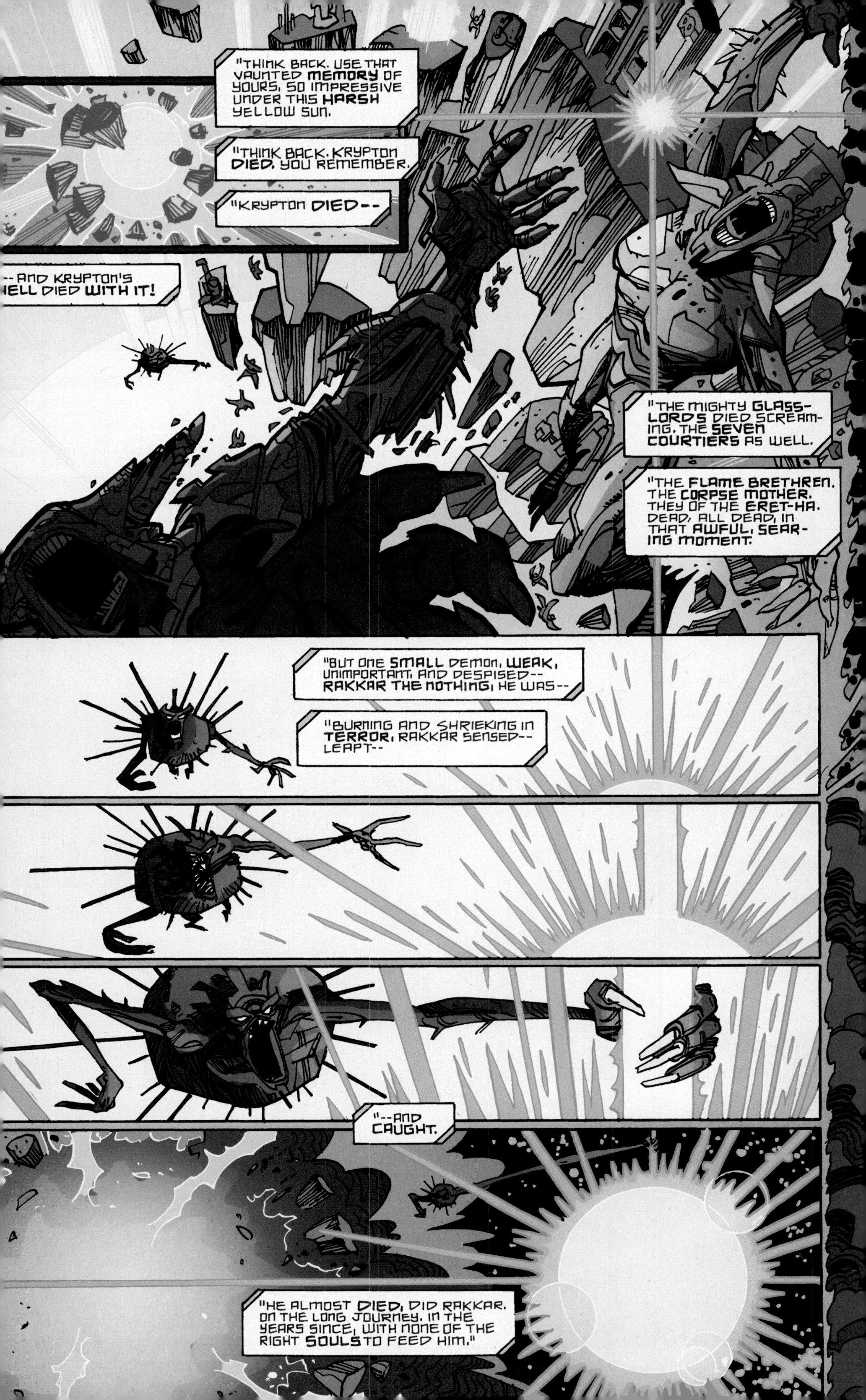
"THINK BACK. USE THAT VAUNTED MEMORY OF YOURS, SO IMPRESSIVE UNDER THIS HARSH YELLOW SUN.
"THINK BACK. KRYPTON DIED. YOU REMEMBER.
"KRYPTON DIED--
--AND KRYPTON'S HELL DIED WITH IT!
"THE MIGHTY GLASS-LORDS DIED SCREAMING. THE SEVEN COURTIERS AS WELL.
"THE FLAME BRETHREN. THE CORPSE MOTHER. THEY OF THE ERET-HA. DEAD, ALL DEAD, IN THAT AWFUL, SEARING MOMENT.
"BUT ONE SMALL DEMON, WEAK, UNIMPORTANT, AND DESPISED-- RAKKAR THE NOTHING, HE WAS--
"BURNING AND SHRIEKING IN TERROR, RAKKAR SENSED-- LEAPT--
"--AND CAUGHT.
"HE ALMOST DIED, DID RAKKAR, ON THE LONG JOURNEY. IN THE YEARS SINCE, WITH NONE OF THE RIGHT SOULS TO FEED HIM."

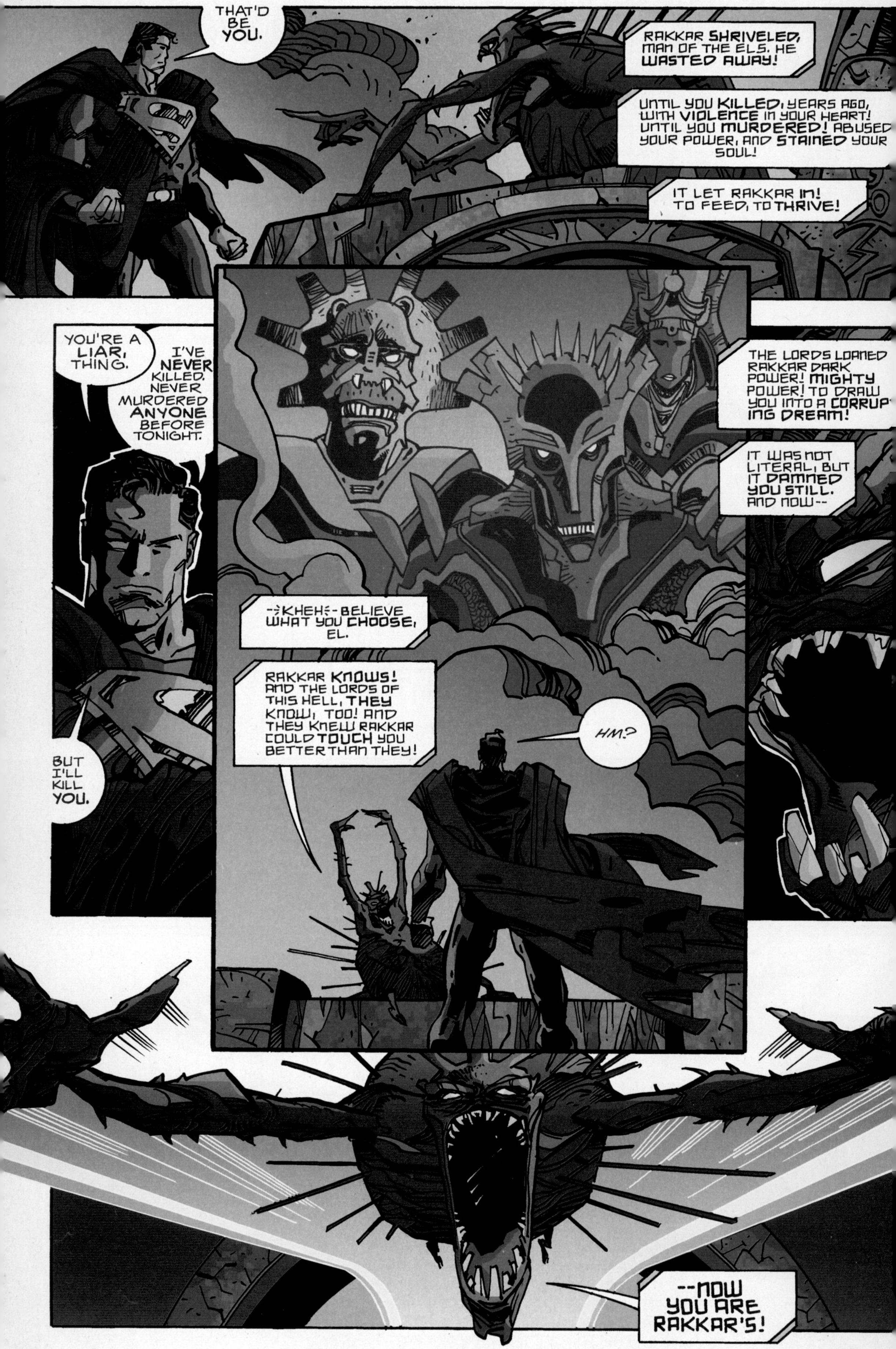

THAT'D BE YOU.
RAKKAR SHRIVELED, MAN OF THE ELS. HE WASTED AWAY!
UNTIL YOU KILLED, YEARS AGO, WITH VIOLENCE IN YOUR HEART! UNTIL YOU MURDERED! ABUSED YOUR POWER, AND STAINED YOUR SOUL!
IT LET RAKKAR IN! TO FEED, TO THRIVE!
YOU'RE A LIAR, THING.
I'VE NEVER KILLED. NEVER MURDERED ANYONE BEFORE TONIGHT.
BUT I'LL KILL YOU.
--KHEH--BELIEVE WHAT YOU CHOOSE, EL.
RAKKAR KNOWS! AND THE LORDS OF THIS HELL, THEY KNOW, TOO! AND THEY KNEW RAKKAR COULD TOUCH YOU BETTER THAN THEY!
HM?
THE LORDS LOANED RAKKAR DARK POWER! MIGHTY POWER! TO DRAW YOU INTO A CORRUPTING DREAM!
IT WAS NOT LITERAL, BUT IT DAMNED YOU STILL. AND NOW--
--NOW YOU ARE RAKKAR'S!

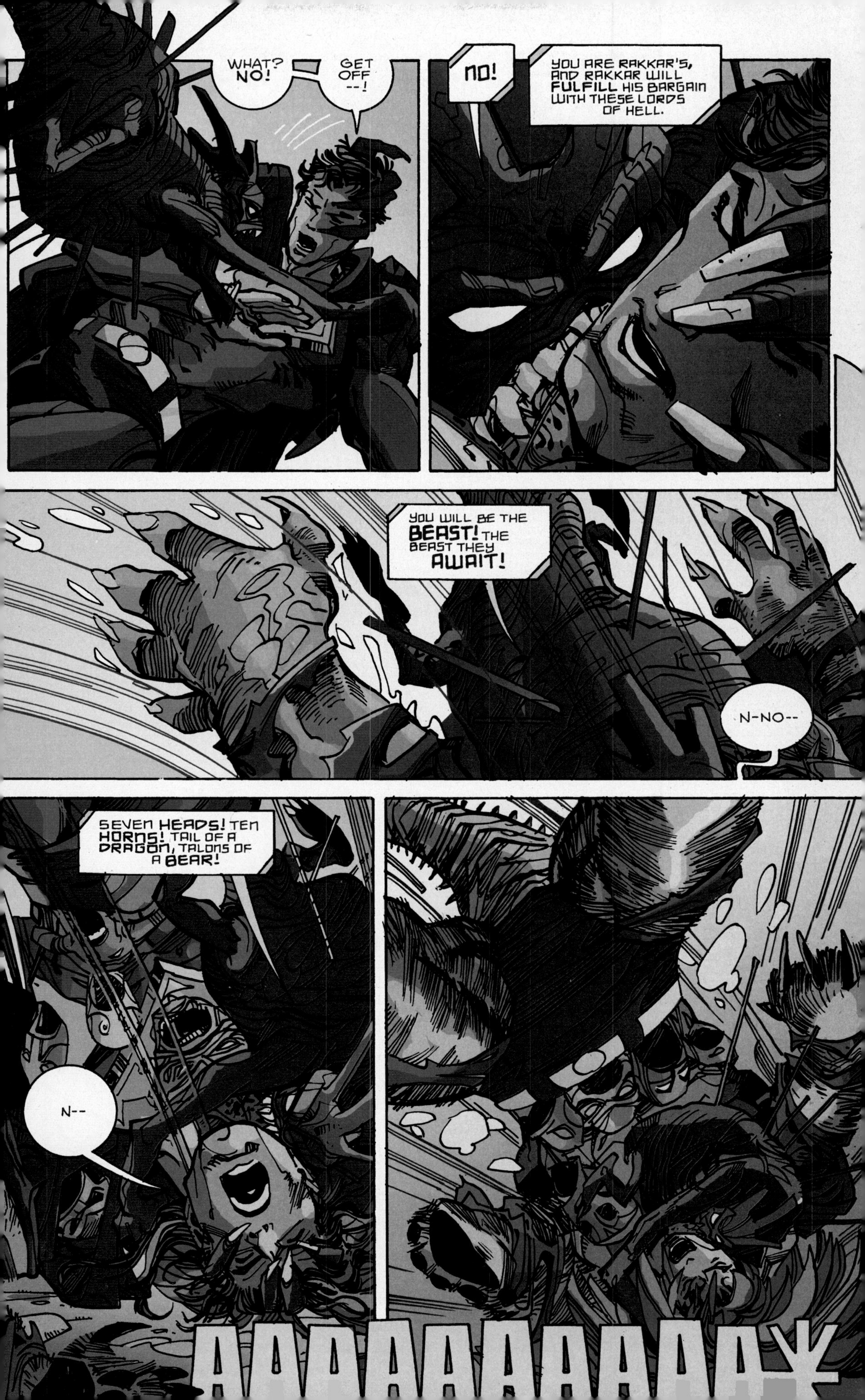
WHAT? NO!
GET OFF --!
NO!
YOU ARE RAKKAR'S, AND RAKKAR WILL FULFILL HIS BARGAIN WITH THESE LORDS OF HELL.
YOU WILL BE THE BEAST! THE BEAST THEY AWAIT!
N-NO--
SEVEN HEADS! TEN HORNS! TAIL OF A DRAGON, TALONS OF A BEAR!
N--
AAAAAAAAAAY

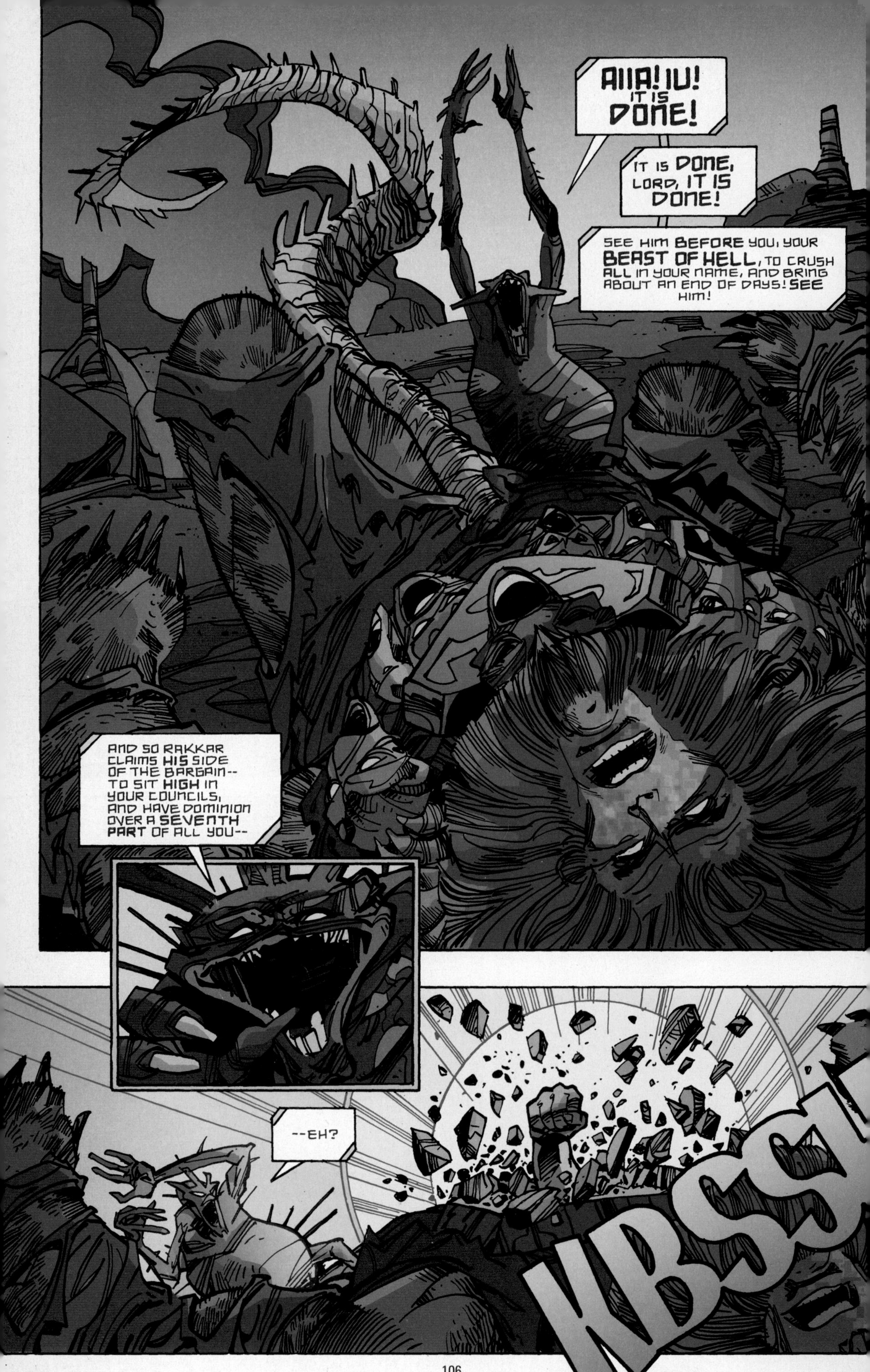
AIIIA! IU! IT IS DONE!
IT IS DONE, LORD, IT IS DONE!
SEE HIM BEFORE YOU, YOUR BEAST OF HELL, TO CRUSH ALL IN YOUR NAME, AND BRING ABOUT AN END OF DAYS! SEE HIM!
AND SO RAKKAR CLAIMS HIS SIDE OF THE BARGAIN-- TO SIT HIGH IN YOUR COUNCILS, AND HAVE DOMINION OVER A SEVENTH PART OF ALL YOU--
--EH?
KBSSH

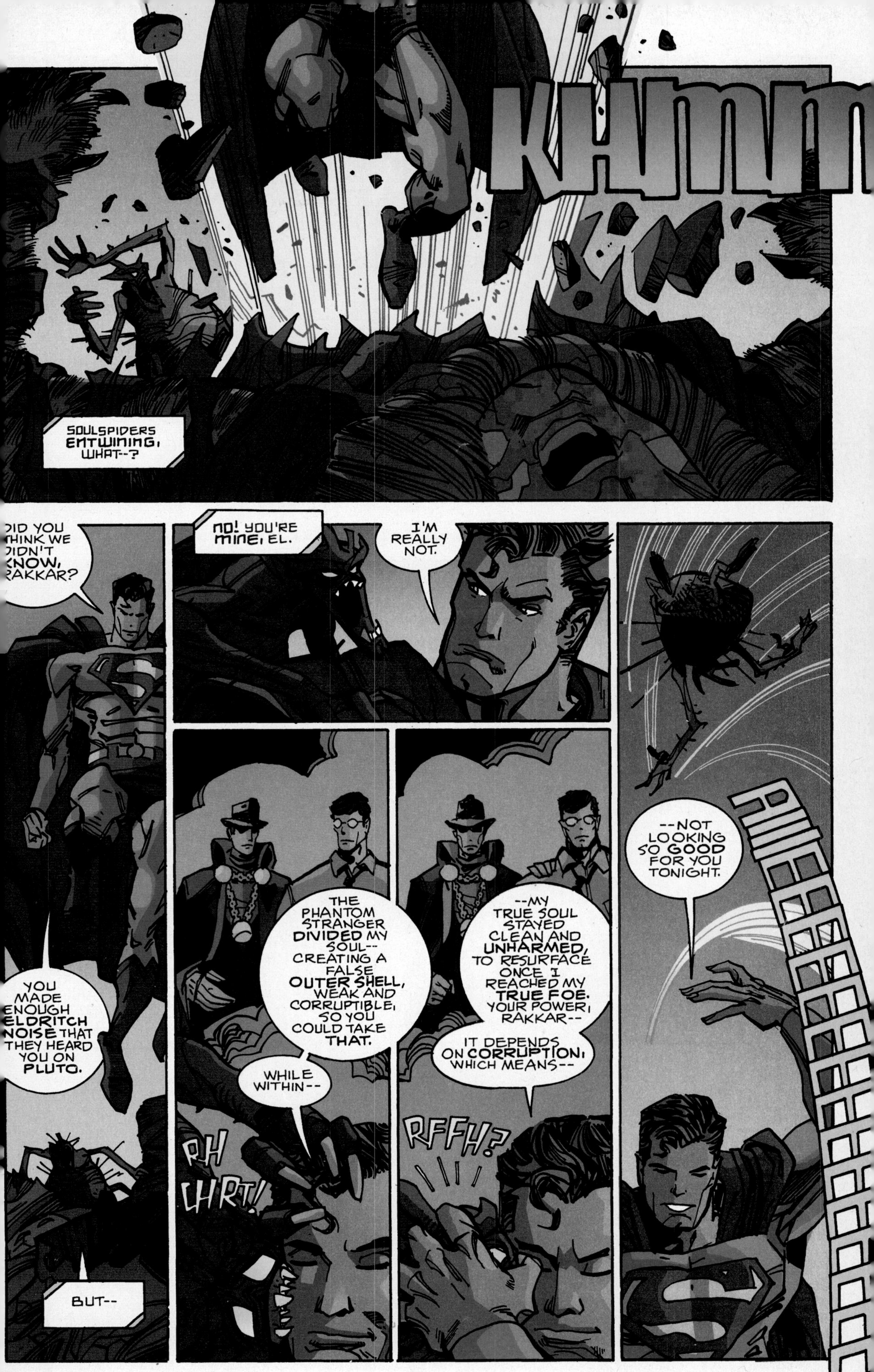

KHMMM
SOULSPIDERS ENTWINING, WHAT--?
DID YOU THINK WE DIDN'T KNOW, RAKKAR?
NO! YOU'RE MINE, EL.
I'M REALLY NOT.
YOU MADE ENOUGH ELDRITCH NOISE THAT THEY HEARD YOU ON PLUTO.
BUT--
THE PHANTOM STRANGER DIVIDED MY SOUL-- CREATING A FALSE OUTER SHELL, WEAK AND CORRUPTIBLE, SO YOU COULD TAKE THAT.
WHILE WITHIN--
RH CHRT!
--MY TRUE SOUL STAYED CLEAN AND UNHARMED, TO RESURFACE ONCE I REACHED MY TRUE FOE. YOUR POWER, RAKKAR--
IT DEPENDS ON CORRUPTION, WHICH MEANS--
RFFH?
--NOT LOOKING SO GOOD FOR YOU TONIGHT.

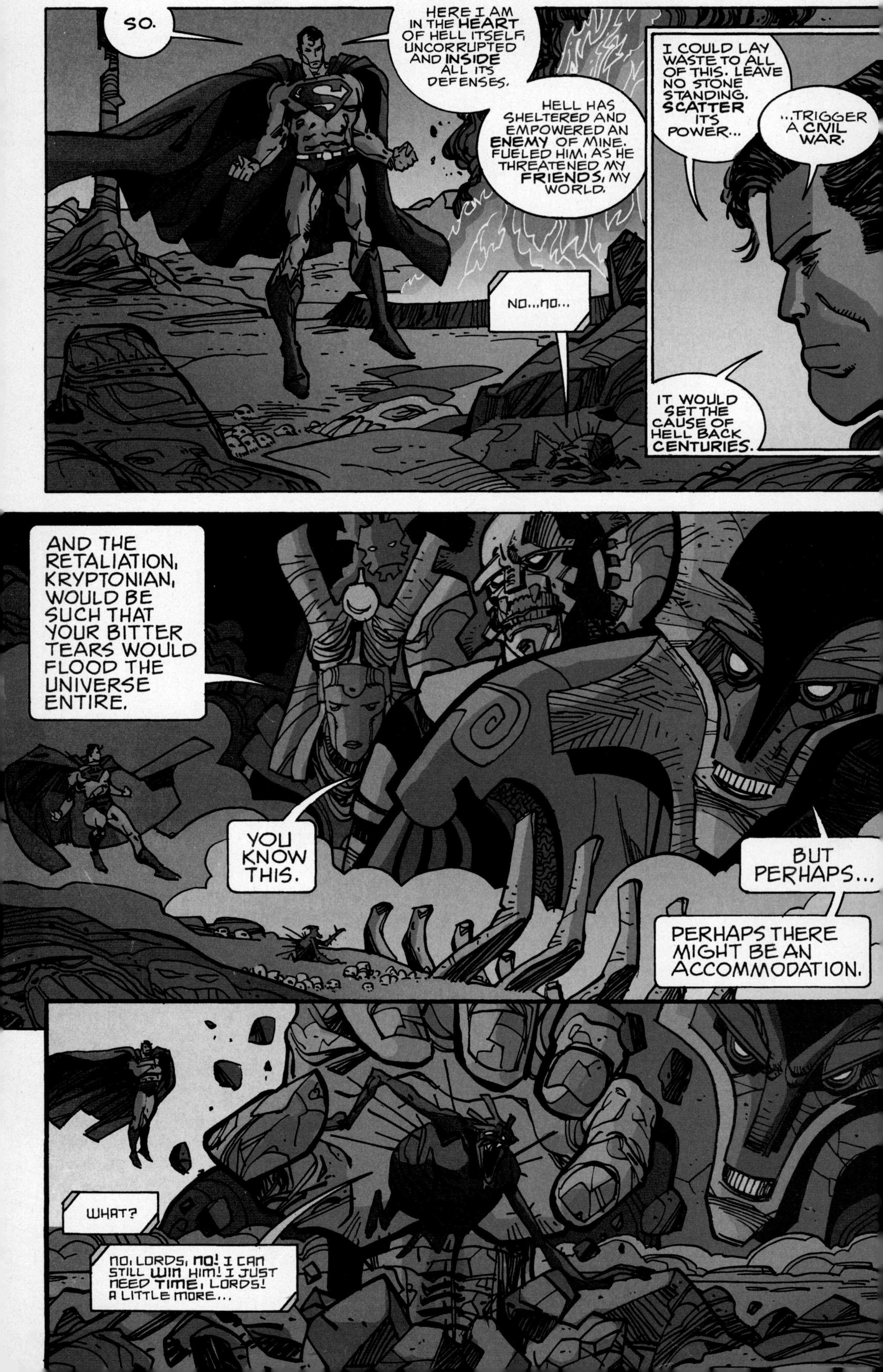
SO.
HERE I AM IN THE HEART OF HELL ITSELF, UNCORRUPTED AND INSIDE ALL ITS DEFENSES.
HELL HAS SHELTERED AND EMPOWERED AN ENEMY OF MINE. FUELED HIM, AS HE THREATENED MY FRIENDS, MY WORLD.
NO...NO...
I COULD LAY WASTE TO ALL OF THIS. LEAVE NO STONE STANDING. SCATTER ITS POWER...
...TRIGGER A CIVIL WAR.
IT WOULD SET THE CAUSE OF HELL BACK CENTURIES.
AND THE RETALIATION, KRYPTONIAN, WOULD BE SUCH THAT YOUR BITTER TEARS WOULD FLOOD THE UNIVERSE ENTIRE.
YOU KNOW THIS.
BUT PERHAPS...
PERHAPS THERE MIGHT BE AN ACCOMMODATION.
WHAT?
NO, LORDS, NO! I CAN STILL WIN HIM! I JUST NEED TIME, LORDS! A LITTLE MORE...

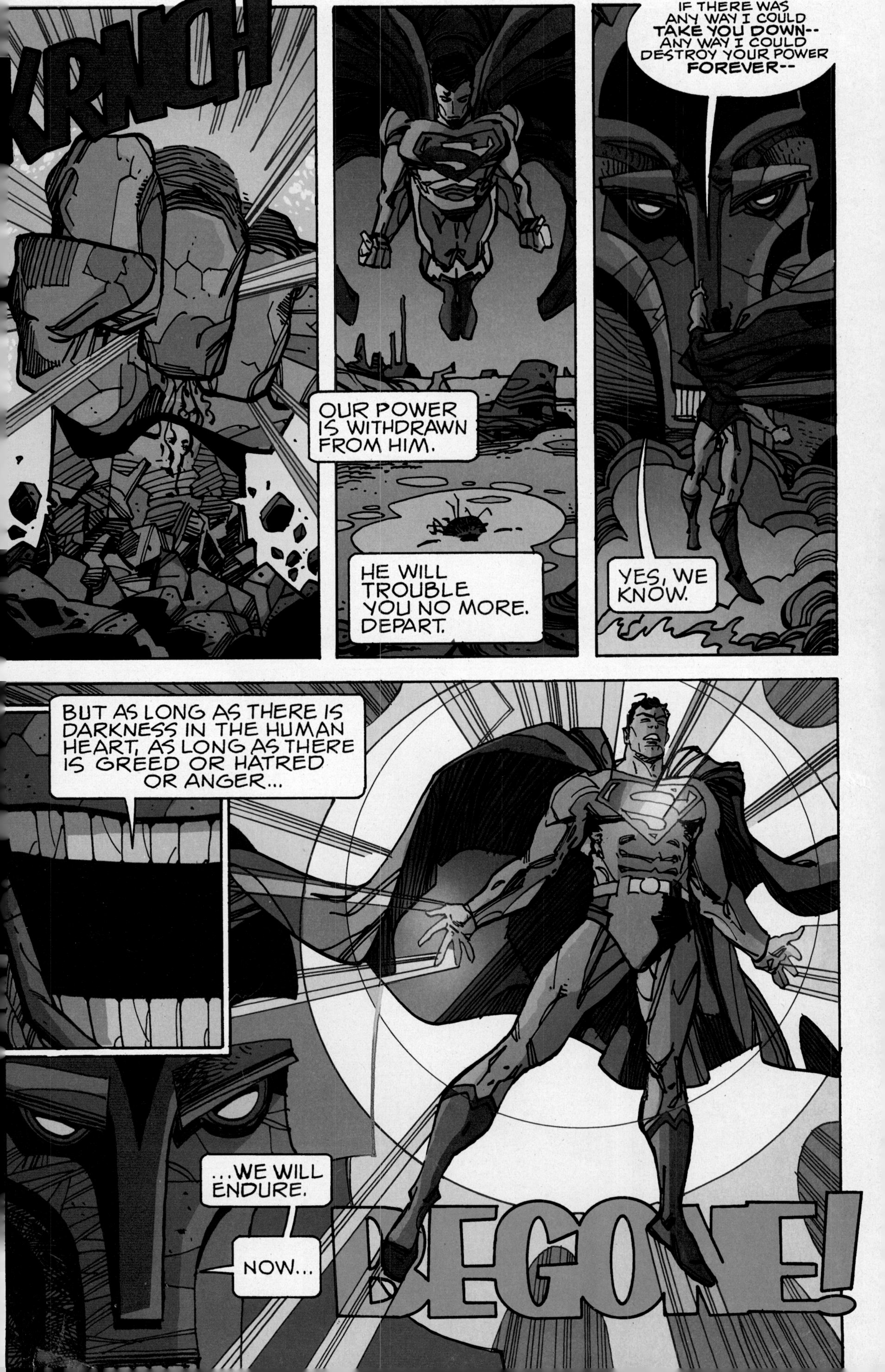
KRNCH
OUR POWER IS WITHDRAWN FROM HIM.
HE WILL TROUBLE YOU NO MORE. DEPART.
IF THERE WAS ANY WAY I COULD TAKE YOU DOWN-- ANY WAY I COULD DESTROY YOUR POWER FOREVER--
YES, WE KNOW.
BUT AS LONG AS THERE IS DARKNESS IN THE HUMAN HEART, AS LONG AS THERE IS GREED OR HATRED OR ANGER...
...WE WILL ENDURE.
NOW...
BEGONE!

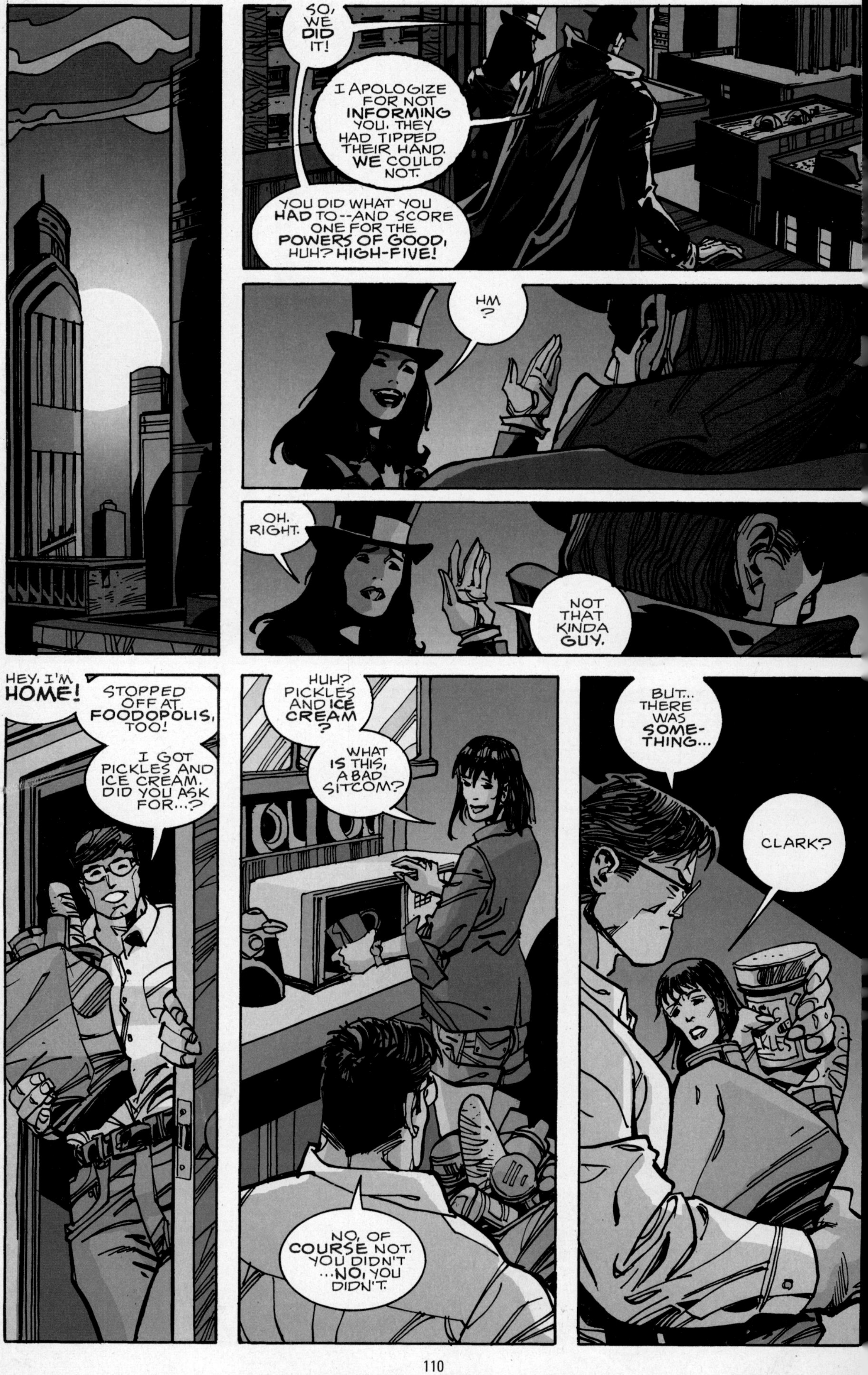
SO, WE DID IT!
I APOLOGIZE FOR NOT INFORMING YOU. THEY HAD TIPPED THEIR HAND. WE COULD NOT.
YOU DID WHAT YOU HAD TO--AND SCORE ONE FOR THE POWERS OF GOOD, HUH? HIGH-FIVE!
HM?
OH. RIGHT.
NOT THAT KINDA GUY.
HEY, I'M HOME!
STOPPED OFF AT FOODOPOLIS, TOO!
I GOT PICKLES AND ICE CREAM. DID YOU ASK FOR...?
HUH? PICKLES AND ICE CREAM?
WHAT IS THIS, A BAD SITCOM?
NO, OF COURSE NOT. YOU DIDN'T ...NO, YOU DIDN'T.
BUT... THERE WAS SOME-THING...
CLARK?

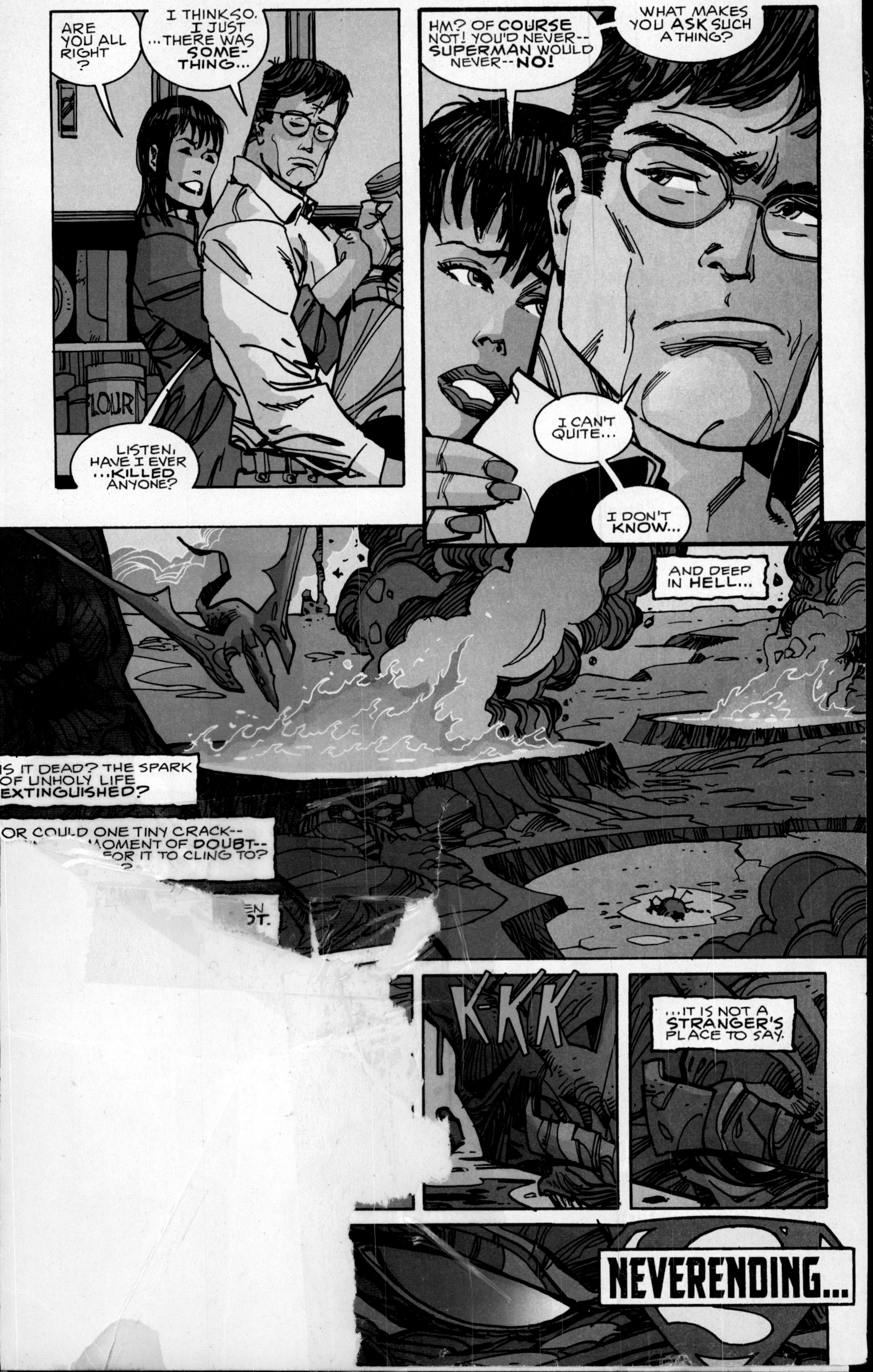
ARE YOU ALL RIGHT?
I THINK SO. I JUST ...THERE WAS SOME-THING...
FLOUR
LISTEN, HAVE I EVER ...KILLED ANYONE?
HM? OF COURSE NOT! YOU'D NEVER-- SUPERMAN WOULD NEVER--NO!
WHAT MAKES YOU ASK SUCH A THING?
I CAN'T QUITE...
I DON'T KNOW...
AND DEEP IN HELL...
IS IT DEAD? THE SPARK OF UNHOLY LIFE EXTINGUISHED?
OR COULD ONE TINY CRACK--
MOMENT OF DOUBT--
FOR IT TO CLING TO?
KKK
...IT IS NOT A STRANGER'S PLACE TO SAY.
NEVERENDING...